MAKING IMMIGR/

MAKING IMMIGRANT RIGHTS REAL

NONPROFITS AND THE POLITICS OF INTEGRATION IN SAN FRANCISCO

ELS DE GRAAUW

CORNELL UNIVERSITY PRESS
Ithaca and London

First published 2016 by Cornell University Press

First printing, Cornell Paperbacks, 2016

Printed in the United States of America

Library of Congress Cataloging-in-Publication Data

De Graauw, Els, author.
  Making immigrant rights real : nonprofits and the politics of integration in San Francisco / Els de Graauw.
     pages cm
  Includes bibliographical references and index.
  ISBN 978-1-5017-0018-7 (cloth : alk. paper)
  ISBN 978-1-5017-0019-4 (pbk. : alk. paper)
  1. San Francisco (Calif.)—Emigration and immigration.
2. Immigrants—Cultural assimilation—California—San Francisco. 3. Immigrants—Services for—California—San Francisco. 4. Immigrants—Civil rights—California—San Francisco. 5. Nonprofit organizations—Political activity—California—San Francisco. 6. Social integration—Political aspects—California—San Francisco. I. Title.
  JV6923.D4 2016
  325.794'61—dc23   2015036174

Cornell University Press strives to use environmentally responsible suppliers and materials to the fullest extent possible in the publishing of its books. Such materials include vegetable-based, low-VOC inks and acid-free papers that are recycled, totally chlorine-free, or partly composed of nonwood fibers. For further information, visit our website at www.cornellpress.cornell.edu.

Cloth printing   10 9 8 7 6 5 4 3 2 1
Paperback printing   10 9 8 7 6 5 4 3 2 1

Contents

Abbreviations

AFL	American Federation of Labor
AFL-CIO	American Federation of Labor–Congress of Industrial Organizations
ALDI	Alianza Latinoamericana por los Derechos de los Inmigrantes
CAA	Chinese for Affirmative Action
CBP	California Budget Project
CPA	Chinese Progressive Association
DABSA	Dymally-Alatorre Bilingual Services Act
DACA	Deferred Action for Childhood Arrivals
DAPA	Deferred Action for Parents of Americans and Lawful Permanent Residents
DCCC	San Francisco Democratic County Central Committee
DLSE	California Division of Labor Standards Enforcement
EASO	Equal Access to Services Ordinance
HERE	Hotel Employees and Restaurant Employees Union
ICE	U.S. Immigration and Customs Enforcement
INS	U.S. Immigration and Naturalization Service
IRC	San Francisco Immigrant Rights Commission
IRS	U.S. Internal Revenue Service
MCO	Minimum Compensation Ordinance
MWIEO	Minimum Wage Implementation and Enforcement Ordinance
MWO	Minimum Wage Ordinance
NCCIR	Northern California Coalition for Immigrant Rights
OCEIA	San Francisco Office of Civic Engagement and Immigrant Affairs
OLSE	San Francisco Office of Labor Standards Enforcement
POWER	People Organized to Win Employment Rights
SEIU	Service Employees International Union
SFLC	San Francisco Labor Council
SFO	San Francisco International Airport

SSA   U.S. Social Security Administration
UFCW   United Food and Commercial Workers Union
ULA   Unidad Latina en Acción
UNITE   Union of Needletrades, Industrial, and Textile Employees
YWU   Young Workers United

MAKING IMMIGRANT RIGHTS REAL

Introduction
The Local Politics of Immigrant Integration

The American political system expects people to stand up for what they believe and advocate the issues important to them. This presents the 41 million immigrants in the United States with a paradox. Advocacy is difficult for many of them: An estimated 22 million were noncitizens in 2013, 11 million had no high school diploma, 20 million had difficulty with English, 8 million were poor, and about 11 million were undocumented (Passel and Cohn 2013; U.S. Census Bureau 2013a). Fewer than half (42%) were voting age citizens eligible to cast ballots, compared with two thirds (68%) of the overall U.S. population, and their turnout rate was nine points below the native population in the 2012 presidential election. At 13 percent of the U.S. population, immigrants made up only 7 percent of the national vote in 2012 (U.S. Census Bureau 2012).

Given this disadvantaged political and socio-demographic profile, immigrants clearly have far fewer resources and opportunities to express their voices in the political process. Yet community organizations—especially immigrant-serving nonprofit organizations—have successfully undertaken a great deal of advocacy on their behalf, effectively promoting the rights of these politically marginalized and economically disadvantaged communities (Andersen 2010; Frasure and Jones-Correa 2010; Gleeson 2012; Theodore and Martin 2007; Wong 2006). This is a substantial departure from the experience of the last great wave of immigrants in the 1880–1920 period, who were slowly integrated into politics and other aspects of U.S. society first through local party organizations and later through the New Deal (Gerstle and Mollenkopf 2001). Why have these new organizations emerged as key agents of immigrants' socioeconomic and political advancement? How did it happen, and what have been their successes and failures? Despite the surge in community-based immigrant rights advocacy over the last several decades, we know little about how nonprofit organizations have shaped government policies and practices to promote immigrant rights and immigrant integration.

The growth of community-based nonprofit organizations was a primary outcome of the civil rights era. Such organizations were relatively rare until the late 1960s, but the long-term legacy of both the demand by communities for locally based services and the shift from direct to indirect public service provision has created a vast array of nonprofit service providers in what Salamon (1981) has called "third-party government." While they are private, nonprofit organizations rooted in urban settings are heavily dependent on government funding as well as their own philanthropic efforts. As such, they have become highly skilled at negotiating local politics.

As immigration surged after the U.S. Congress adopted major immigration reform legislation in 1965, existing and newly developed nonprofits started to pay more attention to political advocacy. They increasingly turned to local politics to advocate measures that help disadvantaged immigrants achieve greater parity with native-born Americans in education, employment, housing, health, and civic and political participation (Andersen 2010; Gleeson 2012; Jones-Correa 2011; Wong 2006).[1] These immigrant-serving nonprofits have succeeded in pushing major immigrant jurisdictions like Houston, New York City, Oakland, Philadelphia, San Francisco, and Washington, D.C., to adopt language access policies that make it easier for limited English proficient immigrants to interact and communicate with city officials. They have prompted New Haven, Los Angeles, Oakland, Richmond (Calif.), San Francisco, and New York City to issue municipal ID cards that allow undocumented immigrants to open a bank account, access basic city services, and identify themselves to police and other local government officials. And immigrant-serving nonprofits routinely work with city immigrant affairs offices to help noncitizens to naturalize and to mobilize them to participate in the civic and political affairs of many big urban centers, including Boston, Chicago, Detroit, Houston, Los Angeles, New York City, Philadelphia, San Francisco, and Seattle.

This phenomenon is particularly interesting because the 501(c)(3) tax-exempt status of nonprofits limits the extent to which they can engage in lobbying and partisan electioneering. Many nonprofits also worry about their reliance on government funding and limited organizational resources (Berry and Arons 2003; Grønbjerg 1993; Pekkanen, Smith, and Tsujinaka 2014; Smith and Lipsky 1993; Wolch 1990). Additionally, an era of stricter federal immigration enforcement and a highly politicized policy environment have severely fractured public support for immigrant rights (Hessick and Chin 2014; Varsanyi 2010b; Voss and Bloemraad 2011). These constraints have typically led civil society scholars to be pessimistic about what nonprofits can achieve in the realm of local politics, often concluding that they can do little (Andrews and Edwards 2004; Baumgartner and Leech 1998; Berry and Arons 2003; Boris and Steuerle 2006; Taylor, Craig, and Wilkinson 2002). Nonetheless, in some instances immigrant-serving nonprofits have driven major changes in local policies and practices that promote the rights and integration of disadvantaged immigrants. Why and how did they succeed?

This book unpacks the puzzle of how immigrant-serving nonprofits successfully navigated these advocacy constraints to influence the local governance of immigrant rights and integration. It draws on case studies in three realms of immigrant rights policies—language access, labor rights, and municipal ID cards—in San Francisco to present a tripartite model of advocacy strategies that nonprofits have used to propose, enact, and implement immigrant-friendly policies. Their first strategy has been one of *administrative advocacy*, where nonprofits advocate with non-elected city officials to influence policy interpretation and implementation in efforts to navigate the lobbying constraints of their tax-exempt status and leverage their contractual relations with city departments and agencies. Second, they have undertaken *cross-sectoral* and *cross-organizational collaborations* by building relationships with public officials and other types of organizations, such as labor unions, which have a more expansive repertoire of political resources and enjoy more advocacy freedoms. Finally, nonprofits have used *strategic issue framing* to counter the growth of anti-immigrant sentiment in the recessionary climate of recent years, when the federal government's enforcement agenda also has put increasing pressure on cities to toe the line.

The following chapters make the case that nonprofit advocates *can* bring about important policy changes in immigrant rights—despite their constraints and weaknesses—when they focus their advocacy on both policy enactment and policy implementation, make collaborations with city officials and other organizations integral to their advocacy, and strategically frame immigrant integration policies as in the interest of *all* city residents. Through use of this tripartite strategy, immigrant-serving nonprofits in San Francisco have helped to create new socioeconomic and political rights for disadvantaged immigrants, including the enactment of language access provisions for limited English proficient immigrants, stronger labor protections for low-wage immigrant workers, and municipal ID cards for undocumented immigrants.

More importantly, they also have consistently shaped the *implementation* of these new rights in ways that institutionalized them into the daily practices of San Francisco government. It is well established that there often is a wide gap between rights on the books and rights in practice, and new rights can remain hollow without effective implementation and enforcement (Epp 2010; McCann 1994; Tilly 1998). Immigrant-serving nonprofits have been instrumental in bridging this gap. They pushed San Francisco government to be accountable to the city's disadvantaged immigrants, to whom elected and appointed city officials are less likely to direct government support (Schneider and Ingram 1993).

This book makes important contributions to the immigrant political incorporation literature. Most explanations of immigrants' integration into the American political system focus on *microlevel* determinants, such as immigrants' resources, skills, and interests (Bass and Casper 2001; Cain, Kiewiet, and Uhlaner 1991; Ramakrishnan and Espenshade 2001; Yang 1994), and *macrolevel* variables, including a range of policy, institutional, and contextual factors (Jones-Correa 2001; North 1987; Portes and Curtis 1987). This book instead underscores the vital role of *mesolevel* structures—namely, local nonprofit organizations that can mediate between immigrant individuals and larger political communities—in the integration process. The book also shifts attention away from the popular focus on electoral participation by highlighting that policy representation and implementation are other key dimensions of immigrants' political integration. It adds to the burgeoning literature on state and local *anti*-immigrant policy activism by demonstrating that nonprofit advocates can play and have played a critical role in helping city officials to make immigrant rights real.

The book also contributes to other debates. It shows that civil society scholarship needs to examine how nonprofit organizations interact with a variety of political institutions beyond the legislature, including executive and judicial officials, other advocacy organizations, and the media. The book also emphasizes just how important nonprofits have become as urban political actors, with a unique ability to advocate for immigrants and other disadvantaged city residents. Finally, the book demonstrates how nonprofits exert influence on the actions of city administrative personnel and how they interpret their professional norms and agency missions.

Immigrant Rights as a Local Government Issue

The United States is a classic country of immigration and has admitted nearly 80 million legal immigrants since 1820 (DHS 2014a). Yet unlike other countries, even those that do not consider themselves countries of immigration, such as Germany, it has no national program to integrate immigrants and few federal laws that establish rights specifically for immigrants. With the exception of refugees, who benefit from programs that promote their short-term settlement and provide a quick route to legal permanent residence, the federal government takes a laissez-faire approach to the immigrants it admits and takes few steps to promote their social, economic, civic, and political advancement (Bloemraad and de Graauw 2012; Jiménez 2011; Schmidt Sr. 2007).[2] While the federal government has recently increased its efforts to promote naturalization and educate immigrants about the rights and responsibilities of U.S. citizenship, it still provides little support for immigrants to learn English or enter into the workforce (Bloemraad and de Graauw 2012; Fix, Zimmermann, and Passel 2001). Instead, federal policy seems to expect immigrants to become part of society through their own hard work, the help of family and friends, and perhaps the assistance of community organizations.

This federal lack of interest in promoting immigrant integration stems from a national individualist ethos that includes skepticism toward government intervention and a "pull yourself up by the bootstraps" mentality to socioeconomic mobility (Pickus 2005). Americans' continued ambivalence about immigration and their growing concern over undocumented immigration also deter federal officials from prioritizing immigrant rights. In 2011, 53 percent of Americans saw immigration more as a problem than an opportunity, 57 percent thought that immigrants take away jobs from natives, and 63 percent saw immigrants as a burden on social services (German Marshall Fund 2011).

More federal support has also not been forthcoming because immigrant rights and integration remain difficult issues for politicians on both sides of the aisle. Those on the right might support immigrant integration to promote societal cohesion, but they oppose the government expansion and economic redistribution implicit in many integration initiatives. Politicians on the left, in contrast, may support government intervention around public policies that promote immigrant rights but are uncomfortable with integration initiatives that seek assimilation and require immigrants to give up their cultural identities.

The federal government does, however, offer some baseline constitutional protections that encompass immigrants and frame their rights and societal integration. The Fourteenth Amendment to the U.S. Constitution enshrines the long-established practice of birthright citizenship, which ensures that all children born on U.S. territory are automatically granted full membership in the American polity. While immigration hard-liners have agitated to end "anchor babies," birthright citizenship still applies to the children of undocumented parents. The U.S. Supreme Court's famous *Plyler v. Doe* decision in 1982 guarantees that all children—including those who are undocumented—have the right to a free and equal K-12 public education. Public schools are important engines for immigrant integration because there children learn English and American history and government, and it is one of the first points at which immigrant parents interact with their larger communities.

Immigrants also benefit from many of the federal policies that seek to increase the life chances for all disadvantaged U.S. residents, and naturalized immigrants can access the same programs as the native born. Federal civil rights laws protect against discrimination in housing and the workplace and seek to promote greater ethnoracial and gender equality through preferential hiring and contracting policies. Originally designed to overcome the pernicious effects of slavery and second-class African American citizenship, these policies have been expanded to cover those immigrants considered to be ethnoracial minorities (Skrentny 2002). Federal labor and employment law protections—including minimum wage and overtime provisions, workplace safety standards, and union organizing rights—generally apply to all workers regardless of citizenship and documentation status (Gleeson 2012; Griffith 2009). Safety net policies—including Temporary Aid to Needy Families, the Children's Health Insurance Program, Medicaid, Medicare, food stamps, Supplemental Security Income, and public housing subsidies—extend to legal immigrants, although the 1996 Welfare Reform Act has instituted a citizenship criterion and limited noncitizens' access to many of these programs for at least five years after their arrival (Fix 2009). While these mainstream policies support many disadvantaged immigrants, they do not amount to a coherent national program of immigrant rights and immigrant integration.

As a result, lower levels of government, and cities in particular, have taken on the de facto responsibility for immigrant rights and integration. The lives of immigrants, including undocumented immigrants, are interwoven with those of native-born city residents in myriad ways. Just like the native born, immigrants work in the city, pay local taxes, own homes and rent apartments in the city, send their children to local schools, use government services locally, and attend city churches. It is thus not practical for city officials to ignore immigrants and their needs and interests, given that they are responsible for devising and implementing public policies that promote a productive local economy and a healthy and safe environment for all. Not surprisingly, then, immigrant rights and integration policies are predominantly local policies (Jones-Correa 2011). Even the media tend to report on immigrant rights and integration as local problems, not a federal responsibility (Abu-Laban and Garber 2005).

These issues are particularly salient in the large urban centers that house the biggest and most diverse immigrant populations. While one in eight U.S. residents is foreign-born, this is true for one in five residents of Chicago, one in four residents of Boston, Dallas, and San Diego, and one in three residents of Houston, New York City, Los Angeles, San Francisco, and San Jose. Immigrants make up more than half the population of Miami (U.S. Census Bureau 2013a). The racial and ethnic diversity of today's urban immigrant population is even more striking than its proportional size. Since the late 1960s, immigrants from Asia, Latin America, Africa, and the Caribbean have dramatically expanded and diversified the minority populations in many cities, and they will continue to do so. Also, relative to the nation and their surrounding suburbs and rural districts, central cities tend to have larger percentages of noncitizens, undocumented immigrants, and immigrants who are limited English proficient, uneducated, and poor (Card 2007; Passel and Cohn 2009; Suro, Wilson, and Singer 2011). In sum, central cities in particular have large concentrations of disadvantaged immigrants who yet have to achieve social, economic, civic, and political parity with the native-born population.

Many localities experiencing an immigrant influx have not moved to promote immigrant integration. In many suburban cities and rural towns in new destination areas in the South, Southwest, and Midwest, this demographic shift has produced anxieties among the native born that have fueled anti-immigrant responses (Hopkins 2010; O'Neil 2010; Ramakrishnan and Wong 2010; Varsanyi 2010b). Given the twenty-year rise in the undocumented population and the federal government's failure to enact comprehensive immigration reform, many suburban cities and rural towns (and new destination states) have curtailed immigrant rights by barring immigrants from working or renting homes in their jurisdictions or by making English the official language (Hopkins 2010; O'Neil 2010; Ramakrishnan and Wong 2010). While targeted primarily at undocumented immigrants, exclusionary policies enacted by jurisdictions like Hazleton (Penn.), Escondido (Calif.), Farmers Branch (Tex.), and numerous copycat municipalities can also hurt legal migrants and native-born minorities (Chavez 2008; De Genova 2004).

The great surge of immigration since 1965 has led many large urban centers, however, to adopt much more pro-immigrant stances. Especially those with a long history of immigration and also strong civil rights movements, like New York City, Chicago, and Los Angeles, have tended to respond much more positively. This book focuses on one iconic case, San Francisco, to understand how immigrant-serving nonprofits have successfully advocated for policies and practices that promote the rights and integration of disadvantaged immigrants.

Immigrant Rights as a Civil Society Issue

Despite the absence of a national integration program and the presence of many disadvantages, contemporary immigrants to the United States are learning English faster than European immigrants did a century ago, and the majority of their children and nearly all their grandchildren speak only English (Alba 2004; Fisher and Hout 2006). Over time and across generations, they improve their educational attainment, income, occupational status, and homeownership, and they tend to live in more integrated urban and suburban neighborhoods (Iceland and Scopilliti 2008; Kasinitz et al. 2008; Park and Myers 2010). Marriages between immigrants and native-born individuals have also sharply increased since 2000 (Qian and Lichter 2011). Finally, more immigrants have been acquiring U.S. citizenship faster since the 1990s, although naturalized citizens are still less likely to register and vote than native-born citizens (de Graauw 2013; Lee 2011). These data suggest that immigrants are passing the litmus test for integration.

This said, patterns of immigrant integration are heavily stratified by immigrants' educational and economic resources, racial inequalities, and legal status, which prevent many immigrants from being fully integrated (Portes and Rumbaut 2001; Portes and Zhou 1993; Telles and Ortiz 2008). First-generation immigrants who belong to an ethnoracial minority group and who do not speak English, have little formal education, are poor, or are undocumented face significant barriers to integration. Immigrant rights policies can expand their life chances and create a first step toward integration. The few studies of the causal relationship between public policies and immigrant integration suggest that helping immigrants learn English and secure better jobs enable them to earn higher incomes and thus contribute more fully to the economy and their children's future (Biles, Burstein, and Frideres 2008; Kymlicka 1998). In the Canadian context, government policies specifically benefiting immigrants also facilitated their naturalization and encouraged their civic and political participation (Bloemraad 2006).

Although disadvantaged immigrants could benefit from public policies designed to help them, they are not in a good position to influence the policymaking process directly. To begin with, they lack the resources to do so. Limited English proficiency makes it hard for them to communicate their needs to government officials. With little formal education, they may lack the skills necessary to succeed in public policy advocacy. And when they are not U.S. citizens, they cannot use their vote to signal their policy preferences to government officials. Many disadvantaged immigrants also lack a sense of democratic entitlement and feel they cannot or should not make demands on the American political system. They may think that they need to get settled economically before they become politically active. Their experiences with government abuse and corruption in their native countries may have made them distrustful and fearful of government. And if they are undocumented, they likely want to avoid contact with government officials for fear of being apprehended.

It is also unrealistic to expect government officials to take the initiative in proposing, enacting, and implementing immigrant rights and integration policies. Elected and appointed officials with conservative views might oppose continued migration and be wary of extending new rights or benefits to immigrants. More progressive officials, on the other hand, may welcome such policies but lack the resources or know-how to address the challenges of immigration-generated diversity. These different outlooks also make bipartisan collaboration unlikely, especially when public officials at all levels of government increasingly confront large budget deficits and are looking for ways to cut, rather than add, programs. Also, because immigrant populations are constantly in flux and have correspondingly changing needs, without direct input from immigrants it can be difficult for government officials to determine how best to help them. Finally, regardless of their political leanings, to the extent that elected officials are rational vote maximizers, they are unlikely to see disadvantaged immigrants—many of whom do not or cannot vote—as a distinct population requiring or deserving government support (Schneider and Ingram 1993).

Immigrant-serving nonprofits have often stepped in to bridge the gap between immigrant communities and city government (Andersen 2010; Bloemraad 2006; de Graauw 2008; de Leon et al. 2009; Jones-Correa 2011; Modares and Kitson 2008; Wong 2006). These organizations have learned how to provide an array of linguistically accessible and culturally appropriate services to disadvantaged immigrants, allowing them to build trust with immigrants, who often are reluctant or fearful to contact government about the help they need (Cordero-Guzmán 2005; Frasure and Jones-Correa

2010). Daily interactions with immigrants have given immigrant-serving nonprofits a deep understanding of those they serve. This gives them an unrivaled expertise on the particular challenges and needs of immigrants and helps them to develop an advocacy agenda (Cordero-Guzmán 2005). Located in neighborhoods where immigrants live, immigrant-serving nonprofits also are strategic sites through which city officials and city agencies can communicate with a large and growing proportion of city residents.

Long experience with local government contracts has enabled immigrant-serving nonprofits to establish lines of communication with a range of city officials and government agencies (Boris et al. 2010; Marwell 2004). This gives them considerable access to advocate immigrants' needs and interests in the public sphere. It also helps city officials to learn about on-the-ground experiences of the successes and shortcomings of government programs and services. All in all, immigrant-serving nonprofits are uniquely situated to represent disadvantaged immigrants and advocate for policies that promote their advancement.

These immigrant-serving nonprofits are the modern-day equivalents of yesteryear's settlement houses and mutual aid societies, which also combined advocacy with service provision to improve the living and working conditions of urban immigrants. A century ago, Chicago's Hull House, Boston's South End House, and New York City's Henry Street Settlement offered social, educational, and cultural programs to immigrants and lobbied city officials to provide public bathhouses, neighborhood parks, better waste collection and disposal, and night classes in public schools in immigrant neighborhoods (Davis 1994; Trolander 1987). Mutual aid societies like L'Ordine Figli d'Italia (the Order Sons of Italy), the Ancient Order of Hibernians, and the Alianza Hispano-Americana (Hispanic-American Alliance) provided relief to immigrants by paying for funerals and helping them survive periods of illness and unemployment (Beito 2000). They also encouraged immigrants to naturalize and protested discrimination against immigrants (Soyer 2006; Sterne 2001).

These past organizations, however, give us a poor guide for understanding how today's nonprofits influence the local politics of immigrant issues. The U.S. Congress did not enact the first federal law limiting the political activities of charitable organizations until 1934 (Scrivner 1990).[3] Yesteryear's settlement houses and mutual aid societies thus had more freedom to undertake advocacy on behalf of disadvantaged immigrants, and many did (see chapter 1). They did not have to fear that their political advocacy might jeopardize their government funding, because they were supported primarily through private donations (Fabricant and Fisher 2002; Smith and Lipsky

1993). Only since the 1970s have nonprofits grown dependent on funding from various levels of government when they assumed a more prominent role in the provision of public services (Grønbjerg 1993; Marwell 2004; Salamon 1995; Smith and Lipsky 1993). Finally, compared with the federal emphasis on immigration enforcement today, federal support for the Americanization movement at the turn of the twentieth century helped to sensitize local government officials to the importance of immigrant integration.

In sum, today's immigrant-serving nonprofits operate in a much more challenging policymaking and advocacy context than did their counterparts a century before. This makes their ability to play an influential role in the local politics of immigrant rights and integration all the more surprising and important.

A Tripartite Strategy to Promote Immigrant Rights

The following chapters present a tripartite model of advocacy strategies that San Francisco–based nonprofits have used to influence the local governance of immigrant rights and immigrant integration. They are: (a) administrative advocacy, (b) cross-sectoral and cross-organizational collaborations, and (c) strategic issue framing. The elaboration of this model investigates how immigrant-serving nonprofits can overcome the constraints posed by their 501(c)(3) tax-exempt status, reliance on government funding, limited organizational resources, and a fractured context of public support for immigrant rights. It will show that nonprofit advocates can and do realize important policy changes in immigrant rights—despite the constraints they face—when they focus their advocacy on policy enactment and policy implementation, make collaborations with city officials and other organizations integral to their advocacy, and strategically frame immigrant integration policies as in the interest of all city residents.

Administrative Advocacy

Scholars often see immigrant-serving nonprofits as social movement organizations that use protests and rallies to pressure government officials to abandon their pursuit of anti-immigrant legislation or strengthen their commitment to policies that expand immigrant rights (Cordero-Guzmán et al. 2008; Pallares and Flores-González 2010; Voss and Bloemraad 2011). Many immigrant-serving nonprofits, however, actually behave more like mainstream political actors and frequently work *with*, rather than *around* or *against*, government officials. Compared with other advocacy organizations like unions, immigrant-serving nonprofits stand out for their sustained advocacy with administrative officials in city departments and agencies. To evaluate nonprofits' impact, we need to consider not only their role in community mobilization and policy enactment—as most scholars do—but also how they influence policy implementation. The chapters that follow argue that non-profits' administrative advocacy is instrumental in transforming immigrant rights on the books into immigrant rights in practice.

Immigrant-serving nonprofits can be successful at administrative advocacy because their 501(c)(3) tax-exempt status has no restrictions about this. Federal regulations limit what nonprofits, including those that cater to immigrants, can do to lobby *legislative* officials, including city council members and county supervisors, and they bar them from doing anything to support or oppose candidates during elections (Lunder 2007). In contrast, they place no explicit restrictions on interacting with *administrators*, who are political appointees or career civil servants. Most of my nonprofit informants had a sophisticated understanding of this aspect of the federal rulebook. They knew that their 501(c)(3) tax-exempt status restricts their legislative advocacy with city legislators to enact new laws, but not administrative advocacy with city departments and agencies to implement existing legislation, and many acted accordingly.

Immigrant-serving nonprofits also have easy and many opportunities to influence city administrative officials. Many work under contract with city departments and agencies to provide social services to immigrants and other disadvantaged city residents. They also have an expertise on immigrant communities that is useful to city administrative personnel, who are under constant pressure to make city services more effective and less costly and whose professional norms and missions motivate them to serve all city residents, even when they lack a good understanding of the rapidly changing needs of immigrant residents. City departments and agencies also rely on nonprofit advocates to provide them with political support when they deal with other government officials, including city legislators. This convergence of interests explains the ongoing interactions and partnerships between immigrant-serving nonprofits and city departments and agencies. It can, however, also blur the public-private divide, especially when nonprofit advocates spin through the revolving door to become better-paid city employees.

In advocating with city administrative personnel, immigrant-serving non-profits seek to highlight immigrants as a distinct and important constituency within the policy implementation process. This is necessary because ordinances can have broad mandates, leaving administrative officials with significant discretion over who ultimately benefits from enacted legislation.

Also, legislators do not always allocate funding or staff resources to policy implementation, making it more likely that enacted policies will languish or become merely symbolic measures without outside help in implementation. My research in San Francisco found that immigrant-serving nonprofits were the only organizations advocating for immigrant rights *after* an ordinance had been enacted. This was the case for legislation specifically targeting immigrants (language access) but also legislation benefiting a range of disadvantaged populations (labor rights and municipal ID cards). Their expertise in administrative advocacy enabled immigrant-serving nonprofits to help local agencies to institutionalize the practice of immigrant rights in San Francisco.

This is a new insight about the process that has come to be called "immigrant bureaucratic incorporation" (Jones-Correa 2008; Lewis and Ramakrishnan 2007; Marrow 2009). Previous studies have analyzed why reputedly unresponsive local administrative officials (Etzioni-Halevy 1983; Lineberry 1977) decide to accommodate newcomers' needs, including those of undocumented immigrants. They highlight the importance of professional norms and inclusive agency missions in this process, but I make the case that they are not sufficient to explain it. External pressure on bureaucratic institutions to serve immigrant populations is also necessary. Even though San Francisco has an ethnically diverse municipal workforce with an overall cosmopolitan outlook, nonprofit advocates still had to apply constant pressure to move city departments and agencies to develop policies and bureaucratic practices that accommodate immigrants' unique circumstances. The book's conclusion discusses the lessons that can be learned about nonprofits' use of administrative advocacy as a strategy to advance the interests of disadvantaged immigrants in cities other than San Francisco.

Cross-Sectoral and Cross-Organizational Collaborations

Immigrant-serving nonprofits operate on tight budgets and cater mostly to noncitizens. Lacking the money or voter base to exert their own pressure, immigrant-serving nonprofits with public policy aspirations must build larger coalitions in support of immigrant rights. Immigrant-serving nonprofits need to collaborate with elected and appointed city officials because they control funding to nonprofits and have the power to enact, implement, and enforce the needed programs and policies. They also need to work with other immigrant-serving nonprofits to pool resources and multiply advocacy voices. Finally, immigrant-serving nonprofits need to work with other advocacy organizations like labor unions, which have more resources and clout and fewer explicit restrictions on their political activities. In turn, government officials and union activists welcome collaborations with immigrant-serving nonprofits, which can help them navigate language, culture, and trust barriers with immigrant communities. The use of cross-sectoral and cross-organizational collaborations is thus another important strategy that immigrant-serving nonprofits can use to overcome resource limitations and legal restrictions on their advocacy.

The nonprofit experience of building coalitions around immigrant rights in San Francisco reminds us of the coalition-building experiences discussed by race and ethnic politics scholars (Browning, Marshall, and Tabb 1984; Sonenshein 1993) and scholars of labor unions (Tattersall 2005; Tattersall and Reynolds 2007). These scholars have argued that coalitions are more likely to form, cohere, and succeed when the individuals participating in them share common interests and ideologies, trust one another, and invest time and resources to realize coalition goals. What the San Francisco experience adds to this literature is that we also need to consider broader questions of organizational structure, resources, and status to understand the dynamics and challenges of collaborations, especially when different types of organizations are involved. Immigrant-serving nonprofits rely heavily on government funding, are legally restricted in the amount and types of advocacy they can undertake, and have few resources to devote to advocacy. This explains why cross-sectoral and cross-organizational collaborations to promote immigrant advancement remain tenuous even when nonprofit advocates, city officials, and union leaders share the key ingredients of an inclusive political ideology, common policy interests, and a commitment to work together. In other words, good intentions and aligned interests may not be enough.

In San Francisco, nonprofits' collaborations with elected and appointed city officials were constantly challenging undertakings. When immigrant-serving nonprofits advocated too aggressively, they worried that city officials might react by endangering their tax-exempt status or government funding. If, in contrast, they were too accommodating of city officials, they risked cooptation and losing the trust of their immigrant base. They thus faced a constant challenge of maintaining support from city officials so as not to compromise their financial support and access to the governmental process while also providing a critical outside voice for the immigrant communities they represent. All three policy case study chapters (chapters 3–5) pay close attention to the complexity and dynamics of the collaborations between city officials and immigrant-serving nonprofits, and this is a central focus of the analysis of nonprofits' advocacy for immigrant language access in chapter 3.

It was also necessary for immigrant-serving nonprofits to work with one another to build coalitions that span different immigrant communities and native-born minority groups. When they were able to pool more voices and resources, they achieved greater political visibility and were more likely to get positive responses from policymakers. Such larger coalitions also gave cover to immigrant-serving nonprofits that were uncomfortable with political advocacy due to their tax-exempt status or government contracts. But building broader coalitions required them to work through differences in organizational structure and size. Chapters 3 through 5 discuss nonprofit coalitional dynamics in the campaigns for immigrant language access, labor rights, and municipal ID cards and examine how disagreements and compromises were addressed in each. These cases highlight how nonprofits that involved immigrant clients in their campaigns were more aggressive in their advocacy, while smaller and newer immigrant-serving nonprofits struggled to be taken seriously by larger and more established ones.

Finally, collaborations between immigrant-serving nonprofits and other types of advocacy organizations are challenging due to differences in organizational resources and tax-exempt status. Cross-organizational collaborations between nonprofits and labor unions, for example, have become more common as unions have sought to revitalize their ranks and organize immigrant workers (Applegate 2007; Dean and Reynolds 2009; Fine 2006; Luce 2004; Needleman 1998). Having unions as their allies puts immigrant-serving nonprofits in a stronger position to influence the decisions of city officials. Unions have more financial resources and can often mobilize their large membership in the political process. Incorporated under section 501(c)(5) of the Internal Revenue Code, unions also have more freedom to engage in political advocacy than 501(c)(3) nonprofits. While these differences make unions attractive coalition partners, they can also frustrate the immigrant-serving nonprofits that collaborate with them. The discussion of the campaigns to promote immigrants' labor rights in San Francisco (chapter 4) shows that such differences can lead to a power imbalance within coalitions and give unions the means to crowd immigrant-serving nonprofits out of the policymaking process.

Strategic Issue Framing

Issue framing is at the center of debates about immigration and immigrant rights. Immigration opponents have used a variety of frames centering on job displacement, welfare abuse, national security threats, environmental destruction and overpopulation, and crime to portray immigrants—and especially undocumented Latino immigrants—as a major social problem and serious public policy failing (Chavez 2008; Cisneros 2008; Mehan 1997; Santa Ana 2002). Supporters have organized around the ideas of "immigrant empowerment" as a new stage in the civil rights movement and "immigrant rights as human rights." They have emphasized immigrants' economic contributions to refute opponents' negative immigration frames (Fujiwara 2005; Smith 2007). Nonprofit advocates in San Francisco also used these themes to talk about the need for immigrant language access, labor rights, and municipal ID cards, but this discourse did not fully resonate with local policymakers, voters, or the mainstream media. Immigrant-serving nonprofits consequently had to recraft their message from one campaign to the next. Their experience suggests that no one set of ideas will always work in today's anti-immigrant environment.

Nonprofit advocacy for immigrant rights is playing out against a national background in which the federal government is focused on national security and immigration law enforcement and in which there is public antipathy toward immigration in the wake of the recent recession. Since the 2001 terrorist attacks, states and local governments have faced increasing pressure to align their policies and practices with federal enforcement objectives. Not only have Homeland Security officials propagated such programs as 287(g), Secure Communities, and the Criminal Alien Program, but they have criticized sanctuary and other local programs that run counter to the federal enforcement agenda. Also, since the mid-1990s and again as a result of the labor market anxieties of the 2000s, federal policymakers have been critical of the notion that immigrants deserve government help. These national trends have made it harder for immigrant-serving nonprofits to convince city officials to enact and implement programs favoring immigrants, particularly undocumented immigrants.

To counter these national trends, nonprofit advocates in San Francisco habitually justified claims by noncitizens and the undocumented on public services by invoking cosmopolitan (Carens 1989) and postnational (Soysal 1994) ideals of membership. They used the language of "immigrant empowerment" and mobilized around the platform that "immigrant rights are human rights" to emphasize that it was improper to exclude noncitizens and undocumented immigrants from government programs and protections. Their advocacy proceeded from the conviction that mere city residence entitled immigrants to have a say in how they were governed. They sought to use these moral and localized conceptions of membership to uncouple immigrants' access to basic rights, services, and civic participation from their formal citizenship or documentation status.

Discursive frames centered on immigrant empowerment and human rights helped to unify and mobilize a diverse group of immigrant-serving nonprofits around a comprehensive immigrant rights agenda. Yet they did not gain much traction with San Francisco government officials, voters, or the mainstream media. In each of the case studies described below, nonprofit advocates had to customize their message to connect with city officials, voters, and the media. Across campaigns, nonprofit advocates sought to emphasize that other city residents also had an interest in legislation benefiting disadvantaged immigrants. They used different advocacy frames to establish this linked fate in each of the campaigns. They framed language access legislation as a civil rights issue and a much-needed local attempt to enforce existing state and federal language access provisions (chapter 3). In contrast, they used the lens of economic justice to frame labor rights legislation (chapter 4), and they framed municipal ID cards legislation as a public safety and civic integration issue (chapter 5). By strategically downplaying that these policies primarily benefited immigrants, immigrant-serving nonprofits successfully navigated a highly politicized environment in which their objectives remained a difficult political sell.

This savvy was necessary even in the relatively favorable conditions of San Francisco. Most San Francisco elected officials appreciated immigrants and understood their needs, but they also wanted to enact policies that would help them get reelected or gain higher office, that would address widely acknowledged public problems, and that would comport with state and federal laws. Given that the prevailing national discourse portrays immigrants as societal burdens and national security threats, enacting policies narrowly tailored to help immigrants or that run counter to federal law could be a political liability. Immigrant-serving nonprofits tried to make immigrant rights policies more attractive by casting them as anti-discrimination, economic justice, or public safety measures from which many city residents would benefit. All three case study chapters delve into how nonprofit advocates struggled to find suitable frames, but this plays a central role in chapter 5's discussion of the campaign to enact and implement a municipal ID card program to benefit undocumented immigrants.

Research Design and Data

This book is based on four years (2005–2009) of research in San Francisco, a traditional immigrant destination that has not received much scholarly attention compared with New York City, Miami, Los Angeles, or Chicago. San Francisco has been continuously exposed to immigration and had a foreign-born population of 35 percent in 2013 (U.S. Census Bureau 2013a). Consequently, it has experienced a demographic imperative for public policies addressing immigrants' needs and interests. A city-county consolidation,

San Francisco bears more responsibility for social welfare functions than most large U.S. cities. This has increased nonprofits' opportunities to obtain service contracts and expanded the range of local policies and programs they can push for but also heightened their awareness of the possible financial repercussions of their advocacy. Finally, San Francisco has a large, diverse, and vibrant nonprofit sector, and the city's progressive political culture provides a good climate for such organizations to advocate on behalf of immigrants. This made it possible to observe a range of nonprofit behaviors and analyze when they became active in city politics, what advocacy strategies and tactics they used to influence the policymaking process, and what factors contributed to their failures and successes.

One might expect that these background characteristics would mean that nonprofit advocates encountered little resistance from government officials, unions, the public, and the media regarding their policy proposals to promote immigrant rights. In fact, immigrant-serving nonprofits in San Francisco faced several challenges and had to innovate to overcome them. Some of these challenges were structural, as already discussed. These included the 501(c)(3) restrictions on nonprofit advocacy, their reliance on local government funding and limited organizational resources, and the hostile national political context. Other challenges, discussed more fully in chapter 2, were specific to San Francisco. The city's social and ethnic diversity, fragmented government, weak political leadership, and partyless milieu all make immigrant rights advocacy difficult. A multitude of competing interest groups and policymakers' orientation toward adopting policies that strengthen the city's economy also make it difficult for nonprofit advocates to promote immigrant interests.

This study zeroes in on nonprofits that are incorporated as 501(c)(3) tax-exempt, not-for-profit organizations and that serve or advocate on behalf of immigrants or promote their cultural heritage, whatever their ethnicity or national origin. Although foundations and churches also enjoy the 501(c)(3) tax-exempt status, they are excluded from the analysis because their missions, funding sources, institutional structures, and IRS requirements are distinct from those of nonprofits.[4] The objects of this study all have offices in San Francisco and have first-generation immigrants as a significant (30% or more) share of their clientele. They were selected based on the assumption that if they serve sizable numbers of immigrants, they are more likely to notice and act on the concerns and interests of immigrants.

To determine the number of immigrant-serving nonprofits in San Francisco, I initially used cues in the organizations' names and mission statements to identify them in the National Center for Charitable Statistics database of 5,217 San Francisco–based nonprofits that had registered with the federal government as 501(c)(3) tax-exempt organizations by the end of 2005. After excluding foundations and churches, this search yielded a group of 433 nonprofits whose name or mission suggested that they catered to immigrants. I next used web searches, interviews with 55 of the most active immigrant-serving nonprofits, and organizations' annual reports (when available online) to enumerate the universe of nonprofits with an immigrant clientele of at least 30 percent. This second search yielded a total of 216 nonprofits (see appendix).[5]

The book presents case studies on six policies grouped in three distinct issue areas: language access, labor rights, and municipal ID cards. These policies all provide tangible resources to disadvantaged immigrants but differ with respect to which political institutions (legislature, executive, judiciary, and initiative process) were responsible for their enactment and implementation. As summarized in table 1, legislators on the San Francisco Board of Supervisors adopted the Equal Access to Services Ordinance in 2001 and amended the legislation in 2009 (and again in 2015, after my research was completed). The Minimum Compensation Ordinance was enacted by the Board in 2000, while the Minimum Wage Ordinance was legislated via initiative in 2003 and then amended by the Board three years later. Finally, the Municipal ID Ordinance was also adopted by the Board of Supervisors in 2007 and survived a court challenge the following year. City-level executive departments and agencies had a role in the interpretation, implementation, and enforcement of all six policies.

This variation in political institutions helps elucidate how tax code regulations and limited organizational resources shape the ways that immigrant-serving

Table 1   Policy cases and decision-making arenas compared

Policy	Language access		Labor rights			Municipal ID cards
	Equal Access to Services Ordinance (2001)	Language Access Ordinance (2009)	Minimum Compensation Ordinance (2000)	Minimum Wage Ordinance (2003)	Minimum Wage Implementation and Enforcement Ordinance (2006)	Municipal ID Ordinance (2007)
Legislature	•	•	•		•	•
Executive	•	•	•	•	•	•
Judiciary						•
Ballot				•		

nonprofits seek to influence the policymaking process. As discussed, these restrictions discourage nonprofit advocacy targeted at the legislature (San Francisco Board of Supervisors). Limited organizational resources also make it challenging for nonprofits to have sway with legislators and other elected officials, who are more likely to respond to interests that aggregate votes and contributions. Given these constraints, immigrant-serving nonprofits reacted rationally by directing their advocacy at branches of government other than the legislature. Since service contracts with city departments and agencies gave nonprofits easy access to administrative personnel, it was particularly rational for them to focus on the city's executive branch (administrative departments and agencies) in efforts to promote immigrant rights and integration.

All six policies eventually became law, but only after nonprofit advocates fought long, hard battles and overcame initial failures by developing new strategies and tactics. Chapter 3 discusses how nonprofit advocates' initial failure to enact a language access ordinance in 1999 drove them to collaborate strategically with key legislative and administrative city officials who successfully stewarded the policy's enactment and implementation in 2001 and subsequent years. Chapter 4 shows how immigrant-serving nonprofits failed to strengthen immigrant labor rights by themselves, driving them to collaborate with labor unions, which enjoyed relatively more legislative and electoral advocacy freedoms to enact the Minimum Compensation and Minimum Wage Ordinances. Finally, chapter 5 highlights how immigrant-serving nonprofits failed to change the critical media coverage on undocumented immigrants but learned to frame the Municipal ID Ordinance as a non-immigrant issue, a strategy that in turn helped them to defeat a legal challenge against the ordinance a year later. By analyzing how immigrant-serving nonprofits overcame these advocacy failures, this book provides concrete examples of how nonprofit advocates can innovate and retool to overcome barriers in the policymaking process.

A variety of data support this argument. The bulk of the evidence comes from 127 open-ended interviews with (a) staff of immigrant-serving nonprofits, (b) elected and appointed officials and other local government employees, and (c) leaders from a variety of community-based organizations with an interest in immigrant rights and integration, such as local labor unions, churches, and grant-making institutions. My sampling frame relied on the directory of 216 San Francisco–based immigrant-serving nonprofits I compiled, augmented by newspaper stories on immigration and immigrant issues in San Francisco and interviewee referrals. Fifty-one interviews were also conducted with nonprofit advocates, local government officials, and other community advocates in Houston, New Haven, New York City, Oakland, San Jose, and Washington, D.C. All but a few interviews were conducted by the author in person and ranged from 45 minutes to four hours in length. To preserve the anonymity of all nonprofit and community advocates and some public officials, they are named by the organization or government office for which they worked at the time of the interview.

These interviews were supplemented with an original survey of all 216 immigrant-serving nonprofits identified early in my research (see appendix). The survey questionnaire contained forty-three mostly closed-ended questions examining (a) organizational characteristics, (b) an organization's general interactions with local, state, and federal government, (c) organizational capacity to engage in advocacy, and (d) an organization's advocacy around immigrant rights and integration issues in San Francisco. The survey was fielded in 2007 through a six-wave set of mailings—alternating copies of the questionnaire with reminder postcards—that took five months to complete. This generated one hundred usable responses, equaling an effective response rate of 46 percent. Census statistics, newspaper reports in the local mainstream and ethnic press, documentary evidence from immigrant-serving nonprofits, two dozen recorded and televised hearings, and an assortment of government reports provided additional material.

Looking Ahead

Chapter 1 examines nonprofit organizations as distinctive contemporary agents of the movement for immigrant rights and immigrant integration. Through cross-historical and cross-organizational comparisons with political parties, labor unions, and churches, this chapter draws on the unique ways in which the activism of immigrant-serving nonprofits can be distinguished from that of other types of civic organizations. Contemporary immigrant-serving nonprofits are set apart by the lack of political and financial resources with which they can influence the political process. They are also subject to federal restrictions on the amount and types of advocacy they can do. Finally, their heavy reliance on local government funding creates dependencies that might make them less willing to engage in policy advocacy. These constraints do not necessarily prevent immigrant-serving nonprofits from taking an active and influential role in local political affairs but do explain the strategies they use to promote immigrant rights and integration policies. This chapter shows that nonprofits' expertise on immigrant communities is their most valuable resource and that city administrative officials are their most common advocacy targets and collaborators.

Chapter 2 contextualizes the role of immigrant-serving nonprofits in promoting immigrant rights and integration in San Francisco. It describes contemporary immigration to San Francisco and demonstrates the need for government policies addressing the needs of disadvantaged immigrants. Even though San Francisco is known as the most left-leaning big city in the United States, immigrant-serving nonprofits had to contend with three challenges embedded in the city's civic and political context. First, San Francisco has a hyperpluralist organizational landscape where immigrant-serving nonprofits must compete with many other interest groups seeking to effect policy change. Second, despite its progressive aura, political elites in San Francisco have put a lot of effort into promoting development policies that strengthen the city's economy, thus making it challenging for immigrant-serving nonprofits to advocate redistributive measures that benefit disadvantaged immigrants. Finally, the city's progressive political culture can be a liability for immigrant-serving nonprofits if the policies they advocate reflect local norms but run counter to federal immigration enforcement goals.

Chapters 3 through 5 elaborate the tripartite model of strategies that nonprofit advocates used to strengthen immigrant rights and integration in San Francisco. Chapter 3 focuses on nonprofits' use of cross-sectoral collaborations and administrative advocacy to enact and implement San Francisco's Equal Access to Services Ordinance. Educating and collaborating with elected and non-elected government officials allowed immigrant-serving nonprofits to have more influence in local politics and to serve the interests of disadvantaged immigrants more effectively, compared with advocacy tactics that relied only on confrontation with city hall. However, nonprofit collaborations with government officials introduced cooptive dynamics that risked blurring the public-private divide in ways that were not beneficial either to public officials or nonprofit organizations and the immigrants they represent.

Chapter 4 turns to immigrant labor rights and nonprofits' use of cross-organizational collaborations and administrative advocacy to enact and implement the Minimum Compensation and Minimum Wage Ordinances. It shows that immigrant-serving nonprofits and labor unions shared a commitment to immigrant rights and understood the need of working together to raise wages for the city's lowest paid workers. Yet, because unions had more resources and faced fewer restrictions on their lobbying and electioneering, these collaborations relegated nonprofits to the legislative and electoral shadows of unions as they sought to promote immigrants' labor rights. Immigrant-serving nonprofits, however, successfully influenced city administrators to implement the Minimum Wage Ordinance with maximum benefit to the city's non-unionized immigrant workforce. Nonprofits' success in administrative advocacy stemmed from the lack of interest in and experience with the public enforcement of wage laws on the part of unions as well as from nonprofits' expertise in dealing with local administrative officials.

Chapter 5 focuses on nonprofits' strategic issue framing to enact and implement the Municipal ID Ordinance that allows San Francisco to issue identification cards to undocumented immigrants. In the face of increased federal immigration enforcement and growing media scrutiny of San Francisco's welcoming treatment of undocumented immigrants, nonprofit advocates understood that it would be difficult to promote an ordinance benefiting only the city's undocumented immigrants. They subsequently framed the ordinance as a citywide public safety measure and policy promoting the civic integration of all city residents who have difficulty obtaining identification documents, including transgender individuals, the homeless, elderly, and youth. To minimize scrutiny of the ordinance still further, nonprofit advocates kept the text of the ordinance silent on the issue of immigration. Nonprofits' strategic approach to framing the issue explains why city officials enacted and implemented the Municipal ID Ordinance despite the political controversy surrounding it. While the media continued to refer to the card as an "immigrant card," nonprofits' strategic use of non–immigrant frames increased city officials' support for the ordinance and helped them to defeat a court challenge to the ordinance shortly after its enactment.

The conclusion draws out the lessons that the case studies hold for scholars and practitioners. It explores the applicability of the tripartite model of advocacy strategies to nonprofit organizations that represent disadvantaged immigrants in cities other than San Francisco. It ends by placing nonprofit immigrant rights advocacy in a national perspective and by underscoring how important it is that officials at all levels of government take more initiative in promoting immigrant integration.

CHAPTER 1

Nonprofit Organizations as Immigrant Rights Advocates

The Chinese Progressive Association (CPA) occupies a small fifth floor office on Grant Avenue, one of the oldest streets in San Francisco's bustling Chinatown. A product of the civil rights era, this immigrant-serving nonprofit was founded in 1972, when social movements for racial equality swept the country. The organization, long run by volunteers, hired its first paid staff person in the early 1990s, when it received funding from the City and County of San Francisco to organize fire prevention workshops for residents of single room occupancy hotels. By 2005, CPA's budget had grown to $500,000, allowing it to support a staff of six full-time employees and nine part-time community members who worked as peer organizers. Throughout its existence, CPA has maintained high levels of grassroots participation in all aspects of the organization.

Today, CPA is a mainstay of the community, offering a strong and progressive voice for low-income and primarily monolingual Chinese-speaking immigrants in San Francisco. It educates immigrants about their rights as tenants and workers, offers them personalized legal services, and organizes them in campaigns to fight substandard housing conditions and illegal employment practices. The organization has boycotted garment factories, restaurants, hotels, and other businesses that have violated immigrants' labor rights and staged protests at city hall to draw public attention to ongoing housing and labor law violations within immigrant communities. CPA also has pressured San Francisco officials into enacting and implementing stronger labor laws targeting employers, including those in the Chinese community who continue to exploit immigrant workers. Its advocacy has helped to secure several local laws that have improved the lives of low-wage immigrant workers, including the Minimum Wage Ordinance (2003), the Minimum Wage Implementation and Enforcement Ordinance (2006), and the Wage Theft Prevention Ordinance (2011). CPA has also won more than $700,000 in back wages for Chinese immigrant restaurant workers since 2004 (CPA 2015).

This type of community agitation on behalf of immigrant rights is no new phenomenon. At the turn of the twentieth century, settlement houses and mutual aid societies promoted the rights and integration of disadvantaged immigrants from Europe. They reached out to immigrants by tapping into gender issues, language, ethnicity, citizenship, or occupation, and they provided much-needed services, including English language training, job referrals, health care, and funeral benefits (Sterne 2001). They also taught leadership skills, got immigrants organized for civic and political purposes, and pressured local, state, and federal officials to address immigrant rights (Beito 2000; Davis 1994; Soyer 2006; Trolander 1987). The immigrant-serving nonprofits analyzed here mirror the tactics and strategies used by settlement houses and mutual aid societies a century ago.

Yesteryear's settlement houses and mutual aid societies routinely collaborated with local party organizations, labor unions, and religious institutions to promote immigrant rights and integration (Sterne 2001). These collaborations are now less common: Today's local party organizations are less able and less willing agents of immigrant integration (Jones–Correa 1998; Wong 2006), and today's unions remain divided over immigration issues (Burgoon et al. 2010; Jacobson and Geron 2008). Contemporary immigrant-serving nonprofits also are far more reliant on government funding and subject to federal restrictions on their advocacy. These restrictions did not exist a hundred years ago when settlement houses and mutual aid societies used mostly private funding to promote immigrant integration. Today's immigrant-serving nonprofits thus play a more central role in helping immigrant communities advance, but they must be far more strategic than their historical counterparts.

We can learn about the unique role of nonprofits that advocate for immigrant rights by comparing them with other types of civic organizations, defined as the totality of organizations that bring people together around shared interests, purposes, and values. They tend to be community-based and are distinct from public agencies and private businesses. Civic organizations include a great many different actors, take on diverse institutional forms, and differ in formality, autonomy, and power. They include political parties, religious institutions, labor unions, social service organizations, self-help groups, neighborhood associations, social movement organizations, women's organizations, and business associations. I juxtapose immigrant-serving nonprofits with political parties, labor unions, and religious institutions because they are all key agents of immigrant integration (Andersen 2010; de Graauw 2008; Gleeson 2012; Heredia 2008; Jones-Correa 1998; Milkman 2006; Mooney 2007; Ramakrishnan and Bloemraad 2008; Wong 2006).

It is instructive to compare civic organizations across time and to compare different types of contemporary civic organizations. When the advocacy of civic organizations on behalf of immigrants who came from Europe between 1850 and 1924 is compared with more recent efforts, it becomes clear that today's nonprofits play a more prominent role. It is also clear that nonprofits today face distinctive constraints but also have unique political resources. The first part of the chapter draws on examples from civic organizations across American gateway cities; the second part focuses on those in San Francisco.

Civic Organizations and Early European Immigrants

Civic organizations can provide services that facilitate immigrants' social, economic, and political mobility. They can help immigrants acquire U.S. citizenship; activate them to vote in local, state, and federal elections; and encourage them to run for political office. Civic organizations can also advocate for local, state, and federal policies and practices that reflect immigrants' needs and interests. Finally, they can get immigrants to participate in informal political activities, ranging from petition-signing campaigns to political rallies and protests. But not all of them have done these things equally.

Political Parties and Urban Machines

Historically, political parties served as the key agents of political involvement for early European immigrants. This was accomplished nationally through a competitive party system and locally through urban machines, namely local party organizations headed by "bosses" who dispensed favors to residents in exchange for their loyalty in the voting booth. Immigrants who arrived before 1880 came mostly from northwestern Europe and received a relatively warm reception from local political cultures (Sterne 2001). Noncitizens could vote in many parts of the country and parties competed intensely for new voters, held frequent elections, and promoted grassroots partisan activism during the 1840s and 1850s (Aylsworth 1931; Gerber 1989).[1] In contrast, southeastern European immigrants arriving between 1880 and 1924 faced more electoral obstacles and a less embracing political context. Noncitizen voting was less common, and the Republicans who dominated national and state politics in the second half of the nineteenth century often antagonized the newer immigrants (McGerr 1986; Sterne 2001).

Urban machines, which governed 75 percent of major American cities between 1890 and 1920 (Reichley 1992: 174), were fueled by the early European immigrant flows. Tammany Hall, the key Democratic Party machine in New York City from the 1790s to the 1960s, is often cited for promoting immigrants' political and economic integration. It opened its own naturalization bureau in 1840 and supplied immigrants with witnesses and sympathetic judges at their naturalization hearings (Schneider 2001; Valelly 2005). It recruited over forty thousand immigrant voters during New York's gubernatorial campaign of 1868, nominated immigrant co-ethnics for office, and lobbied state officials for immigrant-friendly legislation (Allswang 1986; Erie 1988). Tammany political bosses socialized with immigrants on a daily basis to learn about their concerns, created thousands of public-sector patronage jobs held by immigrant voters, and operated their own welfare system by distributing coal and food baskets to poor immigrants (Allswang 1986; O'Connor 1956).

These accomplishments notwithstanding, urban machines were self-interested institutions. They mobilized immigrants when it helped them to gain power in a competitive political environment but suppressed immigrants' votes to preserve the status quo or machines' privileged position (Erie 1988; Schneider 2001; Stone 1996). Also, machine politics were not governed by democratic principles. They were rife with corruption and often manipulated the votes of machine-dependent immigrants who knew little about American political affairs (Plotke 1999; Sterne 2001). Finally, because they sought to increase their hold on elected offices, machines focused on immigrants who could vote, namely solvent white men. They often ignored women, who did not get the right to vote until 1920, and Asian immigrants, who were barred from naturalization and the right to vote between 1790 and 1952.[2]

Labor Unions

Labor unions also promoted the rights and integration of early European immigrants. Union fights for labor protections from an unregulated market—including fights to increase wages, establish grievance procedures, and gain a voice in labor relations—strengthened the labor rights of economically disadvantaged immigrants. Unions representing the garment workers of Chicago, New York City, Philadelphia, and San Francisco—including the International Ladies' Garment Workers' Union and the Amalgamated Clothing Workers of America—actively organized immigrant workers, supported the creation of nationality-based unions, and published union newspapers in several foreign languages (La Luz and Finn 1998). The Knights of Labor and the Industrial Workers of the World also activated immigrants in the electoral arena (Plotke 1999; Sterne 2001).

Relations between labor unions and European immigrants, however, were frequently strained, if not openly hostile. Tensions intensified at the turn of the twentieth century when the old immigrants from northwestern Europe confronted the new immigrants from southeastern Europe. Viewing the new immigrants as economic threats, unions became increasingly divided over immigration and some became hostile toward them, especially immigrants of color (Chen and Wong 1998; Wong 2006). The American Federation of Labor (AFL) supported restrictive immigration measures like the 1882 Chinese Exclusion Act and the racially biased national origin quotas of the 1924 Immigration Act.

Early unions also were highly selective in which immigrants they organized and mobilized, excluding many disadvantaged immigrants from important labor and employment protections. The AFL, for example, was a craft union that protected jobs for union members by reaching out to older and skilled immigrants from Ireland and Germany but not the more recent and unskilled immigrants from southeastern Europe (Mink 1986). Labor unions also tended to be off limits to many immigrant women, and union-induced integration at times was coercive rather than voluntary.[3] Unions and employers pressured immigrants to naturalize during World War I, for example, when U.S. citizenship was a requirement for many union jobs (Gavit 1922).

Settlement Houses, Mutual Aid Societies, and Religious Institutions

Settlement houses, mutual aid societies, and religious institutions operated alongside political parties and unions to promote the rights and integration of early European immigrants. They did so precisely for immigrants who could not vote or lacked access to unions, including women, poor immigrants, and Chinese (Sterne 2001; Wong 2006). Settlement houses and mutual aid societies provided social services and civic education and were a jumping board into the political arena (Beito 2000; Sterne 2001). Religious institutions, especially the Catholic Church, also deepened ethnic ties and political skills among their immigrant congregants (Sterne 2001; Wong 2002).

Settlement houses, which totaled four hundred in 1910, were especially important for immigrant women (Fisher 2005; Lissak 1989). Hull House, perhaps the best known and most influential of all settlement houses, documented the harsh working conditions and bad housing and sanitation in the crowded immigrant neighborhoods of Chicago. First published in 1885 as the *Hull House Maps and Papers,* settlement workers used their findings to pressure city officials to provide public bathhouses, neighborhood parks, libraries, better waste collection and disposal, and night classes in public schools (Davis 1994; Trolander 1987). They lobbied Illinois and federal officials for child labor laws, occupational safety and health provisions, women's pensions, and protections for immigrants (Davis 1994; Elshtain 2002). Similarly, Henry Street Settlement in New York City, South End House in Boston, and South Park Settlement in San Francisco educated immigrants about sanitation and labor issues and lobbied city officials to deliver better city services in poor immigrant neighborhoods (Davis 1994; Koerin 2003; Streiff 2005).

Mutual aid societies, or fraternal orders, performed similar functions. A key difference, however, is that they were organized and run by immigrants, while outsiders operated settlement houses, often college-educated American women (Davis 1994; Sterne 2001). Because employers and governments did not yet provide social insurance, immigrants formed their own associations to pay for funerals and help members survive periods of illness and unemployment. These societies provided more direct relief to immigrants than any other institution, and in 1920, an estimated one in three adults belonged to a fraternal order (Beito 2000; Cohen 1990). Mutual aid societies also connected immigrants with American political life. The L'Ordine Figli d'Italia (the Order Sons of Italy), for instance, encouraged their Italian members to acquire American citizenship and taught them democratic traditions, such as free speech, by involving them in organizational activities (Sterne 2001). The Ancient Order of Hibernians, an Irish mutual aid society, and the Alianza Hispano-Americana (Hispanic-American Alliance), a Mexican mutual aid society, also protested discrimination against their members (Soyer 2006).

The Roman Catholic Church was a notable force promoting immigrant rights and integration. As a result of large-scale Irish migration, the Catholic Church grew from a relatively small denomination in 1815 to the nation's largest denomination, with over 9 million members, at century's end ("Church Growth in 1901" 1902; Dolan 1975). Dioceses operated hospitals, working girls' homes, orphanages, and parochial schools, and local parishes offered charitable assistance to the hungry, poor, and homeless, regardless of gender, citizenship, country of origin, or occupation. Parishes served as social and recreational centers in immigrant neighborhoods (Sterne 2001). At times, the Catholic Church enabled their immigrant parishioners to move from private devotion to public activism (Tentler 1997). Church members also organized naturalization and voter registration drives and advocated against the federal immigration restrictions enacted in the 1920s (Sterne 2001).

The efforts of settlement houses, mutual aid societies, and religious institutions to advance the immigrant cause also had limits. Their tactics could be coercive and prove costly to immigrants. Some settlement houses, for example, discouraged immigrants from maintaining ethnic customs and practices (Sterne 2001; Wong 2006). Also, they did not always have a tangible link with immigrant rights. Mutual aid societies and religious institutions varied in the extent to which they took explicit political positions on immigrant issues or encouraged the civic and political participation of their members (Beito 2000; Sterne 2001).

Despite their shortcomings, these organizations had collectively helped a significant portion of early European immigrants to integrate into American society by the beginning of the twentieth century. The extent to which they worked together to accomplish this is remarkable. In 1920s Chicago, for example, mutual aid societies directed their members and organizational resources to local labor unions and the Democratic Party (Cohen 1990). Ethnic social and recreational clubs in New York City had close connections with local political parties and provided naturalization assistance to immigrants (Peel 1935). Irish immigrants in 1920s Providence used their church organizations to coordinate local political campaigns and to lobby for workplace legislation (Sterne 2001). Both the staff and residents of settlement houses in New York City participated in local party politics and the city's mayoral campaigns at the end of the nineteenth century (Davis 1994). By building thick networks of civic activism, these early civic organizations engendered mutually reinforcing modes of immigrant integration.

Civic Organizations and Contemporary Asian and Latin American Immigrants

The integration of post-1965 immigrants from Asia and Latin America is taking place in a vastly different institutional context. Local party organizations are largely absent from the local mobilization process, and other types of civic organizations—most notably immigrant-serving nonprofits—have taken the central role in advocating immigrant rights and integration (de Graauw 2008; Wong 2006).

Political Parties

The wave of newcomers arriving after the liberalization of immigration policy in 1965 entered urban environments where political parties had long been in decline. Progressive-era reforms at the end of the nineteenth century, including the introduction of the secret ballot, nonpartisan elections, and direct primaries, had begun to weaken local party control over election procedures and election outcomes (Reichley 1992). The movement to merit-based, professionalized local bureaucracies also eroded the system of patronage upon which urban machines relied. More recently, the expanding role of the federal government in the American welfare system since the 1930s, the growth of alternative political organizations prompted by the civil rights movement and the War on Poverty, and the rise of media-driven and candidate-centered politics in the 1960s and 1970s all further weakened city party organizations (Wattenberg 1996, 2001). In 1986, California voters amended the state constitution to require all municipal elections, including those in San Francisco, to be nonpartisan so that candidates' party affiliations are not included on the ballot.

As political parties lost their grassroots organizational vigor and became nationalized, it became *more difficult* for local party organizations to promote immigrant integration in ways they had in earlier times (Sterne 2001; Wong 2006). Local parties, however, have also become *less willing* agents of immigrant integration. In their quest for votes in a low-turnout era, political parties increasingly strategically target voters whose behavior is predictable. These include people who already vote and have better incomes and education and stronger partisanship (Rosenstone and Hansen 1993; Wolfinger and Rosenstone 1980). At the same time, redistricting has created bias in favor of incumbents and reduced competition in a two-party winner-takes-all system.[4] In such electoral environments, the majority party has little interest in activating unpredictable new voters, while the minority party does not want to waste resources on mobilizing voters who will not provide an electoral win. The joint result is that neither party will invest in organizing new immigrants.[5]

Various scholars have documented the diminished role of local party organizations in promoting immigrant rights and integration. Jones-Correa's (1998) study of Latino immigrants in Queens, New York, highlights the local Democratic Party's passivity toward naturalizing or registering Latino immigrants or getting them out to vote, much less recruiting them into the party's political clubs. In that era, the Queens Democratic Party did not mobilize the Latino community because it did not need their votes to win elections. Likewise, Rogers (2006) documents how the Democratic Party in Brooklyn, New York, ignored Afro-Caribbean immigrants, many of whom are recent noncitizen arrivals. Finally, Wong's comparative study of Asian and Latino immigrants in New York City and Los Angeles concludes that "local party organizations—the institutions critical to the mobilization of earlier waves of European immigrants—no longer mobilize newcomers in a consistent and committed fashion" (2006: 10).

In San Francisco, the site of this study, the county party organizations are particularly weak, and they do not enjoy much visibility with the electorate. The dominance of the Democratic Party is overwhelming, and more than 75 percent of San Francisco voters have voted Democratic in every presidential election since 2000. The San Francisco Republican Party has thus become a vestigial institution. In the context of nonpartisan and uncompetitive local elections, Democratic constituencies have become fragmented while third parties such as the Green and Libertarian Parties have little motivation to bring immigrants and other new voters into the civic and political system (DeLeon 1992).

Political clubs are integral to San Francisco's political scene, and the Democratic County Central Committee works with twenty-seven chartered clubs to represent active Democrats throughout the city. These clubs, which initially arose during the 1950s as part of the reformist Adlai Stevenson wing of the Democratic Party, play a key role in candidate recruitment and endorsement. Three clubs—the Asian Pacific Democratic Club, the Filipino American Democratic Club, and the Latino Democratic Club—extend their activities also to newcomer communities. However, they as well as the other twenty-four clubs mostly mobilize already engaged Democrats, who tend to be socioeconomically better off. They pay little attention to disadvantaged immigrants, especially noncitizens without the right to vote.

Nonprofit advocates often commented on how passive San Francisco political parties and clubs are about immigrant integration. An advocate with Partnership for Immigrant Leadership and Action, a nonprofit then located in the Mission district that provided technical assistance to other immigrant-serving nonprofits, observed that "the [San Francisco] Democratic and Republican Parties dutifully gather at Masonic Auditorium twice a month to try to register new citizens as they leave the naturalization ceremony. But I haven't seen a concerted or sustained effort by party leaders to educate new citizens about the political process or to make sure they'll use their vote further down the line."[6] An advocate with CPA noted that local party organizations are especially inattentive to poor Chinese immigrants: "The political parties haven't demonstrated a sincere commitment to the Chinese community. They mobilize the Chinese American middle class in the western part of town, but they ignore the low-income Chinese immigrants in Chinatown and Visitacion Valley."[7] San Francisco political parties are clearly not leading the efforts to promote immigrant rights and immigrant integration.

Labor Unions

After decades of viewing immigrants as economic threats, big city labor unions now pay much more attention to nonwhite and unskilled immigrants. In response to rapidly declining membership rates, they are reaching out to Asian and Latin American workers—including undocumented immigrants—in the expanding service sectors. Some American Federation of Labor–Congress of Industrial Organizations (AFL-CIO) unions have been organizing immigrant workers since the mid-1980s.[8] The AFL-CIO's national leadership, however, changed its official position on immigration only in 2000, when it issued a statement calling for amnesty for undocumented immigrants and repeal of employer sanctions enacted in 1986 with the Immigration Reform and Control Act (AFL-CIO 2001). Additionally, in 2005, seven unions representing sectors of the economy with many immigrant workers broke away from the AFL-CIO and formed the Change to Win coalition with promises to be more aggressive in unionizing low-wage jobs commonly held by immigrants.[9]

Despite these efforts by the AFL-CIO and its rival Change to Win, unions still have limited ability to promote Asian and Latino immigrant integration. The institutionalized labor movement still privileges white, male, and skilled workers in union leadership positions and decision-making processes. It has also been slow to organize immigrant workers in such hard-to-organize sectors as restaurants, retail establishments, and contingent work performed by day laborers (Bobo 2008). Unions also remain divided on a number of immigration issues and struggle to incorporate immigrants into leadership positions. La Luz and Finn (1998) and Gleeson (2012), for example, find that unions can be insensitive to the diversity within immigrant communities and do not conduct union meetings or make union publications readily available in languages other than English. Finally, only 9 percent of today's immigrant workers are unionized, which means that the vast majority of immigrants do not interact with unions (Milkman and Braslow 2011).

The San Francisco labor community has been more attentive to immigrant workers than unions in many other parts of the country. HERE Local 2, which represents city hotel workers and merged with the Union of

Needletrades, Industrial, and Textile Employees (UNITE) in 2004, is one of the most inclusive unions in San Francisco. It has been organizing immigrant workers since the late 1970s. As a first step, Local 2 began printing its materials in Spanish, Chinese, and Tagalog. It hired multilingual organizers and used translators at all union meetings to solicit the input and participation of its immigrant members, and in 1985 it allowed noncitizens to hold union leadership positions. Over time, HERE Local 2 changed union contracts to include an extended leave policy so that immigrants can travel back to their home countries for family emergencies (Wells 2000).

The San Francisco Labor Council (SFLC), which operates as the county-wide federation of local labor unions within the AFL-CIO, has taken some steps to include immigrants, though later than Local 2 and some of its other affiliates. Between 2006 and 2010, the SFLC adopted several resolutions supporting the legalization of undocumented workers and opposing federal workplace raids in the Bay Area (SFLC 2006, 2007, 2009a–b, 2010a–c). The SFLC and local unions with many immigrant members—such as Local 2 and SEIU UHW Local 250, which represents home health care workers—have also battled to improve the labor conditions for immigrant workers. They played active roles in the campaigns to enact the 2000 Minimum Compensation Ordinance and the 2003 Minimum Wage Ordinance, discussed at length in chapter 4, which raised pay for low-wage workers throughout the city, over 60 percent of whom are immigrants ("Long-overdue Paychecks" 2005).

Nonprofit informants applauded unions' increased activism on immigrant rights and integration issues in San Francisco. Yet they also pointed out that unions remain irrelevant for many disadvantaged immigrants, including limited English proficient immigrants, elderly immigrants, and undocumented immigrants. An advocate with the Southeast Asian Community Center located in the Tenderloin district noted that "unions aren't familiar with the languages and cultures of the Southeast Asian community and aren't very active on senior issues. . . . They don't reach out to the clients our agency serves."[10] Likewise, an advocate with La Raza Centro Legal (the Community's Legal Center) in the Mission district mentioned that the most vulnerable immigrant workers remain without union protection:

> The folks that come here for assistance are exactly the immigrants who are not members of unions. They're immigrants without papers and immigrants who work in non-unionized jobs and jobs that are challenging to organize, like restaurant workers, domestic workers, and day laborers. In essence, our work helps to extend labor protections to these

workers. . . . At the same time, an important part of our program is that we educate immigrant workers about their rights in the workplace and we help them develop the skills so they can organize around issues that are important to them.[11]

San Francisco's labor unions also have a hard time addressing the many nonlabor issues that immigrants care about. In her study of HERE Local 2, Wells refers to this as the challenge of unions in "venturing outside the bounds of workplace concerns" (2000: 259). San Francisco's hotel workforce includes immigrants from China, the Philippines, Vietnam, Korea, Laos, El Salvador, Mexico, Nicaragua, and Guatemala. This diversity means that the majority of workers agree on only a few issues, making it difficult for union leaders to speak out on issues that are important only to a segment of their immigrant members. Local 2 has taken stands on issues such as affordable housing, immigration, and foreign policy, but some immigrant members have criticized these positions, thereby weakening union unity and undermining its ability to represent all hotel workers (Wells 2000).

All in all, labor unions—including those in San Francisco—have become more accommodating of contemporary Asian and Latin American immigrants. Their ability to promote immigrant rights and integration has been limited, however, by their difficulty in reaching out to language minority communities, elderly immigrants, and undocumented immigrants as well as their focus on labor issues to the exclusion of other issues relevant to disadvantaged immigrants.

Religious Institutions

Religious institutions continue to be important promoters of immigrant rights and integration. Churches provide services to immigrants, foster their civic skills, motivate their participation in public life, and advocate their interests in the policy arena. The country's religious quilt has become much more diverse with the arrival of large numbers of Asian and Latin American immigrants, who have introduced new faiths and are revitalizing old ones. Muslim mosques, Sikh gurdwaras, and to a lesser extent Jewish synagogues and Hindu and Buddhist temples now join Catholic and Protestant churches as institutional points of entry into economic, civic, and political life in the United States (Foley and Hoge 2007; Levitt 2007; Wong 2006).

Motivated by prospects of attracting new members and guided by the faith-based mandate to help those in need, many religious institutions offer religious services in foreign languages and encourage immigrants to naturalize, register, and vote (Foley and Hoge 2007; Wong 2006). The Catholic Church in particular has taken outspoken positions and advocated for humane immigration policies (Heredia 2008; Mooney 2007). Religious institutions have also used new transportation and communication technologies to act transnationally and engage their immigrant members in civic and political affairs in both their home countries and the United States (Foley and Hoge 2007; Levitt 2007).

Since World War II, Catholic and Protestant churches have worked with federal, state, and local governments to resettle refugees, initially from eastern Europe and later Cuba and war-torn countries such as Vietnam, Bosnia, Sudan, and Iraq. During the 1980s, five hundred congregations nationwide participated in the Sanctuary Movement, which brought refugees to the United States from Central America to offer them sanctuary—or faith-based protection—from U.S.-sponsored civil war violence in Guatemala and El Salvador. The Sanctuary Movement also helped refugees learn English and find jobs. Stung by the Sanctuary Movement's challenge to U.S. foreign policy, the federal government began arresting sanctuary workers and refugees in the mid-1980s. In defiance of these arrests, more congregations offered sanctuary, and local governments declared their cities to be sanctuary cities.[12] A number of sanctuary churches also brought suit against federal officials in 1985, resulting in a settlement agreement in 1991 that offered asylees fleeing civil war in Central America fairer judicial treatment and greater protections in the United States.[13]

A "New Sanctuary Movement" took root in the mid-2000s in response to congressional immigration reform proposals and the much-publicized struggles of Elvira Arellano, an undocumented Mexican immigrant who took refuge in a Chicago church in 2006 but was arrested and deported to Mexico in 2007 (Archibold 2007; Dyrness and Irazábal 2007). It continues to draw strong support from the interfaith community but provides sanctuary to undocumented immigrants generally, not just to Central American war refugees. The New Sanctuary Movement, furthermore, does not take aim at U.S. foreign policy but criticizes the federal government's enforcement tactics to detain and deport undocumented immigrants, including worksite raids and state and local law enforcement collaborations with programs such as 287(g), Secure Communities, and the Criminal Alien Program.

Latin American and East Asian immigrants have swelled membership in the Catholic Church, which today remains the single largest denomination among immigrants.[14] The Catholic Church has been particularly active in debates about immigrant rights. During the 1960s, Catholic leaders supported farm worker strikes and boycotts organized by the United

Farm Workers, a union founded by Cesar Chavez in the early 1960s to organize migrant farm workers (Ganz 2009; García 2005). They also supported amnesty for undocumented immigrants as part of the 1986 Immigration Reform and Control Act and opposed Proposition 187, a 1994 state initiative designed to deny social services to undocumented immigrants in California (Heredia 2008). Finally, in the 1990s, they partnered with labor unions, immigrant-serving nonprofits, and advocacy groups for the poor in campaigns to enact living wage ordinances for immigrants and other low-wage workers in cities nationwide (Luce 2004).

As the U.S. Congress failed to enact comprehensive immigration reform, the Catholic Church has become more vocal about immigrant rights. Nearly eighty dioceses nationwide participated in the "Justice for Immigrants" campaign in 2005, and the Catholic Church helped organize the immigration protests that swept the country in 2006 (Heredia 2008; Voss and Bloemraad 2011). A number of prominent Catholic leaders lobbied the George W. Bush administration against congressional legislation that would criminalize undocumented immigrants and those who provide services to them. Most notably, Cardinal Roger Mahony of the Los Angeles Archdiocese made headlines in 2005 and 2006 when he announced that he would instruct his priests to defy provisions of the ill-fated H.R. 4437 (the Border Protection, Anti-terrorism, and Illegal Immigration Control Act of 2005) that would require them to ask immigrants for residency documents before administering certain kinds of assistance (Allen, Jr. 2006; Heredia 2008).

The San Francisco Archdiocese has also been active. Several Catholic priests advocated for the rights of Filipino immigrant workers at San Francisco International Airport (SFO) after the 2001 terrorist attacks, when the 2001 Aviation and Transportation Security Act required airport baggage screeners to be American citizens. At the time, four-fifths of SFO's two thousand baggage screeners were recent immigrants, including eight hundred Filipinos.[15] To try to protect Filipino screeners' jobs, local parishes helped them to apply for U.S. citizenship, organized protests, and supported lawsuits challenging the law in federal court. This campaign brought good media publicity to the issue and organized the local Filipino community in support of immigrant rights, but many Filipino screeners still lost their jobs. San Francisco–based churches were more successful in advocating with labor unions and immigrant-serving nonprofits to enact the 2000 Minimum Compensation Ordinance and the 2003 Minimum Wage Ordinance (see chapter 4).

Faith-based advocacy certainly is not universal across denominations but depends on religious leaders' theological orientation and willingness to stake out an activist role in politics. While Catholic priests and Lutheran ministers have taken openly pro-immigrant advocacy positions, some religious leaders from theologically conservative Protestant congregations aligned with the Christian Coalition of America have taken anti-immigrant stands (Dart 1996; Wong 2006). Other religious faiths typically do not advocate immigration issues at all. Hindu temples, for example, generally consider themselves to be apolitical institutions. Some Latino and Asian evangelical Protestant churches even have an anti-political orientation and discourage the civic and political involvement of their members, who instead are encouraged to focus inward on personal salvation through participation in an intense community of God (Foley and Hoge 2007; Levitt 2007).

San Francisco churches have not consistently supported immigrant rights either. In the last decade, even as local Catholic priests came forward as immigrant rights advocates, the San Francisco Archdiocese only rarely mobilized for social justice and provided no leadership on immigration issues. Under the conservative leadership of William Levada, archbishop of San Francisco between 1995 and 2006, the Catholic Church of San Francisco had no involvement with the immigration protests of 2006, which were organized entirely by local immigrant-serving nonprofits (Shaw 2006). Archdiocesan leaders in other gateway cities such as Los Angeles and Chicago, in contrast, were at the forefront of organizing the 2006 protests against federal immigration reform proposals in their respective cities (Heredia 2008; Pallares and Flores-González 2010).

Immigrant-Serving Nonprofits

In recent decades, immigrant-serving nonprofits have become more prominent advocates for immigrant rights and integration. Three distinct dynamics have driven this development. First, the renewal of large-scale immigration after 1965 increased the need and demand for newcomer services. With local political parties uninterested in reaching out to immigrants, many labor unions still divided on immigration issues, and religious institutions uneven in their advocacy, a proliferating number of immigrant-serving nonprofits have stepped into the breach. Their numbers increased in not only traditional immigrant metropolises like Chicago, New York City, and Los Angeles but also in the newer immigrant destinations of the South and Southwest (Andersen 2010; Brettell and Reed-Danahay 2012; Cordero-Guzmán 2005; de Leon et al. 2009; Hung 2007; Wong 2006).

Second, federal, state, and local governments have increasingly turned to nonprofit organizations to provide social and human services. This pattern was set by the Great Society programs of the 1960s—including the Urban Renewal, Model Cities, and Neighborhood Development programs that the Nixon administration merged in 1974 to become the Community Development Block Grant program—which awarded funding to community-based nonprofits to provide services to extinguish poverty and foster community development in poor urban areas. The privatization of the American welfare state since the late 1970s further contributed to the expansion of the nonprofit sector by making nonprofits the key vehicles for the provision of social services to the poor and other disadvantaged groups (Grønbjerg 1993; Salamon 1999; Smith and Lipsky 1993). The rise of nonprofits providing immigrant services has been a small but important part of this overall trend.

Finally, the civil rights movement of the 1950s and 1960s legitimized advocacy by African American organizations and created a spinoff that favored advocacy for other racial and ethnic minority groups as well (Minkoff 1995). It opened up the political arena for immigrant-serving nonprofits, with an attendant increase in opportunities for them to advocate the rights and integration of disadvantaged immigrants from Asia and Latin America. Nonprofit advocacy for immigrants is now spread across localities nationwide, including older and newer immigrant-receiving cities such as Atlanta, Boston, Charlotte, Chicago, Houston, Los Angeles, New York City, Phoenix, San Francisco, and Washington, D.C., as well as their surrounding suburbs. This advocacy has addressed a wide range of issues, including immigrants' language access and education rights, labor rights, housing rights, voting rights, identification rights, and interactions with police and other law enforcement officials (Andersen 2010; Bloemraad 2006; Cordero-Guzmán et al. 2008; de Graauw 2014, 2015a-b; de Leon et al. 2009; Frasure and Jones-Correa 2010; Gleeson 2012; Hayduk 2006; Jones-Correa 2008; Lewis and Provine 2011; Modares and Kitson 2008; Odem 2008; Smith and Furuseth 2008; Varsanyi 2007).

San Francisco is an important case in point. Its immigrant-serving nonprofits balance dual missions of service provision and advocacy, and their unique community expertise positions them well to promote immigrant rights and integration policies. At the same time, public policy advocacy has been challenging for them compared with other types of civic organizations. Nonprofits are subject to more government restrictions on their political activities, have fewer resources with which to influence the policymaking process, and have a harder time maintaining autonomy due to their reliance on government funding.

Immigrant-Serving Nonprofits in San Francisco

San Francisco has a large and vibrant nonprofit sector, consisting of public charities, private foundations, and religious institutions that have incorporated as 501(c)(3) tax-exempt, not-for-profit organizations. With 6.9 nonprofits per 1,000 city residents in 2005, San Francisco has almost twice the density of 501(c)(3) organizations than California or the nation, with 2.9 and 3.2 nonprofits per 1,000 residents, respectively (NCCS 2006). San Francisco–based nonprofits are also healthier in terms of net assets and have larger annual budgets (Gammal et al. 2005). The robust nature of San Francisco's nonprofit sector puts it in a good position to develop and incubate new ideas and activities, including those designed to further the rights and integration of disadvantaged immigrants.

This study focuses on 501(c)(3) public charities—not private foundations and churches—that serve or advocate on behalf of immigrants, have offices in San Francisco, and have immigrants for at least 30 percent of their clientele. According to my estimates, the city had 216 such organizations in 2006.[16] Table 2 reports data from my 2007 survey of the one hundred most visible and active immigrant-serving nonprofits. It summarizes the variation in age, size (budget and full-time staff), sources of funding, staff characteristics, and client characteristics. This organizational diversity makes it hard to generalize about immigrant-serving nonprofits and sometimes creates tensions within coalitions of immigrant-serving nonprofits. They nonetheless constitute a coherent group because they all have the 501(c)(3) status and, in one way or another, promote the rights and integration of disadvantaged immigrants.

Dual Missions

Immigrant-serving nonprofits have a dual and sometimes conflicting identity. They provide many types of services, including basic information and referral as well as more specialized employment, housing, health, immigration, naturalization, and translation services. But while services are a key component of what they do, they are increasingly also engaging in advocacy and political activism.

Some immigrant-serving nonprofits voluntarily enter politics because they see public policy advocacy as deeply intertwined with service provision and, indeed, sometimes a precondition for it. As the executive director of La Raza Centro Legal explained:

Table 2 Organizational profile of immigrant-serving nonprofits in San Francisco: Selected statistics, 2007

		Age[a]	Annual budget	Percent private funding	Percent all government funding[b]	Percent local government funding[c]	Full-time[d] paid staff	Percent foreign-born paid staff	Percent bilingual paid staff	Percent foreign-born clients	Percent poor[e] foreign-born clients
N	Valid	100	96	94	94	93	97	88	92	100	85
	Missing	0	4	6	6	7	3	12	8	0	15
Mean		33.9	$3,152,981	62.7	36.1	24.3	25.8	45.6	64.3	64.9	69
Stand. dev.		31.7	$9,278,074	35	34.7	30.1	51.1	32.5	32.8	26.1	30.7
Minimum		5	$0	0	0	0	0	0	0	30	0
Maximum		154	$75,000,000	100	100	100	260	100	100	100	100
Percentiles	25	15	$307,500	30	0	0	3	20	31.5	40	50
	50	27.5	$745,500	70	29	10.2	8	40	76	67.5	75
	75	36	$1,692,000	100	65	45	260	72.5	95	90	95

[a] Based on an organization's founding year.

[b] Funding from the federal, state/CA, and local/SF governments.

[c] Funding from the City and County of San Francisco.

[d] Working 30 or more hours per week.

[e] Living below the federal poverty line.

Our mission is to promote a just and equal society, and the way we do that is through the provision of direct legal services and a community empowerment-style of advocacy. And the reason we do it this way is that we recognize that services alone don't challenge the causes of injustice or inequality; you need advocacy for that as well.[17]

Nonprofits like La Raza see no contradiction in using services to remedy the symptoms of a limited public service system while also using local political advocacy to empower immigrants and fight the injustices that disadvantaged immigrants face.

Other immigrant-serving nonprofits are more reluctant to enter politics, often fearing they might lose their government funding. The executive director of Asian Perinatal Advocates, a Chinatown-based nonprofit, observed:

Ideally, we'd like to focus more exclusively on service provision to the immigrant community, but with all these funding cuts we need to advocate. . . . My trips to city hall and our advocacy for continued funding are simply necessary aspects of what we do.[18]

Government retrenchment has pushed many immigrant-serving nonprofits to advocate for the funding needed to secure their survival and to continue the provision of services that promote immigrant well-being.

Regardless of whether immigrant-serving nonprofits pursue greater involvement in local public affairs actively or reluctantly, the reality is that they are dual-mission organizations that merge service provision with political advocacy. My survey data show that a majority of immigrant-serving nonprofits in San Francisco are dedicated to both missions. Of the 100 immigrant-serving nonprofits surveyed, 24 reported focusing exclusively on service provision, 4 reported advocacy as their primary mission, and the remaining 72 organizations reported both.

As dual-mission organizations, immigrant-serving nonprofits are well situated to connect immigrant communities with city government. Since they typically provide services in a linguistically accessible and culturally appropriate manner, their immigrant clients trust them even when they are reluctant or fearful to contact government directly for the help they need (Cordero-Guzmán 2005; de Leon et al. 2009). Through services and daily interaction with their clients, immigrant-serving nonprofits gain a deep understanding of the immigrant communities they serve. This gives them an unrivaled expertise on the particular challenges and needs of these communities—a valuable commodity for local governments—and helps them to develop compelling advocacy agendas for them. The advocacy component creates and reinforces lines of communication between immigrant-serving nonprofits and various city officials and city agencies. Nonprofits thus become important intermediaries when there are few direct lines of communication between immigrants and city government.

Immigrant-serving nonprofits know they provide important connections between immigrants and city government, and so do local government officials. Several members of the Board of Supervisors—San Francisco's legislative officials—commented that immigrant-serving nonprofits provide them with additional eyes and ears on the ground and help them stay informed about the needs of their district residents. The assessor-recorder summed this up as follows:

> Immigrant rights groups play a critical role in representing a part of the population that at times is so invisible and that many of us—especially those of us who are English speakers and including some of the people I work with here at city hall—don't really come across all that often. It's sad to say, but we live in the same city but often move in separate worlds. I think these immigrant rights groups function like essential bridges between these two worlds.[19]

This bridging function enables immigrant-serving nonprofits to involve their clients in the advocacy process. Nonprofit employees tend to see services as a first and crucial line of contact that enables them to help immigrants develop leadership skills in advocacy campaigns. On this point, an advocate with La Raza Centro Legal commented:

> We explicitly ask immigrants who receive our legal services to participate in our leadership development programs and advocacy campaigns. We want them to understand that their personal problem is often a problem shared by others in the community. . . . It's really a systemic problem, and they can help build community power by becoming community activists. . . . I can give you a specific example of how this works. For example, a while back we mobilized day laborers who benefited from our legal services and we asked them to join the picket lines for other workers to help them recover their unpaid wages. We asked them to give back to the community through activism.[20]

Similarly, a CPA advocate recalled when an employer fired 120 Chinese garment workers without paying severance. CPA legal counsel enabled the affected workers to secure two months' severance pay. Some workers then joined CPA advocacy campaigns, partly because they wanted to reciprocate and partly because CPA had invited them to do so. In sum, immigrant-serving nonprofits can become institutional representatives for immigrant communities and mobilize them in the advocacy process.

Community Expertise

Nonprofits' expertise about immigrant communities also helps them promote immigrant rights and integration. They develop this expertise in several ways. Of the 100 immigrant-serving nonprofits under study, 63 conducted surveys of their immigrant clients. In addition, 34 held focus groups with their clients, 37 regularly organized public meetings in immigrant neighborhoods, and 28 conducted their own research on immigrant issues. Nonprofits' daily interactions with immigrants are most important, however. Sixty-nine relied most on these interactions to collect information about their clients. Organizations lacking such daily interactions, like political parties, labor unions, and religious institutions, clearly have a harder time learning from these immigrant communities.

The city's long immigration history has allowed older organizations to share their knowledge with newer ones. Sixty-eight of the 216 immigrant-serving nonprofits (31%) active in San Francisco in 2006 had acquired nonprofit status before 1980. These older organizations incubated new ones as the city's immigrant population changed. The International Institute of San Francisco, for example, was founded in 1918 to help settle early immigrants from Europe. As large numbers of Asian immigrants arrived after 1965, it helped found the Chinese Newcomers Service Center in 1969, the Filipino Newcomer Service Center in 1972, and the Center for Southeast Asian Refugee Resettlement (which became the Southeast Asian Community Center) in 1975. Older and newer organizations learn from one another, in cooperative and sometimes competitive ways, and staff and volunteers rotate among immigrant-serving nonprofits. Several nonprofit staff interviewed at the beginning of my research in 2005 and 2006 were working for other immigrant-serving nonprofits in the city in 2008 and 2009. Institutional incubation and staff rotation facilitate information sharing and the accumulation of expertise within and across immigrant-serving nonprofits.

Nonprofits translated their community expertise into influence with San Francisco officials who were struggling to learn about the needs and interests of a large and growing portion of city residents. "These immigrant organizations are the main touch points for members of the immigrant community because they have more interaction with the members of that community than the city does," the assessor-recorder said. "They're the ones who'll be representing the voices of many of these immigrant families and households in the political process here."[21] The city administrator even believes that immigrant-serving nonprofits have the responsibility to share their expertise with government:

> [Immigrant-serving nonprofits] play an important role in identifying shortcomings of various city programs. They should be there because essentially they represent people who have yet to gain access to government. And that's the role nonprofits should play, I think, to help us identify where we fall short. Because once you get into government, you have so much bureaucracy to deal with . . . that it's easy to forget we still got to go the extra mile to make sure that the bureaucracy actually meets the needs of immigrants and other constituents we've pledged to serve.[22]

These quotes show that San Francisco officials want to learn about the city's immigrants but lack in-house capacity to do this on their own. District supervisors each have only three aides, and they lack the time or resources to build relations with immigrant constituents. The city bureaucracy is large, with over twenty-nine thousand city employees, but its hierarchical organization makes it challenging for city administrative staff to learn about the evolving needs of immigrants. Finally, immigrants often find government intimidating and do not engage city officials directly. "Immigrants are reluctant to go to city agencies for help," an advocate with CPA said. "This is certainly true of the Chinese immigrants we serve. Many of them are afraid, even when we tell them that these agencies are good guys that are willing to help. . . . But it's understandable given the experiences they've had with government back home."[23]

Immigrant-serving nonprofits, in contrast, are more welcoming and often have immigrants on their staff. They are smaller organizations located in the neighborhoods where immigrants live, and they serve immigrants in linguistically accessible and culturally appropriate ways. As a result, immigrant service seekers find them more trustworthy and more accessible. Nonprofits can also better personalize services and adjust to changing needs. A Zellerbach Family Foundation program officer articulated well the advantage of nonprofits over government agencies:

> Even when large government institutions will miraculously become language accessible and culturally competent, they won't take the place

of smaller nonprofit organizations. These nonprofits act like a home away from home for people and they understand better than anybody else what the needs and challenges of newcomers are. . . . It would be phenomenal if city departments would become fully language accessible, but you'd still need nonprofits because the demographics are always changing. Nonprofits, from my experience, have greater flexibility to respond to these changing demographics.[24]

Several informants added that nonprofit services cost a fraction of what city departments would need to pay to offer comparable services. The executive director of Asian Perinatal Advocates commented:

It's difficult for [the Department of Human Services] to provide our services in a way that's effective and efficient. The Asian population is so diverse that even if DHS hired a Chinese worker, it doesn't mean that this person can work with all the Asian immigrant groups that we work with. . . . There is no way they can offer [services] the way we can. Plus the salary of city workers is a lot higher than our salary, so it's cheaper for DHS to give funding to the community to provide these services than to try to do things in-house.[25]

In sum, immigrant-serving nonprofits fill several niches that city government leaves empty. They are better at providing services than city government. This gives them valuable insights into the needs and interests of the city's immigrant communities. This expertise in turn becomes a resource for nonprofits when they advocate for government policies and practices that promote immigrant advancement.

Nonprofit Advocacy for Immigrant Rights

How do immigrant-serving nonprofits go about promoting immigrant rights and integration? Existing scholarship provides little insight. Scholars like Berry and Arons (2003) argue that government rules and regulations circumscribe nonprofit advocacy and discourage nonprofits from participating in the policymaking process. On the other hand, Wong (2006) recognizes that nonprofits have an important political role but inadvertently clusters immigrant-serving nonprofits with many other kinds of organizations, making it difficult to distinguish their activism from that of labor unions, churches, and other civic organizations. Neither the disenfranchisement thesis of Berry and Arons nor the catch-all approach of Wong adequately captures the complexity of nonprofits' advocacy in city politics.

Immigrant-serving nonprofits differ from other types of civic organizations in three key ways. First, they are subject to more government restrictions on their political activities. Second, they have relatively fewer political resources with which to influence the policymaking process. Third, they have a harder time maintaining autonomy because many rely on government funding through contracts with city departments and agencies. These constraints have led many scholars to conclude that they are therefore unable to effect policy change (Andrews and Edwards 2004; Bass et al. 2007; Berry and Arons 2003; Boris and Steuerle 2006). A better way of thinking about the situation is to ask how these constraints explain the strategies that immigrant-serving nonprofits use to promote immigrant rights and integration policies.

Government Restrictions

The federal Internal Revenue Service (IRS) restricts the political activities of 501(c)(3) nonprofit organizations. Nonprofits pay this price in order to receive exemption from federal income taxes and to secure for their donors the ability to deduct their contributions from income taxation. State and local governments also exempt 501(c)(3) nonprofits from other major taxes, including income, property, and sales taxes. California 501(c)(3) organizations enjoy exemption from state income tax as well as state and local property taxes, but they do not have a blanket exemption from the sales tax. The IRS, however, remains the key source of regulations for 501(c)(3) nonprofits.

The federal restrictions on nonprofit political activities reflect congressional efforts to keep the U.S. Treasury neutral in political affairs and to prevent taxpayers from subsidizing nonprofit influences on legislation (Brody and Cordes 2006). The lobbying restriction was enacted as part of the 1934 Revenue Act. The act states that nonprofits can devote only an "insubstantial part" of their activities to "propaganda or attempting to influence legislation." Twenty years later, the 1954 Revenue Act banned nonprofits from engaging in "any political campaign on behalf of (or in opposition to) any candidate for public office." These federal laws still apply today and form the principal restrictions on both the amount and the types of political activity that 501(c)(3) organizations can undertake. If 501(c)(3) nonprofits do not abide by these laws, the IRS can fine them or retract their tax-exempt status.

The 1976 Tax Reform Act created an alternative standard for ensuring that nonprofit lobbying activities comply with federal law. These newer lobbying rules, which are part of Section 501(h) of the Internal Revenue Code, seek to prevent the subjective enforcement of the "insubstantial part" test enacted in 1934 (Lunder 2007; Scrivner 1990). All nonprofits, except private foundations and churches, can opt to have to 501(h) status on top of their 501(c)(3) status if they want to be covered by clearly defined lobbying rules. Nonprofits with the optional 501(h) status can use up to 20 percent of the first $500,000 of their expenditures for lobbying. For nonprofits with larger budgets, these dollar amounts can increase until they reach a $1 million cap on lobbying expenditures (Lunder 2007). Cost-free lobbying activities, such as those undertaken by volunteers or paid staff on their own time, do not count toward an organization's lobbying limit under the 501(h) expenditure test.

Some suggest that the 501(h) status has created more generous limits on nonprofit lobbying (Harmon, Ladd, and Evans 2000), but there is little evidence that it has increased the advocacy freedoms of 501(c)(3) nonprofits. Most 501(c)(3)s do not elect to be covered by the 501(h) expenditure rules (Berry and Arons 2003). Only 11 of the 100 immigrant-serving nonprofits in San Francisco reported that they had become 501(h) entities, and many indicated that they did not know what the 501(h) election was. Furthermore, case law suggests that nonprofits that do not make the 501(h) election, and consequently are covered by the "insubstantial part" test of the 1934 Revenue Act, can spend between 5 and 20 percent of their annual expenditures on lobbying activities (Lunder 2007). Thus 501(c)(3) organizations with and without the 501(h) election face a similar upper limit on the amount of money they can spend on lobbying.

Nonprofits are more restricted than other types of civic organizations. Civic organizations that work to influence political decisions for the benefit of the people they represent can be registered under other subsections of Section 501(c) of the tax code, most commonly 501(c)(4) (social welfare organizations), 501(c)(5) (labor unions), and 501(c)(6) (trade associations). As table 3 shows, these other organizations also do not pay federal income taxes, but their donors' contributions are *not* tax-deductible. In return for their less favorable tax treatment, these other organizations can lobby as much as they want as long as their lobbying is related to their tax-exempt purpose. They can also engage in political campaigning, again as long as it is consistent with their exempt purpose as well as applicable election and campaign finance laws (Lunder 2007). Thus, 501(c)(3)s, (c)(4)s, (c)(5)s, and (c)(6)s can all legitimately provide political representation for their clients, constituents, and members, but only 501(c)(3) nonprofits face federal limits on the amount and types of lobbying and electioneering they can do.

While nonprofits have more difficulty engaging in political work, it is not impossible for them. Federal law defines lobbying narrowly as advocacy targeting the legislature with the goal of influencing the passage or defeat

Table 3   Advocacy organizations compared

	501(c)(3)	501(c)(4)	501(c)(5)	501(c)(6)
Description	Public charities	Social welfare organizations	Labor unions	Trade associations
Examples	Catholic Charities, International Rescue Committee	National Rifle Association of America, Sierra Club, American Association of Retired Persons	United Farm Workers, Service Employees International Union	National Association of Manufacturing, American Medical Association
Deductible contributions?	Yes	No[a]	No[a]	No[a]
Lobbying?	Restricted	Unrestricted[b]	Unrestricted[b]	Unrestricted[b]
Partisan electioneering?	No	Yes[c]	Yes[c]	Yes[c]

[a] An organization exempt under a subsection of IRC Section 501 other than 501(c)(3) may establish a charitable fund, contributions to which are deductible. Such a fund, though, must itself meet the requirements of section 501(c)(3).
[b] As long as lobbying is related to the organization's exempt purpose.
[c] As long as political campaign activity is consistent with the organization's exempt purpose and applicable election and campaign finance laws.

of a specific piece of legislation. Consequently, it does not restrict nonprofit advocacy before the executive and judicial branches or preclude nonpartisan and educational advocacy, and nonprofits can freely engage in these activities. Federal law also does not restrict legislators from inviting nonprofit advocacy and testimony when they want to be educated on a particular issue.

The electioneering ban means that nonprofits cannot endorse or campaign for a candidate or party, donate money to a candidate or party, or distribute materials aimed at influencing the outcome of an election for public office. These election rules, however, do not apply to the initiative process or issue campaigns, and nonprofits can take positions on city ballot measures and state initiatives. Nonprofits can also undertake voter education and get out the vote campaigns. Immigrant-serving nonprofits thus have several opportunities for political work despite the need to keep their public policy activities within the parameters of federal law.

My informants completed a ten-question quiz measuring their knowledge of the federal tax code.[26] Table 4 lists the wording of each question, along with the percentages of immigrant-serving nonprofits answering the questions correctly. Given that the median nonprofit organization answered eight questions correctly, they have a good understanding of the laws that govern their advocacy. However, they have a better idea about what is *not* permitted than what *is* permitted. Nearly all immigrant-serving nonprofits know that they are not allowed to lobby government using government

Table 4   Knowledge of the federal tax code

Can your nonprofit organization . . . ?	Correct answer	Percent with correct answer
Actively support or oppose government legislation (N=90/100)	Yes	61
Take a policy position without reference to a specific bill (88/100)	Yes	74
Actively support or oppose government regulations, rules, and procedures (89/100)	Yes	77
Lobby if part of your organization's budget comes from government funds (88/100)	Yes	49
Use government funds to lobby government (90/100)	No	98
Endorse a candidate for elected office (91/100)	No	93
Talk to public officials about public policy matters (92/100)	Yes	89
Sponsor a forum or candidate debate for elected office (91/100)	Yes	59
Make campaign contributions to political candidates (92/100)	No	95
Encourage your organization's clients/members to vote in elections (95/100)	Yes	86

Note: Percentages are rounded.

funds, and they know about the electioneering ban, but they are unclear about what they are permitted to do in advocating with legislative officials. They are relatively ignorant, for example, about their right to lobby if only part of their budget comes from government funds; only half of the respondents marked the correct answer to this question. Despite an overall solid knowledge of the law, immigrant-serving nonprofits generally believe that the federal tax code is more prohibitive than it really is.

Interview data echo the survey responses but also reveal that immigrant-serving nonprofits do not see the 501(c)(3) restrictions as necessarily limiting their ability to advocate for immigrant rights and integration policies. An advocate with Chinese for Affirmative Action, a Chinatown-based nonprofit, mentioned that advocacy aimed at city agencies has enabled her organization to serve the needs of disadvantaged immigrants:

> At the local level, we do some legislative advocacy in terms of bills and actual laws, as much as we are legally allowed, but we do a lot more administrative advocacy where we advocate with a particular agency that's in charge of administering a particular program. . . . Administrative advocacy is much more useful in terms of serving the needs of our clients and this isn't considered lobbying in the legal sense of the

word. . . . We work with the school district to make sure they're developing and implementing their translated document services. . . . We also do things with the Employment Development Department, locally and at the state level, which is charged with administering workforce development benefits and training programs, making sure that they're doing that in a way that is accessible for [limited English proficient] workers. And we regularly advocate with the Department of Elections, making sure that when they draft their budget and invest in new voting machines that they're thinking first and foremost that everyone who has the right to vote can vote.[27]

Other nonprofit advocates also felt that they are able to press their interests with a wide variety of city departments and agencies—including the Mayor's Office of Housing; the Human Services Agency; the Department of Children, Youth, and Families; the Department of Public Health; the Police Department; the Juvenile Probation Department; the Recreation and Park Department; the Office of Labor Standards Enforcement; and the Office of Civic Engagement and Immigrant Affairs. They explained that this type of administrative advocacy circumvents federal restrictions and effectively serves their immigrant clients.

Limited Political Resources

Immigrant-serving nonprofits, compared with other types of advocacy organizations, also lack the resources normally associated with political influence, including money and votes. As local governments tightened their belts and private foundations reduced their grants, nonprofits had to learn to get by with shrinking financial resources even though the demand for their services was growing. This bind left most immigrant-serving nonprofits without money to invest in costly forms of advocacy, such as ballot initiatives and get out the vote campaigns. Their resource disadvantage was markedly greater than that of labor unions, which can use pooled membership dues to support political candidates and initiatives as well as finance lobbying activities that benefit union members.

Many immigrant-serving nonprofits cannot fund staff positions dedicated to advocacy. Only two of the one hundred immigrant-serving nonprofits reported having a policy director or advocate whose sole responsibility was to maintain relations with government, develop a public policy agenda, or engage in political advocacy. Twenty-eight nonprofits reported not having any staff whose work includes advocacy. The remaining seventy reported

having some staff capacity to take on advocacy, with several employees sharing the function as an often unwritten part of their job responsibilities. This
suggests that nonprofits want to take up advocacy despite having limited staff
resources for that purpose. This also contrasts with labor unions, most of
which have policy directors responsible for organizing campaigns, determin-
ing unions' policy needs, and promoting policies to improve their members'
working conditions.

Immigrant-serving nonprofits also have difficulty mobilizing voters
among the people they serve, because many lack citizenship. "Many of our
clients have little schooling and can't fully participate in the political process
because they're not citizens and they can't vote," commented an employee
of Wu Yee (Protector of Children), which provides family support services
to low-income Chinese immigrant parents.[28] When immigrant-serving
nonprofits reach out beyond their immigrant clientele, as thirty-six of
the one hundred nonprofits reported doing, federal law requires that their
voter education and voter mobilization activities be strictly nonpartisan.
Immigrant-serving nonprofits cannot direct voters to support the political
candidates they favor. This differs markedly from the experience of labor
unions and special interest groups, which can and do encourage their members to vote for particular candidates.

It is difficult for immigrant-serving nonprofits to bring about
change through the ballot box also because many are client-serving, not
member-serving, organizations. Most people contact a nonprofit because
they need immediate help, not because they want to join a group of
like-minded individuals to effect political change. "Most of our immigrant
parents are not political minded," the same Wu Yee employee explained.
"They are just trying to survive economically. . . . To them it's about bread
and butter issues and not about getting involved in the electoral process."[29]
Even when immigrants repeatedly seek the services from an organization
like Wu Yee, they do not become dues-paying members. Compared with
the relations that, for example, labor unions develop with their members,
nonprofit-client relations are relatively short-lived and less focused on formal
political issues like voting.

Reliance on Government Funding

A final constraint on political advocacy by immigrant-serving nonprofits is that they rely heavily on government funding. Many observers of
the nonprofit sector have commented on the increasing dependence of
community-based nonprofits on government contracts (Chaves, Stephens,

and Galaskiewicz 2004; Grønbjerg 1993; Smith and Lipsky 1993). San Francisco has also experienced the increased privatization of public services. In 1980, nonprofits controlled a third of public services in the city (Hirsch 2005). By 2006, the city administrator estimated that nonprofits' share of government-funded services had increased to 50 percent.[30] Of the one hundred immigrant-serving nonprofits in my survey, sixty-two reported receipt of government funding, with an average of 55 percent of their operating budget coming from government funding in 2006.

San Francisco–based immigrant-serving nonprofits receive funding from all levels of government, but twice as much comes from local government than from state and federal governments.[31] Fifty-seven of the one hundred immigrant-serving nonprofits reported getting grants or contracts from the City and County of San Francisco, compared to thirty-one from the state of California and twenty-six from the federal government. Also, twenty-one nonprofits reported that all their government funding in 2006 came from San Francisco. This dependence on local government funding reflects both the increasing reliance on local government to finance nonprofit services and the steady shift toward "third-party government" (Salamon 1981). It also reflects San Francisco's status as a city-county consolidation, which bears more responsibility for health, welfare, and social services than most large U.S. cities.

Contracting data from the San Francisco Office of the Controller indicate that 85 of all 216 immigrant-serving nonprofits in San Francisco received one or more grants from city departments and agencies in fiscal year 2007–2008. This totaled $72.9 million, or 15 percent of the $488 million the city paid out to all its nonprofit vendors that year. In fiscal year 2009–2010, that amount increased to $84.7 million to 86 immigrant-serving nonprofits, equaling 18 percent of the $478 million given to nonprofit vendors. While these contract percentages are less than immigrants' share of the city population (37% in 2007), immigrant-serving nonprofits nonetheless have captured a significant amount of the city's discretionary budget distributed to nonprofits. They even managed to increase their share of contracts slightly at a time when public expenditures on nonprofit vendors in San Francisco declined overall.

These financial ties can make some immigrant-serving nonprofits reluctant to engage in advocacy. Nonprofit advocates mentioned that government funding ties their hands because city officials who fund them do not always welcome advocacy—especially advocacy that criticizes city government. Few had experienced the wrath of city officials themselves, but many recounted the misfortune that befell La Raza Centro Legal to confirm that government can exact real retribution when a government-funded nonprofit is too aggressive or too antagonistic. Mayor Willie Brown froze La Raza's city funds between 2002 and 2004 after it brought a First Amendment lawsuit against the city to protest the police department for ticketing day laborers who had gathered at public street corners. Eventually, La Raza reached a settlement with the city and had its city funds reinstated when Mayor Brown left office. The funding freeze, however, forced La Raza to lay off a third of its staff and significantly cut the pay of remaining staff.

Not all immigrant-serving nonprofits, however, felt that city funding holds them back, even on very contentious political issues. In one telling instance, an advocate with Chinese for Affirmative Action (CAA) explained that his organization openly promoted supervisor district lines that differed from the mayor's redistricting vision, yet suffered no backlash:

> The fact that CAA gets government funds for our employment program could have been a potential challenge for us. But it's because we've been in the community for so long and we've had these relationships with the city that go beyond individual mayors and members of the Board of Supervisors that nobody ever threatened to take away our funding because of our advocacy work. They would look absolutely terrible if they'd tried. The most challenging moment was when we helped to redraw the Board of Supervisors map as part of redistricting [in 2000] in direct opposition to the districts as articulated by [Mayor] Willie Brown, and I thought that that would be one situation where he'd feel angered. But to his credit he never raised the issue with us. In fact, I think we got increased funding shortly afterwards because his department heads liked some of the work we were doing with direct services and the suggestions we gave them for how they could improve services. So, I don't think it should be a problem for a nonprofit to get involved in politics when they receive government funding. I know a lot of nonprofits raise this as an issue. But advocacy can be done in a straightforward professional manner so those concerns are lessened.[32]

Other publicly funded immigrant-serving nonprofits even thought that city funding made their advocacy easier. "When our clients tell us that they have difficulties finding jobs and affordable housing in San Francisco," an employee of the African Immigrant and Refugee Resource Center commented, "we'll get in touch with our contracting agency and let them know how our clients would benefit from additional programs in these areas."[33] An employee of the Vietnamese Community Center of San Francisco similarly stated, "I'll call our contacts in the Mayor's Office of Community Development and our [district] supervisor, especially about our computer training and employment services, but also to make a plug for more youth services and health services for immigrants . . . [Interviewer: Why do you contact them?] . . . Because they've funded us and because I've worked with them before."[34] Relations with government funders provide immigrant-serving nonprofits with valuable contacts to whom they direct their advocacy.

These different perspectives show that government funding plays a complicated role in nonprofits' decisions to become involved in politics. This echoes the unsettled scholarship on the topic. Some scholars argue that government funding suppresses nonprofit advocacy by showing that nonprofits shy away from politics for fear of biting the hand that feeds them (Berry and Arons 2003; Salamon 1995; Schmid, Bar, and Nirel 2008; Wolch 1990). Others add that nonprofits' misunderstanding of the anti-lobbying rules attached to government funding reduces their advocacy, even though nonprofits may engage in lobbying that is supported by other funds or that nonprofit staff do on their own time (Berry and Arons 2003). Still others find that government funding transforms nonprofits into professionalized and formalized organizations with a greater focus on the administrative duties necessitated by government funding and less on advocacy (Grønbjerg 1993; Piven and Cloward 1977; Smith and Lipsky 1993). Others claim that government funding actually enhances nonprofit advocacy; they show that government-dependent nonprofits have self-interested incentives to advocate for continued government support and that government funding bolsters organizational resources, enabling nonprofits to commit other resources to advocacy (Chaves, Stephens, and Galaskiewicz 2004; Donaldson 2007; Mosley 2010).

My data are inconclusive on this question. In the course of my research, the city terminated funding to two immigrant-serving nonprofits because of financial malfeasance, but La Raza Centro Legal seems to have been the only nonprofit punished for its brazenly provocative advocacy. A half dozen immigrant-serving nonprofits had clear political aspirations but stayed away from advocacy because they feared losing their government funding. Yet many other nonprofits, similar to CAA, advocated controversial political issues and suffered no backlash from government funders. Based on these findings, it does not seem that government funding suppresses nonprofit advocacy, but it certainly tempers it. Reliance on government funding forces immigrant-serving nonprofits to scrutinize the tone as well as the strategies and tactics they use in the advocacy process.

Navigating Constraints

Immigrant-serving nonprofits in San Francisco have found ways to overcome these constraints and influence local government policies concerning immigrant communities. Chapters 3 through 5 show how immigrant-serving nonprofits successfully advocated the enactment and implementation of legislation concerning immigrant language access, labor rights, and municipal ID cards. Their tripartite strategy focused on (a) administrative advocacy, (b) cross-sectoral and cross-organizational collaborations, and (c) strategic issue framing. In each campaign, immigrant-serving nonprofits carefully negotiated the constraints facing them due to their 501(c)(3) tax-exempt status, limited organizational resources, and reliance on government funding. They discovered ways to succeed even when facing fractured public support for immigrant rights in an era of federal immigration enforcement.

San Francisco is a progressive city where one would expect little opposition to immigrant rights advocacy. Yet all my informants commented that the city's advances in immigrant rights and integration would not have been possible without their consistent advocacy. One CAA advocate commented that "nothing moves in this city unless there is some sort of community impetus."[35] A La Raza Centro Legal activist added that "immigrant rights become viable, they become real only when immigrants and their community organizations fight for them."[36] And a Young Workers United staffer who works with young immigrant workers in San Francisco's low-wage service sector reflected that "city leaders sometimes are armchair progressives. We *have* to get up in their business to get them actively involved in the fight for greater worker justice and immigrant rights."[37] Nonprofit advocates know that even though city officials may be appreciative of immigrants and understanding of their needs, they need to apply constant pressure to get them to act on their inclusive political philosophies. The next chapter further examines how San Francisco's civic and political context has influenced how immigrant-serving nonprofits have promoted immigrant advancement.

CHAPTER 2

Immigrants and Politics in San Francisco

San Francisco has long been one of the nation's most liberal big cities, repeatedly bending the curve on important social, economic, and political issues. Well known for promoting neighborhood interests in the face of downtown growth and redevelopment during the 1980s, the city was also in the forefront of expanding medical marijuana rights in the early 1990s. It was among the first to offer a citywide minimum wage exceeding the federal and California minimum wages in 2003, same-sex marriages in 2004, and universal health coverage to uninsured city residents in 2007. In 2007, San Francisco also outlawed large supermarkets from using plastic checkout bags, and since 2011, it prohibits restaurants from providing free toys with kids' meals that do not meet certain nutritional standards. Yet despite the city's track record of tolerance and progressivism, San Francisco politics are still hotly contested. It would be wrong to assume that this "left coast city" (DeLeon 1992) would automatically favor immigrant rights and immigrant integration policies.

San Francisco has come a long way in how it treats immigrants. During the second half of the nineteenth century, racial discrimination was rampant, and San Francisco led the nation in anti-Asian agitation that climaxed in 1882 with the enactment of the Chinese Exclusion Act. This federal law prohibited the immigration of Chinese laborers and was in place until World War II. Today, in contrast, no city official takes an openly anti-immigrant stance, and the city provides a relatively welcoming environment to immigrants, including undocumented immigrants. Recently enacted immigrant rights and integration policies, however, have had to contend with the many hurdles built into San Francisco's kaleidoscopic decision-making process. Nonprofit advocates successfully navigated those hurdles to enact and implement several policies that advance immigrants' needs and interests.

San Francisco has a progressive political culture, yet immigrant-serving nonprofits have had to contend with several major obstacles as they advocate for local immigrant rights and integration policies. San Francisco's fragmented government, weak political leadership, partyless milieu, and social and ethnic diversity make any kind of democratic change difficult and slow. Additionally, a multitude of competing interest groups, the tendency of policymakers to promote business development policies that strengthen the city's economy, and the national focus on immigration enforcement have all impeded nonprofit advocacy to expand immigrant rights.

San Francisco's Immigrants

San Francisco's long experience with receiving immigrants has earned it the designation of a continuous gateway city (Singer 2004). When California joined the Union in 1850, more than half of San Francisco's inhabitants were foreign-born. As figure 1 shows, that percentage declined in subsequent decades as a result of federal restrictive immigration laws enacted at the turn of the twentieth century, reaching a low point of 17.7 percent in 1950, and increased again after liberalization of immigration policy in 1965. Soaring rents and housing prices have slowed immigration to San Francisco since 2000, driving more immigrants to the surrounding suburbs (Begin 2011). The city's foreign-born population grew only 4 percent between 2000 and 2013, compared with 16 percent in the 1990s and 28 percent in the 1980s. In 2013, San Francisco was the nation's fourteenth-largest city with about 827,000 residents, 36 percent of whom were foreign-born (U.S. Census Bureau 2013b). Given their sustained and large numbers, immigrants made an imprint on the city in the past and continue to do so today.

As in the country as a whole, the national origins of San Francisco's immigrants have changed over time. Initially, the city housed many Mexicans and Asian immigrants. The 1848 Treaty of Guadalupe Hidalgo, which ended the Mexican-American War and required Mexico to cede the present-day Southwest to the United States, made Mexicans in San Francisco foreigners in their native land (Heizer and Almquist 1971). The Chinese arrived in the 1850s and 1860s to escape war and famine at home and to mine for gold and build railroads in California. They were succeeded by Japanese laborers in the 1880s and Filipino

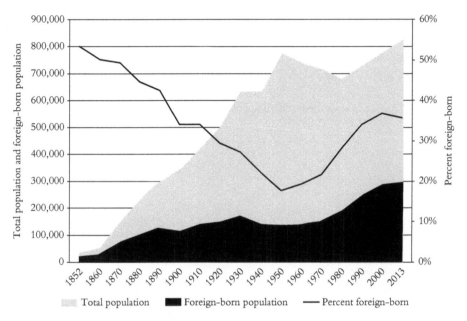

FIGURE 1   San Francisco's foreign-born population, 1852–2013
Source: The 2013 data are from the American Community Survey, three-year estimates (2011–2013). The 1860–2000 data are from Gibson and Jung (2006). The 1852 data are from the California Census.

students and agricultural workers in the 1920s (Laguerre 2000). European migration increased in the late nineteenth century, bringing large numbers of Irish and Italians as well as Russian émigrés and German Jews to the city. Following the 1965 Hart-Celler Act, which removed restrictions on non-European migration, San Francisco once again drew large numbers of immigrants from Asia and Latin America. They included refugees fleeing brutal wars in Vietnam and Central America, economic migrants searching for a better life, and immigrants joining family members already living in the United States. These successive immigrant waves have changed the ethnoracial composition of San Francisco's population in dramatic ways. While almost completely white before 1940, San Francisco was a majority-minority city by 1990 with a combined population of ethnoracial minorities exceeding the white non-Hispanic population.

San Francisco's immigrants are a diverse lot, as summarized in table 5.[1] The majority (64%) hail from Asia, mostly China (36%), the Philippines (9%), and Vietnam (6%). The second-largest group (19%) comes from Latin America, mostly Mexico (8%) and El Salvador (4%). San Francisco continues to attract immigrants from Europe (13%) as well, with the largest number coming from Ukraine (2%). The city's foreign born vary in the year of entry, but one in three (34%) has arrived to the United States since 2000. Many foreign-born San Franciscans (40%) have not acquired U.S. citizenship, and an estimated 30,000–45,000 (10–15%) are undocumented (Hill and Johnson 2011; MPI 2014).[2] Finally, San Francisco's foreign born speak a range of languages at home, vary notably in their educational backgrounds, and work in both high- and low-skilled occupations.

Table 5   San Francisco's foreign-born population, 2013

Foreign-born population	296,342
Region of birth (%)	
Europe	13.2
Asia	63.7
Africa	1
Oceania	0.9
Latin America	19.5
Northern America	1.7
Period of entry (%)	
2010 or later	8.1
2000 to 2009	26.1
Before 2000	65.8
Citizenship (%)	
Naturalized U.S. citizen	60
Not a U.S. citizen	40
Language spoken at home (%)	
English only	14.6
Spanish	17.7
Indo-European language	11.8
Asian language	54.1
Other language	1.8
Education (%)	
No high school degree	26.6
High school degree	17.6
Some college	18.5
Bachelor's degree	22.7
Graduate or professional degree	14.5
Occupation (%)	
Management, business, science, arts	38.6
Service	27.4
Sales, office	19.7
Natural resources, construction, maintenance	6.1
Production, transportation, material moving	8.3

Note: Occupation data is for individuals sixteen years and over who are employed in the civilian labor force (169,680); education data is for individuals twenty-five years and over (270,573); language data is for individuals five years and over (295,248). Percentages may not add up to 100% due to rounding.

Source: American Community Survey (three-year estimates, 2011–2013).

This diversity makes it hard to generalize about San Francisco's immigrant population. The focus of much of the activism described in this book, however, is on disadvantaged immigrants, a group that includes mostly noncitizens and recent arrivals. Table 6 shows that immigrants—regardless of citizenship status—are more likely than the native born to lack a high school degree, experience difficulty with English, work in the service sector, and have lower median household incomes. It also shows that noncitizens have the weakest socio-demographic profiles. Table 7 highlights how all of San Francisco's immigrants—regardless of length of stay—have trouble with the English language. It also shows that immigrants who arrived since 2010 have better educational profiles than earlier arrivals and are more likely to hold a professional job, yet they have lower median household incomes, and a much larger percentage lives in poverty. Noncitizens and newcomer immigrants, in sum, are more socioeconomically disadvantaged than immigrant citizens and longer-term residents. They face significant integration challenges.

Table 6   Selected socioeconomic characteristics of San Francisco's native- and foreign-born populations, 2013

	Native	Foreign-born citizen	Foreign-born noncitizen
Population	530,284	177,745	118,597
Educational attainment (%)			
No high school degree	4.1	26.1	27.5
Graduate or professional degree	25.3	12.6	17.8
Language (%)			
Speaks English less than "very well"	2.9	54	54.8
Economic characteristics (%)			
In the civilian labor force	72.5	59.6	69.8
Unemployed	5.3	3.8	6.8
Managerial/business occupation	60.1	39.6	37.2
Service occupation	11.5	23.5	32.7
Lives below the federal poverty line	13	12.7	21.9
Median annual household income ($)	85,896	59,861	51,154
Median annual earnings for a full-time male worker ($)	80,123	53,452	47,605

Note: Education data is for individuals twenty-five years and over, language data is for individuals five years and over, and employment and earnings data is for individuals sixteen years and over.

Source: American Community Survey (three-year estimates, 2011–2013).

Table 7   Selected socioeconomic characteristics of San Francisco's foreign-born population, by period of entry, 2013

	Period of entry		
	Since 2010	**2000–2009**	**Before 2000**
Foreign-born population	23,903	77,387	195,052
Naturalized U.S. citizen (%)	3.9	28.2	79.4
Educational attainment (%)			
No high school degree	15.2	25.1	28
Graduate or professional degree	25.7	17.3	12.7
Language (%)			
Speaks English less than "very well"	53.3	56.3	53.7
Economic characteristics (%)			
In the civilian labor force	56	74.4	60.4
Unemployed	8.6	6.2	4.1
Managerial/business occupation	52.6	34.5	39.1
Service occupation	23.4	33.3	25
Lives below the federal poverty line	35.4	19	13.1
Median annual household income ($)	35,403	53,719	58,434
Median annual earnings for a full-time male worker ($)	81,500	43,690	53,544

Note: Education data is for individuals twenty-five years and over, language data is for individuals five years and over, and employment and earnings data is for individuals sixteen years and over.

Source: American Community Survey (three-year estimates, 2011–2013).

Limited English Proficient Immigrants

Most immigrant-serving nonprofits in San Francisco are well aware of how difficulties with English hamper immigrants' integration. "I see language as a gateway integration issue that affects everything else," an employee of the Southeast Asian Community Center commented, "and when immigrants don't know English, it hurts them in school and on the job and makes it difficult for them to receive government services, become a citizen, and participate in the political process."[3] An employee of the African Immigrant and Refugee Resource Center said that language is such an important integration issue also because it affects so many immigrants, regardless of national origin or ethnoracial background. "Language barriers are color-blind. They affect immigrants from Mexico, they affect immigrants from China, and they affect immigrants and refugees from Africa."[4] An employee of Chinese for Affirmative Action perhaps put it most succinctly when she remarked that "language is a quintessential immigrant issue. . . . Who else experiences English language barriers like they do?"[5]

English is not the home language for many San Franciscans today. Of the foreign born aged five and over, 85 percent (252,189) speak a language other than English at home, and only 15 percent (43,059) speak only English. One out of three (34%, 99,149) speak English "not well" or "not at all," leading them to be classified as limited English proficient. Most of them speak an Asian language at home (74%, 73,012), followed by those who speak Spanish (20%, 19,563) and then those who speak other languages, including other Indo-European languages (7%, 6,574). Limited proficiency in English makes it hard for them to get an education, improve their job, or participate in American civic and political life (Alba 2004).

Despite some who worry that immigrants will never learn English (e.g., Huntington 2004), immigrants are well aware that knowing English will help them get ahead, and most want to become proficient. Yet learning English remains difficult for many. Those who migrated to the United States as adults find it particularly hard. Learning English can take years for low-skilled immigrants working multiple jobs with little time for English classes. Housing segregation and labor market segmentation force many immigrants to live and work in ethnic enclaves where use of English is uncommon (Chiswick and Miller 2005). At the same time, the availability of English as a Second Language classes falls woefully short of demand, and community colleges and adult schools in San Francisco have long waiting lists for immigrants wanting to enroll (Hendricks 2009; Tucker 2006). The absence of suitable opportunities to learn English helps explain why 54 percent of immigrants in San Francisco speak English less than "very well" even after having lived in the United States for fourteen or more years (see table 7).

The continued tempo of migration to San Francisco means that there will always be many individuals who do not speak English as their native language. The majority of their children and nearly all their grandchildren—regardless of national or ethnic origin—will be English monolinguals (Alba 2004), but first-generation immigrants will continue to struggle with English and thereby risk exclusion. English language training and public accommodation to language diversity will thus be important issues for San Francisco now and into the future. Not surprisingly, some immigrant-serving nonprofits have continuously pushed San Francisco officials to improve immigrant language rights since the 1970s (CAA 2015).

Recent decades have seen a surge in policies nationwide that address immigrant language rights. While there is no single nationwide language policy, federal, state, and local authorities have adopted a patchwork of policies regulating the use of English and other languages in education, government, and business. The restrictive "English-only laws" effective in twenty-eight states (including California) and over forty cities seek to protect the status of English against the multicultural influences of especially the growing number of Spanish speakers (English First 2015; Schmid 2001). Many English-only laws (like the one in California) are symbolic, but others officially bar government officials from providing services and information in foreign languages. Symbolic or not, state and municipal English-only activism sends immigrants the message that those who do not speak English well are not welcome to participate in the community, thereby discouraging their integration (Linton 2009).

Other policies—including "English-plus laws"[6] enacted in four states and more than a dozen municipalities as well as policies providing for bilingual education and voting ballots—allow people to use foreign languages alongside English in the public sphere (Linton 2009). These policies do not diminish the importance of English but make it easier for limited English proficient immigrants to function in an English-dominant society. Chapter 3 considers a San Francisco ordinance related to this larger family of inclusive language measures. This policy mandates city departments and agencies to provide language translation and interpretation in Chinese, Spanish, and Tagalog, thereby making it easier for the biggest non-English-speaking groups in San Francisco to access government information and public services.

Low-Wage Immigrant Workers

Many immigrant-serving nonprofits in San Francisco focus on the plight of immigrant workers. Disadvantaged immigrants often work in low-wage service jobs where wage violations, lack of benefits, and poor working conditions are common (Bernhardt et al. 2009; CPA 2010). Immigrants "come here with dreams of economic success," an employee of the Chinese Progressive Association commented, "but many never find stable employment that pays a livable wage."[7] An employee of Instituto Laboral de la Raza (the People's Labor Institute) mentioned that many immigrants work under precarious conditions and that "unscrupulous employers take advantage of them and most workers don't fight the abuse for fear of retaliation."[8] An employee of the Day Labor Program also explained that immigrant labor rights are important because employment issues are tied to other aspects of immigrant integration. "We want to empower immigrant workers because economic empowerment also promotes their social and political empowerment."[9]

Noncitizens and immigrants who arrived between 2000 and 2009 are economically most disadvantaged among San Francisco residents, as tables 6 and 7 show. Their median household incomes are markedly lower ($51,154 and $53,719, respectively) than for the native born ($85,896), but this is not because they do not work. In fact, 70 percent of noncitizens and 74 percent of immigrants who arrived between 2000 and 2009 are in the civilian labor force, compared with 73 percent of natives, though higher percentages report being unemployed. A substantial earnings gap drives the income difference: The median income of a full-time male noncitizen worker is $47,605 and for a male immigrant who arrived between 2000 and 2009, the figure is $43,690, compared with $80,123 for an American-born male worker. The lower levels of schooling among disadvantaged immigrants likely explain part of the gap, but its sheer size raises questions about employment equity and labor market segmentation.

The economic profile of foreign-born San Franciscans who arrived after 2010 is more of a mixed bag. Their median household income is lower compared with that of earlier immigrant arrivals and a much larger percentage lives in poverty. Yet the median income of a full-time immigrant male worker who arrived after 2010 is $81,500, nearly double that of a male immigrant who arrived between 2000 and 2009. These statistics reflect a growing economic divide also within the immigrant community, with both high incomes for some new immigrant arrivals and high poverty for others. This is the result of the economic bifurcation that has occurred in San Francisco in recent decades.

Since the onset of national economic restructuring in the early 1970s, San Francisco's economy has increasingly specialized in advanced corporate services in management, law, finance, and communications (DeLeon 1992). The shift to a postindustrial economy, which was accelerated by the rapid internationalization of economic activities during the 1980s, transformed San Francisco into a regional center in the global economy with marked occupational and income polarization (Sassen 2001). San Francisco's late-1990s dot-com bubble and current tech boom have polarized its economy even further (Onishi 2012). The city's restructured economy has produced many more professional and managerial jobs but also more demand for the service workers who make life easier for those in the new economy. These economic changes coincided with the post-1965 influx of low-skilled immigrants from Asia and Latin America, who have become the backbone of the growing low-wage service sector and hospitality industry in the lower tiers of San Francisco's postindustrial economy (Wells 2000).

This new occupational order contains fewer channels of upward mobility from its bottom rungs than did the industrial economy of a century ago. Unskilled immigrants from Europe, who made up a significant part of

America's industrial labor force at the end of the nineteenth century, were able to secure a good measure of economic mobility and attain living wages and a comfortable middle-class life style within their lifetime (Bean, Leach, and Lowell 2004). In contrast, much of today's service work and many hospitality jobs performed by low-skilled immigrants are dead-end jobs that do not pay a livable wage in the context of San Francisco, one of the most expensive cities in the country. They also offer little job security and few benefits and present their own postindustrial health risks (Bernhardt et al. 2009; CPA 2010).

San Francisco's dot-com bubble of the late 1990s and its current tech boom have taken a vast economic toll on low-wage immigrant workers (Lovett 2014; Nieves 1999). An influx of well-to-do tech workers employed by Silicon Valley companies like Apple, Google, and Facebook have been pouring into the Mission district and North Beach, forcing a ruthless gentrification on these heavily immigrant neighborhoods. Real estate and rental prices have soared to unseen heights and evictions have spiked as landlords eject tenants to sell their units in the booming housing market. For many immigrant San Franciscans, including those statistically well above the federal poverty line, economic conditions have become untenable. Some have moved to the surrounding suburbs, where housing is more affordable. Others have stayed but moved into overcrowded single room occupancy hotels in the Tenderloin district and Chinatown, where landlords routinely violate health and safety codes (CJJC 2014).

Because many low-wage immigrant workers struggle with English and have little formal education, they find it difficult to participate in government-sponsored and employer-provided job training programs that could improve their career mobility and help them obtain better-paying jobs (Tumlin and Zimmermann 2003).[10] Undocumented immigrants are altogether ineligible for such programs. A range of policies can possibly improve the economic position of immigrant workers with disadvantaged skill sets. Chapter 4 examines one such policy and considers how raising the minimum level of pay provides government with a tool to improve the well-being of disadvantaged immigrant workers whose economic mobility has been constrained by an increasingly segmented labor market.

Undocumented Immigrants

Finally, undocumented immigrants in San Francisco confront tough barriers in conducting their daily lives. The federal government's increased emphasis on immigration enforcement certainly can prevent undocumented immigrants from even taking the first steps to integrate. "The immigration raids [in 2007] sparked so much fear," a staff member with the Alianza Latinoamericana por los Derechos de los Inmigrantes (Latin American Alliance for Immigrant Rights) commented, "and many immigrants didn't want to leave their homes and were afraid to send their kids to school."[11] A St. Peter's Housing Committee worker added that the difficulty of undocumented immigrants to obtain a government-issued form of identification is particularly problematic. "It's such a huge barrier to being integrated. . . . Being able to prove who you are is just so basic for so many things, like renting an apartment or getting a job or getting help from a social service agency or traveling."[12]

An estimated 30,000 to 45,000 undocumented immigrants make up 10 to 15 percent of the city's foreign-born population (Hill and Johnson 2011; MPI 2014). We have no detailed breakdown for them, but data on undocumented immigrants nationwide and San Francisco's foreign-born population can provide insights.[13] The majority likely come from Mexico, elsewhere in Latin America, and Asia. However, a sizable number—estimated at 2,500—reportedly come from Ireland (Shaw 2007). Since California shares a land border with Mexico, many of San Francisco's undocumented immigrants likely entered the United States by jumping a fence and hiking through the desert or paying someone to help them sneak into the country. Undocumented immigrants from Asia and Ireland likely include many individuals who overstayed legal visas for tourism, study, or temporary work. Undocumented immigrants are likely to be overrepresented in low-skilled and low-wage jobs in the city's service sector and hospitality industry (Passel 2006).

Undocumented immigrants live in the shadows of the law. While San Francisco is a sanctuary city and limits cooperation with federal immigration authorities in all but a few explicit circumstances, undocumented immigrants still fear that interacting with local government officials will increase the likelihood of federal detention and deportation. Their hidden existence undermines their integration and hurts their well-being. When undocumented immigrants do not go to health clinics for preventative checkups, they will end up in costly emergency care when they become critically ill (Berk and Schur 2001). By avoiding police, they become easy targets for crime and inadvertently make the larger community less safe by not reporting crime (Davis, Erez, and Avitabile 2001). When undocumented parents do not interact with schoolteachers, they miss opportunities to improve the academic performance of their children (Delgado-Gaitan 2004). Finally, unscrupulous employers can easily exploit undocumented workers who are reluctant to report abusive labor practices (Gleeson 2012). The overall effect is to condemn those living in the shadows to the underclass.

How to deal with the country's estimated 11.3 million undocumented immigrants remains a controversial issue (Passel et al. 2014). Given the prolonged impasse over federal immigration reform, many states and municipalities have taken immigration matters into their own hands. State officials in Arizona (S.B. 1070), Alabama (H.B. 56), Georgia (H.B. 87), Indiana (S.B. 590), South Carolina (S.B. 20), and Utah (H.B. 497) enacted tough laws in 2010 and 2011 in efforts to drive undocumented immigrants away by excluding them from the civic sphere. Following the 2006 enactment of the Illegal Immigration Relief Act in Hazleton (Penn.), more than 130 municipalities have passed or considered similar ordinances that bar undocumented immigrants from working and renting homes in their cities (Varsanyi 2010a). These policies clearly retard integration and only push undocumented immigrants further into the shadows of American society. San Francisco provides a sharp contrast to such reactions. Chapter 5 considers a 2007 ordinance that allows the city to issue identification cards to undocumented immigrants with the goal of improving their local civic participation.

Government, San Francisco–Style

The view from afar may be that San Francisco is a harmonious melting pot where it is easy to enact and implement immigrant rights and integration policies, but the reality is quite different. San Francisco's city charter makes it difficult to employ government as an instrument for social change. At the same time, the city's economic and social diversity prevents a natural majority from emerging around any type of policy change, much less one benefiting a disadvantaged immigrant minority. In a city where "democracy is hard work" and "majorities are made, not found" (DeLeon 1992: 13), those advocating immigrant rights have their work cut out for them.

The Mayor and the Board of Supervisors

San Francisco is a city-county consolidation, a status it has had since 1856. As a result, the mayor is also the county executive, and the city council doubles as the county Board of Supervisors. The Constitution of California allows for municipal "home rule," allowing cities to develop and ratify a charter that regulates all aspects of city governance and administration. San Francisco voters approved their first home rule charter in 1898, providing for a mayor, an eighteen-member Board of Supervisors (elected at large), the initiative and referendum processes, and a civil service. However, this system was initially marked by bribery and corruption as well as serious conflicts of authority between executive and legislative officials (Keesling 1933; McDonald 1987).

In 1932, San Francisco voters approved a new charter to try to root out political corruption. It succeeded at that and more. The authors of the second charter were convinced that a divided and fragmented government would produce a more honest government. They consequently separated executive and legislative powers, partitioning government into many pieces and isolating powerful politicians (DeLeon 1992; Wirt 1974). The new charter split executive power among an independently elected mayor, a chief administrative officer, innumerable boards and commissions, a controller, an assessor, and a city attorney. The eleven members of the Board of Supervisors were elected at large to staggered four-year terms and part-time positions. Supervisors were expressly prohibited from interfering in executive functions and exercising oversight in the implementation of city ordinances. The fragmentation of power was so effective that it rendered local politicians "impotent" and deprived them of the coordination and discretion necessary to solve the city's urgent problems (Wirt 1974: 11).

Amid continuing criticism of the 1932 charter, San Francisco voters approved a new charter, which took effect in 1996. The main goal of the city's third charter was to make government officials more accountable to the public by reeling in the power of unelected officials and by placing more executive authority with the mayor (Mullin, Peele, and Cain 2004). The new charter also aimed to make San Francisco government more rational and efficient. Finally, the new charter promised to be more accessible to the public. In contrast to the 1932 charter, which at 370 pages was more than fourteen times longer than the U.S. Constitution and had been amended over 250 times between 1971 and 1995, the 1996 charter was only eighty pages long, well organized, and simple and clear in its language.

The 1996 charter created a more unified executive, yet retained its multi-layered character. It eliminated the position of chief administrative officer and put the mayor—assisted by a professional city administrator appointed by the mayor for a term of five years—in charge of the day-to-day management of city departments and agencies. It also gave the mayor appointive, budgetary, and veto powers. The city's numerous boards and commissions, designed to maximize citizen participation in government, continue to influence the plans, policies, and goals of individual departments and agencies, although they have less autonomy than before and now are subject to the authority of both the mayor and the Board of Supervisors. The mayor appoints the controller—the city's chief financial officer—for a ten-year term. The assessor-recorder and city attorney, typically staffed by appointment in other cities, are highly prized elective positions in San Francisco.

Executive power in San Francisco is now more centralized than under the 1932 charter, but the mayor still has a hard time exerting top-down influence. The 1996 charter gives the mayor more administrative and legislative powers, but a thicket of boards and commissions continues to filter his executive leadership. With over twenty-nine thousand civil servants (in 2005), the mayor also experiences bureaucratic hurdles in exercising control. To get things done, the mayor consequently needs to build coalitions, negotiate deals with powerful interest groups, and mobilize the energies of the administrative staff under his authority (DeLeon 1992).

San Francisco's multi-layered executive structure provides multiple access points for immigrant-serving nonprofits with public policy aspirations. With a municipal workforce that is diverse in terms of race and ethnicity (see figure 2), immigrant-serving nonprofits can generally find public employees who are amenable to accommodating the needs and interests of their immigrant co-ethnics. Yet community groups of all sorts have limited access to the mayor and his closest staff, both by charter design and mayoral decision. As San Francisco's top elected official facing citywide demands, the mayor is likely to heed the interests of individuals and groups with the most voting power and the greatest ability to affect his political fortunes. These do not often include immigrant-serving nonprofits and their clients. To secure policy benefits for the city's disadvantaged immigrants, nonprofit advocates must therefore develop a variety of strategies targeting a wide range of administrative officials.

The 1996 charter vests legislative authority in the eleven full-time members of the Board of Supervisors, who are elected by district to staggered four-year terms. Supervisors are limited to two terms. They initiate and enact legislation, share budget authority with the mayor, and can place proposed initiatives on the ballot. They can also override a mayoral veto with a two-thirds majority vote and have the power to confirm some mayoral appointments. The Board of Supervisors is also required to provide public access to its meetings, documents, and records. While supervisors still cannot intervene in administrative affairs, they now are allowed to testify at public meetings of executive boards and commissions as well as adopt legislation on administrative matters other than contract and personnel issues.

Nonprofit advocates enjoy relatively easy access to their supervisors, who by law must invite the public to testify during regular Board meetings. Given that immigrant communities are geographically dispersed, it can be challenging to advocate immigrant rights policies with some legislators (see figure 3).

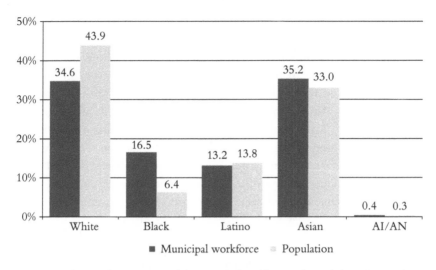

FIGURE 2 Ethnoracial composition of the municipal workforce and population: San Francisco, 2005

Source: Population data are from the 2005 American Community Survey (one-year estimates). San Francisco workforce data are from the San Francisco Department of Human Resources (2008).

Note: AI/AN = American Indian/Alaska Native; SF population (estimate) = 719,077; SF municipal workforce = 29,079.

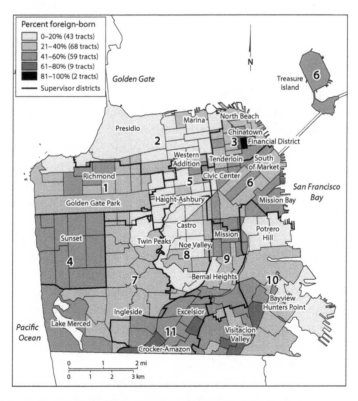

FIGURE 3 San Francisco's foreign-born population by supervisor district, 2009

Source: American Community Survey (five-year estimates, 2005–2009).

Each supervisor, furthermore, represents over seventy-five thousand residents and has only three legislative aides. Minimal Board resources can make it difficult for advocates to get immigrant rights issues on the city's legislative agenda. Legislators also have limited ability to interfere in administrative affairs. Even if nonprofit advocates succeed in engaging a majority of legislators on immigrant rights issues, they cannot count on them to watch over the implementation and enforcement of these policies. For this, they have to turn to administrative officials. Nonprofit advocates thus have to be long-term participants in the policymaking process if they want to influence immigrant rights policies and practices in San Francisco.

The Immigrant Rights Commission and the Office of Civic Engagement and Immigrant Affairs

The Board of Supervisors does not have a committee dedicated to immigrant issues, but San Francisco does have an Immigrant Rights Commission (IRC). The IRC's mission is "to improve, enhance, and preserve the quality of life and civic participation of all immigrants in the City and County of San Francisco" (IRC 2008). Created by ordinance in 1997, the IRC is charged with providing supervisors and the mayor with advice and policy recommendations on issues affecting the city's immigrants. The IRC consists of fifteen volunteer commissioners, who are jointly appointed by the Board of Supervisors and the mayor for two-year terms and who hold public meetings once a month. At least eight commissioners must be immigrants to the United States and a director, who reports directly to the city administrator, leads the IRC's day-to-day operations. Many IRC commissioners are involved in the city's immigrant nonprofit sector as paid employees, board members, or volunteers.

Nonprofit advocates have been frustrated in their attempts to use the IRC to advance their agendas. A Chinese for Affirmative Action employee described the IRC as a "weak commission" that "means well, but doesn't have the staff, resources, and authority to make a difference."[14] An employee with St. Peter's Housing Committee similarly remarked that "the commission isn't the go-to entity for us" because "it doesn't have any real power."[15] Several aides to members of the Board of Supervisors echoed these sentiments. As a result, many immigrant-serving nonprofits bypass the IRC in seeking to influence the policymaking process and go directly to the city's legislative and administrative officials.

Since 2009, San Francisco has also had the Office of Civic Engagement and Immigrant Affairs (OCEIA). Similar to the mayoral offices of immigrant affairs in New York City, Boston, Chicago, Detroit, Houston, Philadelphia, and Seattle, this executive-level office seeks to foster language access and immigrant civic participation. Creating OCEIA was a more serious attempt by the mayor to institutionalize San Francisco's commitment to immigrant integration, but it is not yet clear how this new office will affect nonprofit-government relations. Nonprofit advocates have a variety of perspectives on OCEIA: Some are optimistic that it can support and promote their advocacy, while others are more cynical and fear that it will crowd out civil society initiatives on immigrant rights and integration.

Partisanship, Parties, and Elections

San Francisco politics have long been nonpartisan, but the city is not without parties. Local party organizations do not enjoy much visibility with the electorate, and every local official is elected without a party label. Yet voters in San Francisco have strong partisan leanings. "The Democratic Party imbues the partisan air that San Franciscans breathe," a leading chronicler of San Francisco politics commented, "and in state and local elections the city belongs to the Democrats" (DeLeon 1992: 22). This still is the case, even in national elections, and more than three-quarters of San Francisco voters have supported Democratic presidential candidates in recent years.

The Democratic County Central Committee (DCCC) is the official voice of the local Democratic Party. Most rank-and-file voters do not know about it, however, and the DCCC has made few efforts to get out the vote in local elections. Even politicians in DCCC leadership positions admit that their organization has not done enough to register and turn out new Democratic voters (Hogarth 2008a–b). The DCCC lacks internal discipline, makes few efforts to bind fellow Democrats to a common program, and seldom takes public stands on policy issues (Knight 2008b; Wirt 1974). All in all, the DCCC does not fulfill parties' traditional roles in mobilizing voters and structuring the policymaking process.

The DCCC, however, is important to candidates for local office since its endorsement virtually guarantees an election victory. Since 1989, when the U.S. Supreme Court ruled unconstitutional California's ban on party endorsements in nonpartisan elections, 40 of 47 DCCC-endorsed candidates have won contested supervisor races (Nevius 2010). The DCCC can also boost candidates' fundraising operations and thus increase their electoral success. Local campaign finance rules limit donations to candidates seeking city office to $500 per donor but do not cap contributions to those running for a DCCC seat. Taking advantage of this loophole, political candidates have run simultaneous campaigns for the DCCC and the Board of Supervisors. The money raised and spent on their DCCC races has helped candidates to increase their visibility with voters, thereby improving their chances to get elected to the Board of Supervisors (Hogarth 2010).

While San Francisco is a one-party town, local Democrats disagree on a range of issues. In fact, the factional power struggles within the DCCC are not unlike those taking place between different parties in cities with more party competition and partisan elections. For many years now, a bloc of reform-minded and left-leaning progressives, led by former supervisor Aaron Peskin, has battled the city's "moderate" or old-time Democrats, including former mayor Gavin Newsom and U.S. Representative Nancy Pelosi, for control over the DCCC. The progressives won a majority of DCCC seats in 2008 and added four new DCCC-endorsed progressives to the Board of Supervisors, locking in a majority they have held for nearly a decade. The progressives dealt another blow to the moderates when they removed Newsom, now lieutenant governor of California, from the DCCC in July 2011.[16] Immigrant-serving nonprofits need to tread carefully when searching for political allies in a city known for its Democratic infighting.

The recent progressive insurgency has a lot to do with the city's switch from at-large back to district elections in 2000. For most of its history, San Francisco had at-large elections, and all supervisor candidates appeared on the voting ballot together and were elected to represent a single citywide constituency. In 1977, the city installed district elections where voters choose one supervisor to represent their district. After the assassinations of Mayor George Moscone and Supervisor Harvey Milk by former supervisor Dan White, however, moderates argued that district elections were divisive, and voters approved a return to at-large elections in 1980. Perhaps surprisingly, the Board of Supervisors initially grew more demographically representative under at-large elections. In 1992, for example, the eleven supervisors included five women, two African Americans, one Latino, one Asian, and three gays or lesbians.

By the mid-1990s, however, African Americans, Latinos, and Asians complained that at-large elections failed to represent the city's ethnoracial diversity, pointing out that it was difficult for supervisors of color to get elected to the Board in at-large elections without first having been appointed by the mayor to fill pre-election vacancies (DeLeon, Hill, and Blash 1998). The local Republican Party, Green Party, and local labor unions similarly complained that at-large elections had given Mayor Willie Brown too much influence over the Board. These frustrations charged a grassroots electoral reform movement to mount a successful ballot campaign to restore district elections in 1996. First implemented in 2000, district elections dramatically changed the composition of the Board of Supervisors. Voters replaced the Board aligned with the administration of Mayor Brown with a more progressive Board with greater independence from the mayor's influence (DeLeon 2003).

The reinstatement of district elections in 2000 redrew the political landscape of San Francisco. It changed the way in which supervisor candidates run for office, the role that local organizations play in elections, and ultimately the way that city hall makes decisions. Local organizations with interests tied to a particular geographic area (such as neighborhood associations) now find it easier to identify the specific supervisor who will represent their interests. The switch from at-large back to district elections has forced immigrant-serving nonprofits to rethink how they engage supervisors in discussions about immigrant rights and integration in San Francisco. This is highlighted in the discussion in chapter 3 of the campaign to expand immigrant language access in San Francisco, which nonprofit advocates started in the late 1990s and continued into the 2000s.

Voter Initiatives

San Francisco voters can make laws through the ballot. The twenty-five elections that took place in San Francisco between March 2000 and November 2010 featured 193 local measures, an average of eight per election. San Franciscans find themselves voting on a long list of local ballot measures (and state initiatives) in every election because charter amendments and bond measures require voter approval and because both the Board of Supervisors and city residents can place policy proposals and charter revisions on the ballot. Because ballot measures have a prominent role in shaping San Francisco governance and politics, they are similar to a fourth branch of government. Chapter 4 discusses nonprofit efforts to strengthen immigrant labor rights through a ballot campaign.

Progressive and conservative groups in the city have both used the initiative process to circumvent elected officials who are unresponsive to their policy demands. Progressive groups relied extensively on initiative campaigns during the 1980s to force elected officials to slow the development of high-rise buildings in San Francisco's downtown area (DeLeon 1992; Hartman 2002). To address the city's homeless problem, more conservative groups used the ballot in 2002 (the "Care Not Cash" initiative) to replace existing cash grants for homeless San Franciscans with food, shelter, and health services, in 2003 to ban aggressive panhandling, and in 2010 (the "Civil Sidewalks" initiative) to make it illegal to sit or lie on sidewalks during the day.

Efforts by immigrant-serving nonprofits to use this means to promote immigrant rights and integration have had little success so far. In 2002, for example, they backed Proposition C, a ballot measure that would have allowed noncitizens to serve on the city's boards, commissions, and advisory groups. In 2004 and 2010, they also campaigned for similar measures (Propositions F and D, respectively) that would have allowed noncitizens with children in the San Francisco school district to vote in school board elections. All three measures lost, although the margin was slim for the 2004 noncitizen voting measure (51% no, 49% yes).[17] These failed ballot campaigns show that a majority of San Francisco voters do not necessarily support pro-immigrant measures, even though survey data show that public opinion is sympathetic toward immigrants.[18]

Advocating Immigrant Rights in San Francisco

Immigrant-serving nonprofits seeking to influence the policymaking process in San Francisco have to contend with three additional challenges. San Francisco has a multitude of interest groups, each pressuring government officials to act on their policy demands. Immigrant-serving nonprofits compete with many other organizations for politicians' attention in this hyperpluralist environment. San Francisco policymakers also tend to favor pro-growth development policies, which makes it difficult for immigrant-serving nonprofits to advocate for redistributing scarce resources to disadvantaged immigrants. Finally, San Francisco's progressive political culture can actually limit immigrant-serving nonprofits when they push policies that reflect local norms but run counter to federal immigration enforcement goals.

Hyperpluralism

Urban scholars have called San Francisco's organizational landscape "hyperpluralist" (Coyle 1988; DeLeon 1992; Ferman 1985). Tony Kilroy (1999), a longtime neighborhood activist, created a directory of politically active groups in the city. It contained over nine hundred listings in 1999, covering local political clubs, labor unions, business associations, nonprofit organizations, neighborhood associations, and other collectives of individuals who share and act on a common purpose. Some groups have small constituencies with highly specialized interests and few resources, while others are multi-issue organizations with large memberships and substantial clout, such as labor unions and chambers of commerce. According to Kilroy, about a third of these groups are "always" politically active. My San Francisco government informants agreed that local groups frequently contact them to try to influence their policies and decisions.

Scholars of San Francisco politics have concluded that the many activists and organized groups lobbying city hall challenge policymakers' ability to consolidate power and govern the city's diverse population. They disagree, however, on how debilitating this hyperpluralism is. Coyle (1988) thinks that the city's hyperpluralism is unmanageable, concluding that San Francisco is a "Balkans by the Bay." Ferman (1985), in contrast, contends that skillful mayoral leadership can create order out of hyperpluralist chaos. Sharing Ferman's optimism that this hyperpluralism is workable, DeLeon (1992: 13) comments that democratic policymaking is "hard work" in San Francisco.

Subsequent chapters examine how immigrant-serving nonprofits have navigated this hyperpluralism. Because they have limited resources to devote to advocacy, these nonprofits are at a disadvantage compared with better-resourced advocacy organizations with more political clout, such as labor unions and business associations. To build power and influence, they therefore have to collaborate with other types of advocacy organizations. In theory, the city's rich organizational infrastructure should provide them with an array of possible coalition partners. In practice, however, building such cross-organizational coalitions is complicated. Differences in organizational structure, resources, and status between immigrant-serving nonprofits and unions, for example, make it challenging for these organizations to collaborate on supporting immigrant rights.

It is also challenging to build coalitions of nonprofits that span different immigrant communities, such as when nonprofits serving Latino immigrants collaborate with those serving Asian immigrants. DeLeon (2003) used San Francisco voting data to show that the city's major ethnoracial groups have different ideologies on economic and socio-cultural issues. Whites are ideologically polarized between those who are progressive and conservative on both economic and socio-cultural issues. Latinos tend to be progressive on both economic and socio-cultural issues. Asians tend to occupy a middle position on both issues but frequently align with conservatives. Finally, most African Americans are progressive on economic issues and conservative on socio-cultural issues. Because Latinos and Asians—the city's largest foreign-born groups—have divergent ideologies on economic and socio-cultural issues, nonprofits representing these groups cannot necessarily count on working together. Later chapters show that when immigrant-serving nonprofits do work together in multiracial and multicultural coalitions, tensions can arise due to differences in advocacy strategies, organizational age, and size.

Urban Redistribution

Peterson (1981) explains that cities' primary concern must be to maintain and enhance their economic activity. Because cities are subject to stiff economic competition from other cities and have few powers independent from state and federal governments, they depend heavily on their own tax revenues. To create and maintain wealth and revenue, cities must attract and retain businesses and jobs. According to Peterson, this explains why they favor business development policies that yield fiscal resources over redistributive polices that drain such resources and hurt cities' competitive positions. Extending Peterson's logic, it is easy to imagine why city officials would resist enacting and implementing immigrant rights and integration policies. Such policies arguably help only a small segment of the population, including non–U.S. citizens. They simultaneously impose costs on other city residents and create the perception that the city is an expensive place to do business.

San Francisco does not fully conform to the Peterson model, but redistributive policies still compete with developmental ones. As a peninsula city, San Francisco exercises near-monopolistic control over its land area. This makes it easier for San Francisco to retain mobile capital and, in theory, also gives city officials more freedom to enact redistributive policies. The city's small size (47 square miles) and scarcity of developable land, however, produce fierce competition over land use. Community activists who oppose greater densities in their neighborhoods and demand that land be used to build affordable housing have long battled large-scale developers who want to attract new capital to the city (DeLeon 1992, 2003; Hartman 2002; Mollenkopf 1983). The recent progressive majority on the Board of Supervisors is more open to policies that benefit workers, the poor, and minorities. Yet San Francisco officials—and the mayor in particular—are still keen to improve the city's economic vitality, as was true in earlier decades.

Between the early 1960s and mid-1980s, San Francisco's transformation to a postindustrial service economy went hand in hand with extensive urban redevelopment. With the stimulus of federal urban renewal grants, a pro-growth coalition of business, labor, and political leaders set about to improve the city's physical conditions. Together, they cleared "blighted" areas around the downtown business district by removing undesirable populations (including immigrants), improving regional transportation, and constructing high-rise office buildings, ultimately giving San Francisco its Manhattanized skyline (DeLeon 1992; Hartman 2002; Mollenkopf 1983).

When the federal government retreated from urban renewal in the 1970s, cities increasingly privatized their economic policies and created partnerships with business interests to fund urban development (Luce 2004; Peterson

1981). In the 1980s and 1990s, San Francisco officials developed tax breaks for businesses and public subsidies for development projects so that the city could compete for mobile capital.[19] They also provided infrastructure to reduce the costs of doing business in the city[20] and lowered the cost of providing public services by contracting with nonprofit organizations, including those serving immigrants.

In this context, immigrant-serving nonprofits have found it challenging to convince San Francisco officials to spend scarce resources on disadvantaged immigrants. Opponents of immigrant rights and integration policies often couched their opposition in terms of cost and expressed concern about the effects on the city's already strained budget. Certain business interests strongly opposed raising wages for the city's lowest-paid workers, who include many immigrants. They felt that measures like the San Francisco Minimum Wage Ordinance would transfer money from the hands of businesses to those of the poor, undermining the city's competitive position. Nonprofit advocates therefore had to convince city officials that such policies would not just benefit deserving immigrants but would also advance the interests of other city residents and city government.

Federal Immigration Enforcement

The U.S. Supreme Court has declared repeatedly since the late nineteenth century that power over immigration and citizenship rests exclusively with the federal government. This position is known as the plenary power doctrine, which holds that only the federal legislative and executive branches can decide which foreigners may enter and legally reside in the United States, when they can be expelled from the country, and when and how they can acquire U.S. citizenship (Aleinikoff, Martin, and Motomura 2008). States and municipalities have no authority over these questions. When states and municipalities do attempt to enter the immigration domain, as many have in recent years, courts have often declared their policies—regardless of whether they restrict or expand immigrant rights—unconstitutional.

While states and municipalities cannot control their borders and regulate the flow of immigrants in and out of their jurisdictions, they can draw on their power to protect the health, safety, and welfare of their residents to adopt measures that affect immigrants. Since the U.S. Congress failed to enact comprehensive immigration reform in 2006–2007, more and more state and local governments have used labor regulations, housing policies, local land use provisions, identification requirements, and access to health and education services to affect immigrant settlement (NCSL 2013). Many of these policies have been restrictive, seeking to drive immigrants away. But others, like those enacted in San Francisco, intend to provide immigrants with new rights and benefits.

San Francisco's immigrant-serving nonprofits have developed the normative orientation that immigrants, regardless of their citizenship and documentation status, can and should make claims on city government. The larger national political context, however, has made it harder for them to advocate immigrant rights policies, especially if they accommodate undocumented immigrants. The terrorist attacks of 2001 increased public opposition to undocumented immigration and engendered federal laws, administrative practices, and court decisions limiting the rights and freedom of movement of undocumented immigrants (Jones-Correa and de Graauw 2013). The media, anti-immigrant groups from outside San Francisco, and federal officials have all pressed for federal preeminence in regulating undocumented immigration when San Francisco has considered initiatives to protect and benefit undocumented immigrants.

These mounting pressures on San Francisco officials to align their policies and practices with federal enforcement objectives have hindered nonprofit advocates in their quest for immigrant rights and integration policies. The increased federal scrutiny of the city's lenient treatment of undocumented immigrants drove a political rift between the mayor and the Board of Supervisors. Federal immigration enforcement activities in the Bay Area also caused undocumented immigrants to retreat from public life and avoid contact with local government officials. All in all, federal intervention soured the advocacy context in San Francisco and weakened the existing consensus among key city officials in support of new immigrant rights and integration policies. This has pressed immigrant-serving nonprofits to be more strategic in framing their advocacy so as to minimize media and political scrutiny and to ensure that the champions of federal immigration preeminence do not reverse their policy gains.

Strategic Local Advocacy

San Francisco is home to a large number of disadvantaged immigrants who face significant integration hurdles. Immigrant-serving nonprofits have promoted their social, economic, civic, and political rights with San Francisco officials. They have had to contend with challenges stemming from San Francisco's fragmented government, weak political leadership, partyless milieu, and social and ethnic diversity. San Francisco's hyperpluralist organizational landscape, policymakers' propensity for business development policies that strengthen the local economy, and the city's progressive political culture in a nation focused on immigration enforcement present them with additional challenges.

The following case studies on language access, labor rights, and municipal ID cards in San Francisco show how nonprofits have adopted a tripartite strategy focused on (a) administrative advocacy, (b) cross-sectoral and cross-organizational collaborations, and (c) strategic issue framing. These advocacy strategies show how nonprofit advocates navigated and negotiated these local contextual challenges as well as the challenges stemming from their tax-exempt status and limited organizational resources. Chapter 3 examines what nonprofits' tax-exempt status and dependence on government funding meant for how they interacted with elected and non-elected city officials and the kind of influence they wielded on language access. Chapter 4 investigates how immigrant-serving nonprofits fared in building advocacy coalitions on labor rights with labor unions, which have more political resources and enjoy more advocacy freedoms. And chapter 5 examines how nonprofits coped with the challenges of framing municipal ID cards for undocumented immigrants at a time when San Francisco officials were under increasing pressure to toe the line of the federal government's enforcement agenda.

CHAPTER 3

Providing Language Access through Nonprofit-Government Collaborations

In July 2008, La Raza Centro Legal (the Community's Legal Center), the Central American Resource Center, St. Peter's Housing Committee, and the Bay Area Immigrant Rights Coalition brought out two hundred community members to the steps of city hall to rally San Francisco officials to reaffirm the city's sanctuary ordinance, a law protecting undocumented immigrants from federal immigration officials. Waving signs, raising fists, and chanting "no one is illegal" and "sí se puede" ("yes, we can"), nonprofit advocates faced off with a dozen members of the Minuteman Project, an anti-immigrant group that patrols the U.S.-Mexico border to keep undocumented immigrants out. The Minutemen had come to San Francisco to demand the repeal of the sanctuary ordinance after an undocumented immigrant from El Salvador had committed a triple murder in the city earlier that summer. The demonstration was overall peaceful, but tempers flared and the police arrested two immigrant rights supporters for disorderly conduct (Knight 2008c).

It is not uncommon for immigrant-serving nonprofits in San Francisco to organize and participate in demonstrations to push their agenda. Media coverage of such demonstrations—along with scholarship on the nationwide immigration protests in 2006 (Cordero-Guzmán et al. 2008; Pallares and Flores-González 2010; Voss and Bloemraad 2011)—have popularized the image that these nonprofits are social movement organizations that rely heavily on confrontational tactics to bring about policy change. In reality, however, the interactions between immigrant-serving nonprofits and government are much more multifaceted and complex: Many nonprofit advocates also work *with*, and not just *around* or *against*, government officials, and they adjust their approach to advocacy accordingly. In other words, immigrant-serving nonprofits can be strategic political actors.

Nonprofit–government relations are complex in large part because nonprofit organizations rely heavily on government funding and are legally restricted in the amount and the types of advocacy they can undertake. These constraints make civil society scholars pessimistic about what nonprofits can do to bring about policy change (Andrews and Edwards 2004; Berry and Arons 2003; Boris and Steuerle 2006; Taylor, Craig, and Wilkinson 2002). Yet the immigrant-serving nonprofits under study here managed to overcome these constraints, and they influenced the enactment and implementation of immigrant rights and integration policies. They did this by asserting their expertise about the issues facing their communities within ongoing collaborations with city legislators and city administrative officials. While these cross-sectoral collaborations produced clear policy benefits for disadvantaged immigrants, they can also coopt nonprofits and blur the public-private divide in ways that can compromise both sides of the relationship and limit the benefits for immigrants.

In San Francisco, immigrant-serving nonprofits proposed, won enactment of, and helped to implement and enforce the Equal Access to Services Ordinance (EASO). This 2001 law, which was amended in 2009 and 2015, requires city departments to offer information and public services in several foreign languages, including Chinese, Spanish, and Tagalog. Because immigrant-serving nonprofits already monopolized the issue of language access and did not have to share the spotlight with other types of organizations, EASO is an archetypal case of how nonprofits collaborate with local government. Nonprofits were able to use their expertise on language access problems to advise and enlighten San Francisco government officials at every stage of the policymaking process. As a result, immigrants with limited English proficiency in San Francisco enjoy stronger language access rights today than ever before.

Language Access Expertise

It took some time and a number of battles over both inclusive and restrictive language access policies for immigrant-serving nonprofits in San Francisco to develop the policy expertise that was key to their subsequent success with

EASO. In the late 1960s, San Francisco went through a legal battle for bilingual education when it came to light that city schools had failed to assist Chinese and Latino students who did not speak English. In 1971, lawyers for non-English-speaking Chinese students brought a class action lawsuit against the city school district. In its landmark *Lau v. Nichols* decision of 1974, the U.S. Supreme Court overturned lower courts and ruled unanimously that San Francisco schools had not provided equal educational opportunities to about 1,800 students of Chinese ancestry. The city had thereby violated Title VI of the 1964 Civil Rights Act, which bans discrimination on the basis of race, color, or national origin in any program or activity receiving federal financial assistance. The court also mandated that state and local governments craft a remedy. This sparked a long struggle between local school officials and a coalition of immigrant-serving nonprofits that wanted greater input in school administration decisions (Moran 2007; Wang 1994).

Even as this court case made civil rights history in 1974, a new generation of restrictive language measures germinated in San Francisco less than a decade later. In 1983—when the city used trilingual voting ballots in English, Chinese, and Spanish in accordance with Section 203 of the 1975 amendments to the 1965 Voting Rights Act—62 percent of San Francisco voters approved Proposition O. This advisory initiative directed city officials to urge the federal government to provide ballots and voting materials in English only. Initiated by Supervisor Quentin Kopp, a conservative independent, the proposition's campaign received backing from U.S. English, the recently established lobbying organization dedicated to making English the official language of the United States. Most leading city and state officials at the time, including San Francisco mayor Dianne Feinstein and State Assembly Speaker Willie Brown, joined immigrant advocacy groups in opposing Proposition O. The measure, however, enjoyed support from Republican, Democratic, and independent voters alike, people from all socioeconomic and ethnic backgrounds, and the *San Francisco Chronicle* (Woolard 1990).

Because Proposition O was nonbinding and local voters could not overturn federal voting rights legislation, San Francisco election officials continued to provide election materials in English, Chinese, and Spanish. The success of Proposition O in the liberal climate of San Francisco did, however, help to diffuse similar and more substantive restrictive language policies to the state of California and beyond (Diamond 1990; Woolard 1990). Encouraged by the success of Proposition O, U.S. English launched a statewide test of voter sentiment on bilingual ballots (Proposition 38 in 1984) and a statewide initiative to make English the official language of California (Proposition 63 of 1986).[1] The passage of these two restrictive language policies in California in turn boosted the English-only movement nationwide, and many other states considered legislation to declare English the official language in the late 1980s and 1990s. Twenty-eight states still had such laws in effect in early 2015 (English First 2015).

Over the next decade, as San Francisco's electorate continued to change and nonprofit organizations evolved their forms of advocacy, San Francisco officials became more accommodating of language diversity. Even when the state's voters approved Proposition 227 in 1998, which virtually banned bilingual education in California public schools, the San Francisco Board of Education voted unanimously to continue bilingual education programs (Jorae 2009). In 2001, San Francisco became the first city to consider, and after Oakland the second to adopt, a local language access policy. San Francisco's proposed EASO served as a model for the Oakland ordinance enacted in May 2001 and similar policies adopted in Philadelphia (2001 and 2008), New York City (2003 and 2008), Minneapolis (2003), Washington, D.C. (2004), Seattle (2007), and Houston (2013).

San Francisco's mixed history with language access led immigrant-serving nonprofits to develop deep expertise in this area. To begin with, nonprofits serving Chinese immigrants—including the Chinese Six Companies, Chinatown Neighborhood Legal Services, and Chinese for Affirmative Action—supported the *Lau v. Nichols* case in several ways. They recruited families to join the class action lawsuit, filed amicus curiae (friend of the court) briefs in support of the Chinese students, talked with San Francisco school administrators about how to develop the court-ordered relief plan, and trained teachers in bilingual education (Moran 2007; Wang 1994). Chinese and Latino organizations campaigned against Proposition O and subsequently lobbied local election officials to reduce language barriers to voting (CAA 2015). By the time these organizations began to push for EASO in the late 1990s, they had become an authoritative voice on these matters and demonstrated a willingness to confront and engage local policymakers.

San Francisco's back and forth on language access issues shows that local immigrant rights initiatives do not happen in a policy vacuum. Local policies often respond to, yet can also drive, federal and state policy dynamics. Initially, actions by San Francisco's immigrant-serving nonprofits, voters, and policymakers on bilingual education and multilingual voting assistance responded to federal civil rights legislation. The 1964 Civil Rights Act triggered the 1974 *Lau v. Nichols* case, which in turn influenced federal and state education policies.[2] Voters' adoption of Proposition O in 1983 was a reaction to the 1975 amendments to the 1965 Voting Rights Act and prompted later state initiatives. Clearly, local immigrant rights initiatives unfold within a context in which no one level of government has exclusive power over immigrant integration. Federalist dynamics also influenced the politics surrounding EASO and allowed nonprofits to use a civil rights frame to promote a language access ordinance in a period in which immigrant rights issues had been sharply politicized in California.

Language Access as Civil Rights

Enacted in 2001, EASO sought to overcome the language barriers that prevented limited English speakers in San Francisco from understanding government information and receiving services. EASO requires fourteen Tier 1 Departments—those city departments that have the most public contact and responsibility for public safety—to translate their informational materials and regulations and hire bilingual staff if a substantial portion of their clients do not read or speak English.[3] Under EASO, these departments had to make adjustments when at least ten thousand city residents or 5 percent of a department's clients primarily spoke a language other than English. As a result of EASO, these departments need to offer information and services in English, Chinese, Spanish, and Tagalog citywide.[4] Branch offices of city departments in areas with concentrations of Russian and Vietnamese immigrants also have to offer oral translation in Russian and Vietnamese. EASO also requires these fourteen departments to develop annual compliance plans and establish a complaint procedure to address alleged violations of the ordinance.

EASO replicates language access provisions in federal and state civil rights laws. As table 8 summarizes, EASO builds on Title VI of the 1964 Civil Rights Act, which offers protections from national origin discrimination and provides the legal foundation for language access legislation, and federal Executive Order 13166 issued by President Clinton in 2000 and reaffirmed by the Bush administration in 2002 to improve the implementation of Title VI. Executive Order 13166 requires administrative agencies at various levels of government to offer translation and interpretation services to limited English proficient individuals consistent with Title VI regulations. EASO also emulates Section 203 of the Voting Rights Act, added in 1975, which mandates language access in voting, and California's 1973 Dymally-Alatorre Bilingual Services Act, which mandates state and local agencies to provide bilingual information and services.

EASO has more robust enforcement mechanisms than these federal and state language access provisions. It establishes specific language thresholds for covered city departments, covers a larger number of city departments,

Table 8   Federal, state, and local language access policies compared

Level	Federal	Federal	Federal	California	San Francisco
Policy	Title VI of the Civil Rights Act (1964)	Section 203 of the Voting Rights Act (1975)	Executive Order 13166 (2000)	Dymally-Alatorre Bilingual Services Act (1973)	Equal Access to Services Ordinance (2001)
Covered entities	All government agencies that receive federal financial assistance	All electoral districts	All federally conducted or federally assisted programs and activities	State and local agencies that serve a "substantial number of non-English-speaking people"	Tier 1 city departments
Language threshold	In education: when 5% or more of the student population belongs to a language minority group	When 10,000 or 5% or more of voters in a district belong to specific language minority groups (Spanish, Asian, Native American, Alaska Native)	None	• State agencies: languages spoken by 5% or more of non-English-speaking clients • Local agencies: none	Languages spoken by 10,000 city residents or 5% or more of the non-English-speaking clients served by a Tier 1 city department
Covers translation?	Yes	Yes	Yes	Yes	Yes
Covers interpretation?	Yes	Yes	Yes	Yes	Yes
Enforcer	Office for Civil Rights, Department of Education	Department of Justice can litigate enforcement	None, but Department of Justice provides technical assistance	None, but State Personnel Board provides technical assistance	Immigrant Rights Commission
Right of private action?	Only in situations where intentional discrimination can be shown	Yes	No	No	No, but individuals and organizations can seek a writ of mandate from state courts
Administrative review?	Yes	Yes	No	Yes	Yes
Noncompliance penalty?	Possible termination of federal financial assistance	None, but attorney's fees are recoverable for private citizens who enforce Section 203	None	None	None

and identifies a local government entity to monitor the implementation and enforcement of EASO. Individuals and organizations cannot directly sue the city for failure to provide language access, but they can seek a writ of mandate from state courts to compel city officials to implement and enforce EASO.

Immigrant-serving nonprofits in San Francisco sought to provide full and forceful implementation of federal and state civil rights protections. To do so, they designed a local law that expanded and strengthened language access rights for limited English speakers and held city officials responsible for realizing those rights. Immigrant advocacy organizations have used the same strategy in other municipalities. In Washington, D.C., and New York City, for example, the D.C. Language Access Coalition, the New York Immigration Coalition, and Make the Road New York relied on Title VI regulations and Clinton's Executive Order 13166 to advocate passage of the D.C. Language Access Act of 2004 and New York City's Local Law 73 of 2003 and Executive Order 120 of 2008—all local language access policies similar to San Francisco's EASO.

EASO Fails in 1999

EASO was years in the making. Nonprofit advocates made two attempts to convince San Francisco legislators to enact it. The first attempt in 1999 failed, but the effort conveyed lessons that led to the success of the next attempt in 2001. The second time around, advocates altered their campaign by emphasizing their issue expertise and by taking advantage of the city's restoration of district elections in 2000, which brought in a new slate of district supervisors. The initial failure of EASO taught advocates that they would face real opposition even in a progressive city like San Francisco and that they could not assume the support of the city's racial and ethnic minority legislators. They learned to act more strategically by working much harder to educate city officials, the media, and the larger community of the need and merits of a language access ordinance and by framing EASO as a civil rights issue, not an immigrant rights issue.

Setting the Agenda

The lack of language access first surfaced as a salient issue in the 1990s, when immigration to California was at a peak and immigrant-serving nonprofits received complaints from immigrants across the state who were unable to access city, county, and state services due to their inability to speak English. "At our organization and at a number of other organizations across the state, lots of folks were coming into the office," a Chinese for Affirmative Action (CAA) advocate commented. "And a lot of the difficulties were the same, that they were finding it difficult to navigate public services because of language barriers. It emerged as a consistent problem that limited

English speaking immigrants were facing, and these immigrants were turning to us for help."[5] It was through their interactions with primarily Asian immigrants—the largest foreign-born group in San Francisco—that CAA first learned of language access barriers in San Francisco and elsewhere in California.

The language access gap affected organizations like CAA in direct and negative ways. They had to use their own resources to translate and help clients fill out forms, processes that were government responsibilities according to federal and state civil rights laws. In theory, Title VI of the 1964 Civil Rights Act and the 1973 Dymally-Alatorre Bilingual Services Act should have required government agencies to provide limited English speakers with access to information and services. In reality, noncompliance was common and no one enforced either law. "The Dymally-Alatorre Bilingual Services Act was passed back in 1973, but it was as if the issue was forgotten for two decades," the same CAA advocate noted. "It wasn't until the mid-1990s that people started paying attention to the fact that we actually had laws on the books. And that's when we figured maybe that's the way to go, that we should start enforcing these civil rights protections or close loopholes so that people can get meaningful access to public agencies and services."[6] Such widespread complaints led fifteen immigrant-serving nonprofits from across the state to form a coalition to advocate stronger measures. They moved initially to politicize the issue around state compliance with federal and state civil rights laws.

In the late 1990s, however, a preponderance of California voters had shown strong hostility to immigrants and strong opposition to language access. In 1994, 59 percent of them voted yes on Proposition 187, which denied social services, health care, and public education to undocumented immigrants. Four years later, 61 percent of California voters approved Proposition 227, the "English for the Children" initiative, which virtually ended bilingual education in public schools. In efforts to achieve change within these hostile political waters, the coalition decided to ask for an audit of the Dymally-Alatorre Bilingual Services Act (DABSA). "We were trying to figure out what's the best strategy for getting better enforcement and better access to services for immigrants at a time when the political environment was *really* unfriendly," commented a second CAA advocate who participated in the coalition's deliberations. "We decided that at the state level we ask for an audit. . . . It allowed us to talk about immigrant language rights as civil rights, and the audit was a way for us to change things by documenting first the lack of enforcement and implementation of existing laws."[7] State Senator Martha Escutia (D-Montebello), one of the few legislators interested in working on language access legislation at the time, helped advocates to get approval from the Joint Legislative Audit Committee of an audit of DABSA.

The state auditor's seventy-five-page report, published in 1999, confirmed what nonprofit advocates already knew: that only a minority of state and local officials knew of DABSA, that implementation of the law had been consistently poor, and that the law's enforcement was practically nonexistent. The report urged state and local agencies to do more to address their clients' needs for bilingual services but contained only vague recommendations as to how to accomplish this (California State Auditor 1999). Nonprofit advocates used the report to give language access public visibility and convinced state officials to try to put more teeth into DABSA. State Senator Escutia (S.B. 987) and Assemblyman Leland Yee (D–San Francisco, A.B. 2408) carried legislation in 2002 and 2004, respectively, that would introduce enforcement mechanisms and require all state agencies to develop implementation plans. The bills passed both houses, but governors Gray Davis (D) and Arnold Schwarzenegger (R) vetoed them, citing budget constraints. While immigrant-serving nonprofits failed to change state policy, they did succeed in getting an audit that thoroughly documented language barriers in California at a time when the mood in the state was decidedly anti-immigrant.

Avoiding Divisive Issue Frames

Although the coalition's initial intent was to ensure state compliance with federal and state civil rights laws, immigrant advocates in San Francisco decided to push simultaneously for a new local law. One of my three CAA informants explained their decision to take the campaign local:

> We decided that a local ordinance would be a good strategy because it did three things from our perspective. One, it was a way to mobilize some support for this issue within our own communities, at the grassroots. Second, it was a public education tool to inform policymakers—the Board of Supervisors and department heads—that the existing laws were already there and that the city wasn't fully complying. And related to that, we were trying to come up with new standards, more specific standards and guidelines for implementing those laws. And the last thing we wanted to do was build some political support for this concept of language access, because we felt that without political support there would be no implementation of any of these laws.[8]

A local campaign would allow immigrant-serving nonprofits to deploy tactics near and dear to their organizational missions. It would give them the opportunity to design a new law with clear benefits to immigrants while educating policymakers and the general public about the importance of language access and mobilizing the immigrant grassroots to action.

CAA, a member of the statewide coalition that sought to amend DABSA, led the campaign to enact EASO in San Francisco. CAA has advocated language rights since its founding in 1969 and dedicated two of its eleven employees to language access advocacy during the 1990s. Throughout the policymaking process, CAA collaborated with seven other San Francisco–based immigrant-serving nonprofits: La Raza Centro Legal, the Asian Women's Shelter, the Chinatown Community Development Center, Self-Help for the Elderly, the Day Labor Program, the Asian Law Caucus, and the Interfaith Coalition for Immigrant Rights. These organizations also worked with the Employment Law Center, a San Francisco–based nonprofit that advocates on behalf of low-wage workers, and the Lawyers' Committee for Civil Rights of the San Francisco Bay Area, a nonprofit that protects and promotes the rights of communities of color, immigrants, and refugees. Finally, they enjoyed support from SEIU Local 790, a local public employees union with an immigrant membership. Other labor unions, however, remained aloof throughout the policymaking process, largely because language access was not a primary concern to their members. Immigrant-serving nonprofits dominated the enactment of EASO, from agenda-setting to implementation and enforcement, giving them an effective monopoly on policymakers' attention.

In their advocacy, immigrant-serving organizations emphasized the uncontroversial nature of a local language access policy. During public hearings of the Board of Supervisors, they testified that EASO would simply bring San Francisco into full compliance with federal and state civil rights laws, thereby making the city a safer and healthier community. They mobilized dozens of their immigrant clients to testify to the urgent need for EASO and share real-life stories of the consequences of language discrimination. They included stories of battered women who had to rely on their batterers for translation when communicating with police. Elderly immigrants related how they were abused by family members or taken advantage of by businesses and could not ask public officials for help. Limited English proficient parents told how their children had to accompany them to hospitals and translate their conditions to medical staff. Also common were stories of immigrants who did not report crime to police or experienced excessive police force at the hands of officers unable to communicate in Chinese or Spanish. Finally, immigrants described how they did not seek out preventative medical care because of their inability to speak English and instead relied on costly emergency room care when they became critically ill. By giving language discrimination a human face, immigrant advocates positioned EASO on the city's political agenda as a practical solution for concrete problems as well as a way to secure the civil rights of limited English proficient individuals.

It is equally important to note how advocates chose *not* to frame EASO in public fora. While the proposed policy would benefit immigrants struggling with English, advocates avoided framing language access as an outright immigrant rights issue. One CAA advocate explained that they did this to minimize scrutiny of EASO. "We thought the Board of Supervisors was open to the idea of the policy," he said, "but they needed so much assistance in gathering language statistics, gathering stories, and framing the argument in such a way that they're not playing into the hands of possible detractors and immigration opponents . . . making it about meeting real needs, improving government service delivery, and strengthening civil rights protections. That's what the community groups provided them."[9]

Framing EASO as a practical solution to problems generated by language discrimination was also a good move because it enabled advocates to play on policymakers' eagerness to claim credit for improving the way the city runs. Supervisor Mark Leno, the policy's lead sponsor later on in the campaign, supported EASO because of its practical benefits:

> Nonprofits briefed me and my staff on the issue and the history of it, and we recognized some startling facts. About a quarter of San Franciscans are less than proficient in English. Nearly half of all San Franciscans speak a language other than English at home, which is just stunning, and the entire city is at potential risk if the government cannot communicate with the citizenry in times of emergency certainly, but on an ongoing basis we have services. That is after all why government exists, to provide services. And if we can't communicate with a quarter to a half of our citizenry, then what are we doing? . . . Our collective opponents, mostly Republicans, use language policy as a political weapon, but we're more interested in the delivery of government services in an efficient fashion and keeping our city safe and vibrant.[10]

Nonprofit advocates consciously chose this set of framings to maximize support for EASO and minimize opposition. They were savvy in tailoring their strategies to the political context.

What Went Wrong?

The push for EASO nonetheless failed in 1999. This was not for lack of preparation. CAA and other immigrant-serving nonprofits got the San

Francisco Immigrant Rights Commission to hold hearings to document language barriers in accessing government agencies and services. They researched the issue, drafted the language of the bill, and secured sponsorship from Supervisor Mabel Teng, an immigrant from Hong Kong for whom language access, according to one CAA advocate, was an issue "very central to her identity."[11] The Board of Supervisors nevertheless did not hold a hearing on the EASO bill, and neither local legislators nor the Mayor's Office gave it strong support. These developments caught nonprofit advocates by surprise and led them to reconsider their tactics.

Some nonprofit advocates thought the policy had succumbed to machine-like dynamics between Mayor Willie Brown and the Board of Supervisors. Brown initially expressed support for EASO. After his 1999 reelection, however, he was less receptive to it and expressed concerns over how much the policy would cost. "The mayor did not want to expend money on this," one CAA advocate commented, "because he felt it would tie the hands of city agencies in a way he didn't want to."[12] Advocates also thought that Brown, an African American, feared that EASO's mandate for bilingual personnel would hurt African American civil servants who often lack proficiency in foreign languages. "The mayor was a very strong supporter of putting African Americans in civil service jobs," the same advocate added, "and he likely viewed the ordinance as a threat to that."[13] Brown's substantial influence over the Board of Supervisors in 1999—he had appointed six of the eleven sitting Board members through pre-election vacancies—explains why Teng and other supervisors also retracted their support for EASO.

Advocates also believed that Mayor Brown and City Controller Ed Harrington had fomented union opposition to EASO. This would not be surprising given the uneasy relationship that existed between public-sector unions and nonprofits in San Francisco in the 1990s (as described in the next chapter). Initially, unions were concerned that EASO's requirement to hire bilingual staff would have a negative effect on unionized civil servants unable to speak Chinese or Spanish. Unions eventually endorsed EASO, but only after receiving assurances that no existing city employees would lose their jobs and that bilingual staff would only be phased in over time as positions opened up through attrition. Mayor Brown, though, clearly had strong reservations about EASO and used his sway with the Board of Supervisors to stop the policy from moving forward in 1999.

In hindsight, immigrant advocates also thought that they had not leveraged their issue expertise to build enough broad-based support for the ordinance. "We had done all this research and gathered many compelling stories about the need for more language access," one CAA advocate reflected, "and we thought we had a strong case for the new ordinance."[14] They came to the conclusion, however, that they had not shared their expertise widely enough or engaged a sufficient range of policymakers, the media, and other community groups. "Mabel [Teng] really took to the issue and made it her own, but we should have done more to talk to other supervisors about [EASO] and get their support," the same advocate admitted. "We also didn't navigate the media to our advantage . . . so that they understood the issue and they were able to paint the human story behind the issue."[15] A second CAA advocate added that they had done insufficient outreach to nonprofits catering to Latino immigrants. "Obviously, language discrimination was a problem also for Latino immigrants. . . . In retrospect, we should have been more proactive in reaching out to groups in the Latino community, to have them sign on to the campaign."[16]

Clearly, nonprofit advocates occupied an outside status in 1999 and lacked inside information on the progression of the policy. They were not able to develop reliable cost estimates, which would have required coordinating communication between Teng, the budget analyst, the legislative analyst, and various city departments. Additionally, Teng had agreed to be the policy's sponsor, was personally committed to the issue, and benefited from advocates' expertise on the issue. But she was not readily available for meetings with nonprofit advocates and never told her allies why she did not schedule a Board of Supervisors hearing on EASO. Finally, nonprofit advocates never knew where Mayor Brown really stood on the issue. One CAA advocate commented on nonprofits' outside status, concluding that "we just couldn't tell from the outside what concerns the Brown administration had and why Mabel [Teng] wasn't actively pushing the ordinance despite her support for it."[17] The collaborations between nonprofit advocates and city officials broke down early on in the legislative process, causing the EASO bill to die prematurely.

The early failure contained valuable lessons for immigrant-serving nonprofits. One CAA advocate reflected on the miscalculations they and their allies made in their efforts to enact EASO in 1999:

> Going in, we thought the politics of the situation were easier than they were. We thought we had a key supporter in Mabel Teng and Mabel had gotten the mayor to actually endorse the measure. We had those two combinations together and it looked like it was not something that would require a great groundswell. But in retrospect, it's clear that there were internal oppositions to the ordinance. There certainly was resistance at the very top level of the city, including the Mayor's Office. We never had those candid conversations, because when we talked to

the Mayor's Office at the time, they said, "You know, we're interested in it," and we got the company line, which was that they were looking into how to implement [the policy] because it was so complicated. In reality, I don't think anybody was looking into it.[18]

Nonprofit advocates realized they had assumed there was more political support for EASO than there really was. They also realized they had to work much harder to get legislators, city administrators, the media, and the local community engaged with the language access issue. All these lessons influenced how they took up EASO the second time in 2001.

EASO Passes in 2001

Immigrant-serving nonprofits waited until after the 2000 elections to make a second attempt to enact EASO. One CAA advocate explained the wait:

After [the 1999 failure], we tried to figure out what was the best way of overcoming resistance. What we ultimately decided was that since San Francisco's Board of Supervisors was going to a district election system, we were likely to have an entirely new Board. We saw no point in pushing forward something that the Mayor's Office not only seemed opposed to, but the mayor had very close relations with the old Board of Supervisors. He probably had a veto-proof majority, and it was a calculation on our part that it wasn't worth the fight. Could we have succeeded? Possibly, but it would have taken an incredible amount of resources and we would have burnt our bridges with people, because there were people who felt very sympathetic to us, who would have been torn had the mayor decided that he didn't want the measure. So, we waited until 2001, because that was the new Board of Supervisors.[19]

In 2000, San Francisco switched from citywide, at-large elections back to district elections, which dramatically changed the composition of the Board of Supervisors. A more progressive Board with greater independence from the mayor's influence replaced the one aligned with the Brown administration (DeLeon 2003). Nonprofit advocates anticipated this change and hoped that the new slate of supervisors would be more receptive to enacting EASO.

The precise outcome of the 2000 elections, however, caught advocates off guard. "What surprised us," one CAA employee commented, "was that Mabel Teng was not reelected, and neither was Michael Yaki. They were our key supporters, and then we thought we really had to come up with a new strategy."[20] Without being able to rely on these two Asian American supervisors to provide a straightforward entrée into San Francisco politics, CAA instead asked Supervisor Mark Leno to become EASO's lead sponsor. Leno chaired the Finance Committee, which the bill had to clear; he had a reputation of being easy to work with and someone who saw his commitments through to the end; he was considered a rising star on the Board; he maintained a good relationship with the mayor; and he used to own a sign company that had exposed him to multilingual messages. Nonprofit advocates thought that Leno would be able to provide strong leadership on the issue and was personally engaged with the proposal. The added benefit, as Leno himself articulated, was that, as a white legislator, he could give "credibility to the language issue beyond the confines of immigrant communities of color."[21]

Nonprofit advocates could have secured the sponsorship of a supervisor with an immigrant background, who could relate on a personal level to the language barriers faced by Asian and Latino immigrants. However, they passed over supervisors Leland Yee (an immigrant from China), Matt Gonzalez (whose mother is an immigrant from Mexico and whose father is Mexican American), and Gerardo Sandoval (a second-generation immigrant from Mexico) to work with an openly gay male and a third-generation descendant of Jewish Russian immigrants. One CAA advocate further underscored how important it was for them to find a powerful legislative ally when he mused about another supervisor they had considered for EASO's lead sponsor: "We thought about Gavin Newsom at the time, too, and maybe in retrospect we should have gone with Gavin."[22] Newsom, then supervisor for District 2, went on to become mayor of San Francisco in 2004 and lieutenant governor of California in 2011.

Immigrant-serving nonprofits reintroduced EASO to the Board in 2001. The second time around, one CAA advocate commented, they left nothing to chance:

> We certainly didn't take for granted that we had political support the second time around. We already did a full court process of talking to all the supervisors, talking to the Mayor's Office, engaging them. . . . We developed cost estimates and addressed the issue of resources. We reached out actively and early on to labor unions and the media. We did the community building and grassroots outreach that we didn't think was necessary the first time around because we thought we had political support. . . . That's where the other community groups helped us. All these groups have different relations with politicians. Some were close to Willie Brown and we tried to get them involved.[23]

Advocates pursued a much more proactive approach: They readily shared their language access expertise with legislators and the media, reached out to address legislators' concerns about EASO, and built broad-based support for the policy proposal.

The same coalition of eight immigrant-serving nonprofits active in 1999 banded together again in 2001. They met regularly to organize the campaign and divide the labor among coalition members. CAA—the nonprofit with a noted expertise on language access and staff capacity dedicated to advocacy—took the lead in researching the issue and redrafting the EASO bill. CAA also maintained communications with Leno, participated in Board negotiations regarding EASO's details, and conducted outreach to the mainstream media. Other immigrant-serving nonprofits engaged individual supervisors as the bill traveled first through the Finance Committee and then the full Board of Supervisors. Their staffs met with individual supervisors to share personal stories of the problems that occur when government business is conducted in English only. They and their clients also testified during public hearings, answered supervisors' questions about the proposal, and did outreach to other nonprofits and the ethnic media.

These coalitional dynamics show that nonprofits with different strengths and varying inclinations to engage in politics can complement one another and become a cohesive political force. CAA is a mature organization with language access expertise and a relatively sophisticated understanding of city politics. It is not afraid to engage policymakers, even in a confrontational manner if necessary. By itself, however, CAA could not speak for all immigrant communities in San Francisco, and it lacked the staff resources to carry out a successful advocacy campaign on its own. CAA's allies also had access to local policymakers, but one CAA advocate explained that "some dropped out of that process because either they weren't interested in being the issue's torchbearer or felt they couldn't participate because of their big contracts or restrictions against lobbying."[24] Instead, these other nonprofits identified ways in which language barriers create problems for both immigrants and city officials, mobilized immigrants' testimony, and presented compelling human stories that earned EASO a place on legislators' agenda.

These coalitional dynamics also help explain why nonprofits feel comfortable engaging in politics in other ways even when they are hesitant to lobby government. "The other groups," one CAA advocate commented, "brought the language issue to us not because they thought it was just our issue, but because they thought we were in the best position to take the heat for it."[25] CAA's advocacy with Leno and other legislators constitutes lobbying and is subject to federal lobbying restrictions. Since CAA needed only little face time with supervisors to communicate their policy priorities, their advocacy remained within permissible limits. CAA's lobbying, however, provided other immigrant-serving nonprofits with a cover for their advocacy and protection from unwanted exposure. Their activities included educating policymakers about the need for better language access, providing policymakers with technical assistance, and giving invited testimony. These activities similarly aimed to enlist legislators' support, but they are not necessarily restricted by federal law and are less likely to attract public scrutiny. By acting as the coalition's chief lobbyist, CAA removed some of the reservations that other nonprofits had about advocating in support of EASO as well.

Addressing Criticisms

Supervisor Leno's sponsorship of EASO developed into a mutually beneficial partnership between his office and the coalition of immigrant-serving nonprofits. Through Leno, one CAA employee explained, nonprofit advocates were able "to overcome their outside status" by having ready access to "communication channels to stay informed about developments related to the ordinance that were taking place inside city hall."[26] Leno in turn explained that nonprofits "brought expertise and firsthand knowledge of the need for the ordinance,"[27] which insured him that he could claim credit for a well-researched policy that would ultimately win approval. Leno and nonprofit advocates also worked together to successfully debunk criticisms of EASO from several supervisors during public hearings on the ordinance in May 2001.

Advocates helped Leno neutralize opposition to EASO in three ways. First, CAA helped calm the concerns that Board President Aaron Peskin and Supervisor Tony Hall continued to have about the fiscal impact of a policy that called for translating government documents into Chinese and Spanish and hiring bilingual staff. Budget Analyst Harvey Rose estimated that the city would incur $600,696 in payments for document translation in the first year of EASO's implementation, with significantly lower translation costs in subsequent years, and an ongoing annual cost of $99,979 for the Immigrant Rights Commission to enforce the policy. Additionally, certified bilingual city employees in public contact positions would receive additional pay ranging from $70 to $120 per month.[28]

During the EASO hearings, Leno publicly thanked the coalition for helping collect the data that the budget analyst had used to estimate the costs. However, he thought that Rose had overestimated the cost of EASO, which could be accomplished "for less than what the budget analyst points out in his report."[29] Leno noted that translations could be done more cheaply in-house, rather than by using outside contractors, as Rose had assumed. Leno also commented that critics had overstated the policy's fiscal impact, and he quipped that for a city with an annual budget of over $4.5 billion the policy has only "a very modest price tag for the tens of thousands of individuals it'll serve."[30]

CAA staff also tipped off Leno about Hall's attempt to undermine the policy and helped Leno prepare a response to Hall's criticisms. One CAA advocate recounted how they learned of Hall's opposition to EASO only at the last minute:

> On the day of the vote of the full Board of Supervisors, [Hall] introduced an amendment to the ordinance that would hinder our ability to hire sufficient numbers of staff that are proficient in Chinese and Spanish. . . . I only found out about it because I heard they were cooking something up when I ran into his staffer. . . . I asked, "What's going on?" and he talked to me in the hallway and said, "Let's talk about this," and I said, "That amendment is not acceptable to us." And he said, "Well, that's what they're going to introduce." We immediately went over to the office of Mark Leno, we scrapped the process and strategized about how to essentially acknowledge Tony Hall's issue, but assure that it got voted down.[31]

Hall, a fiscally conservative independent, was reputed to have an unaccommodating ideology toward immigrants.[32] He criticized EASO for being a poorly crafted policy amounting to affirmative action for Asians and Latinos who—in violation of the city's Civil Service Code—would be given preferential treatment for the bilingual public contact positions specified in the ordinance.

During public hearings, Hall belabored the contentious point that the mandate to hire bilingual staff would discriminate against the vast majority of San Franciscans who are not bilingual. He proposed an amendment that would strip EASO of the bilingual staff requirement. Aware of his intent, Leno openly countered Hall's criticism in the full Board of Supervisors:

> This is not about ethnicity. This is not about race. It's about skills. The assumptions that have been made that only certain people have either the interest or the ability to learn a second language completely confounds me. We're talking about a skill that is learned and perfected and is a marketable skill that we have as requirements for service. . . . If the

job requires it, we put that into the job description. . . . I'd like to suggest that we vote down this amendment and I'll be putting forward a slight amendment to the definition of public contact position instead.[33]

Armed with information from CAA, Leno steered the discussion away from divisive race and ethnicity issues. CAA's advance notice of Hall's criticism also gave Leno time to prepare an amendment with only a definitional clarification that swiftly replaced Hall's more invasive amendment.

Immigrant-serving nonprofits had anticipated that other supervisors would also oppose the bilingual staff requirement. EASO could have become a political wedge pitting the city's African Americans against Asians and Latinos. African Americans, who are primarily English-speaking, comprised 18 percent of San Francisco's full-time public employees in 2000 but only 5 percent of the city's civilian labor force (San Francisco 2008). African American city workers could have been mobilized around the fear of losing their jobs to bilingual individuals of Asian or Latino descent. Yet early and repeated clarifications by Leno and nonprofit advocates that no city workers would be fired to implement EASO likely put these concerns to rest and prevented EASO from being framed in racial terms.[34] Some advocates speculated that Local 790's endorsement of EASO also helped to keep the contentious race issue off the table.

Finally, the nonprofit-Leno partnership effectively addressed supervisors' concerns about the city's ability to implement EASO. Some supervisors feared that EASO would become unwieldy given the many languages spoken in San Francisco. Hall, for example, wondered about how many additional staff his office would need to hire if he were to comply with EASO. "In District 7, I can think of five different groups that automatically qualify right now under the ordinance," he commented. "I'm going to need five staff positions in District 7: Spanish, Chinese, Russian, Yiddish, and Tagalog."[35] Also, EASO's demand for translations and the hiring of bilingual personnel were clear and straightforward. However, several supervisors pointed to the logistical complexity in implementing the law across a large number of city departments whose primary mandates and clientele varied significantly.

With the help of its nonprofit allies, CAA had conducted extensive research on the state of language access in San Francisco as well as best language access practices elsewhere in the country. Leno used this research to convince fellow supervisors that EASO was doable. He pointed out that the San Francisco Department of Public Health was already doing what the law asked for. Leno also told his Board colleagues that if the California Department of Motor Vehicles, reputed to be "one of the most dysfunctional state departments,"[36] could provide driver's license tests in thirty different languages, then San Francisco surely could implement EASO and provide information and services in Chinese and Spanish. Ultimately, all eleven supervisors except Hall approved EASO on June 4, 2001. Facing a veto-proof Board majority, Mayor Brown signed EASO into law eleven days later.

Collaborating in Policy Implementation

After EASO's enactment, nonprofit advocates morphed into stewards of the law. Implementation was no easy task, according to one CAA advocate. "The ordinance looked great on paper," she commented, "but it was an entirely different thing to get it institutionalized into the daily practices of the departments that needed to comply. It required constant, and I mean *constant* advocacy from pressure groups like us."[37] For EASO to really work, the covered city departments had to commit fully to making their services and information available in other languages.

Many departments, however, were reluctant to do this. This stemmed not from outright opposition to the ordinance but rather from lack of interest and an unwillingness to make a departmental priority of language access. Department administrators' "knee-jerk reaction" to EASO, the same CAA advocate explained, was that "they claimed not to have the funding to implement it, but we knew they hadn't actually looked into how much it would really cost."[38] The Immigrant Rights Commission, the office charged with implementing and enforcing EASO, also lacked the staff, issue expertise, and political power to do its work effectively. A final challenge was that Leno, the policy's champion, could do little to hold departments' feet to the fire given city charter rules that forbid legislators from interfering in administrative affairs. To implement EASO, immigrant-serving nonprofits thus had to create goodwill toward the idea of language access among a large and diverse group of city administrators.

To achieve this, nonprofit advocates eventually became administrative aides with a regularized role in carrying out EASO. They shared their expertise over language access with department heads, the Immigrant Rights Commission, and the Mayor's Office. In so doing, they built on their existing relationships with city departments, including those that had contracted with them to provide public services. Advocates felt free to engage administrative officials, knowing that administrative advocacy is not restricted by law. But while their collaborations with administrative officials improved EASO's implementation, it also exposed nonprofits to the danger of cooptation by government.

Advocacy with City Departments

The Immigrant Rights Commission (IRC), officially responsible for implementing and enforcing EASO, initially was ineffective at this. It had neither the staff nor the expertise to analyze departments' compliance plans, identify their shortcomings, or provide technical assistance to departments. "I won't be the first to tell you that the Immigrant Rights Commission doesn't have the infrastructure support or resources to do this monitoring," one CAA advocate commented. "They are not structured that way. They're in essence an all-volunteer commission, and [the director] is largely in a coordinating or convening position. His background is not in compliance review or program implementation."[39] At the time, only the IRC director was a funded full-time position, and the Board of Supervisors had not allocated funds for the IRC to hire a compliance officer to monitor and enforce EASO's implementation. Furthermore, the IRC commissioners serve two-year terms (which are renewable), often not long enough to develop expertise in policy implementation and enforcement.

City departments subject to the ordinance also did not take the IRC seriously. As a consultative body, the IRC has no real political power vis-à-vis city departments. This frustrated the IRC director at the time. He commented that more than once "city departments ignored the communications [about EASO] we sent them" and that the IRC lacked "the institutional authority to force them to comply."[40] Without staff, expertise, and institutional standing, the IRC was ill suited to monitor and enforce EASO's implementation.

In the months following EASO's enactment, nonprofit advocates learned from department heads that they were frustrated with the IRC's inability to provide them with guidance on how to address implementation issues. The Metropolitan Transportation Agency, for example, struggled to determine whether MUNI bus drivers fell within EASO's definition of "public contact positions." Other departments, including the Rent Stabilization and Arbitration Board, required help figuring out which forms to translate. Still other departments, including the Human Services Agency and the Department of Public Health, provided language access prior to EASO but wanted to do this more efficiently. Continuing implementation gaps also became glaringly clear to nonprofit advocates when they sent their staff to test particular city departments to see if they could get information and services in Chinese and Spanish. These developments prompted CAA to take action.

CAA worked to educate department heads about the importance of language access and provide them with technical assistance on implementation. CAA headed this administrative advocacy but also brought to bear various nonprofits' knowledge of different immigrant communities and their relationships with different city departments. One CAA advocate provided a specific example of how this worked:

> We assembled coalitions and targeted each of the city's most critical agencies. We had meetings with them to talk about how they're going to implement the ordinance. . . . With each agency the coalition was slightly different. For example, with the Rent Board, which overseas disputes between landlords and tenants, we worked with St. Peter's Housing Committee, which really represents primarily a Spanish speaking community in the Mission, and we worked with the Chinatown Community Development Center and they represent the Chinese community. We worked with those two organizations in particular because they have a history of representing their clients before the Rent Board. They really understood the Rent Board well and had strong relationships with the guy who was the director of the board at that time. . . . We were effective in bringing together groups that have that kind of relationship with the Rent Board, understood what the forms were that were most critical to immigrant clients, and what the process was. Then what CAA brought to the table was an understanding of the requirements of the ordinance and ideas for how it could be implemented successfully. That was a very effective team that we had going for a while. . . . Similarly, we cobbled together different coalitions for different city agencies.[41]

CAA also developed a checklist for city departments to use in developing annual compliance plans and helped city administrators find vendors for their written and oral translation needs.

Despite their support to city departments in the years immediately following EASO's enactment, advocates continued to hear that immigrants were unable to receive city services in their languages. Immigrant-serving nonprofits, however, filed only two official complaints: one directed at the Rent Stabilization and Arbitration Board in 2002 and another at the Metropolitan Transportation Agency in 2004. Nonprofit advocates never took legal action against city departments, even though they believed they had a credible case against them and could ask state courts to intervene and mandate departmental compliance.

In reflecting on why they chose not to litigate, one CAA advocate commented that they preferred collaboration to confrontation. "We're not out there to say 'I got ya!' to public agencies. We're not in the business to file public lawsuits," he explained. "What we do is educate public agencies. . . .

We want them to develop their own infrastructures . . . so that they respond to immigrants and honor their rights all by themselves, without intervention by community groups."[42] Using more confrontation, he added, also would "undermine the trust and collaboration" that they have established with city officials over the years and is a tactic that CAA and other nonprofits use only as a "measure of last resort."[43] The fact that immigrant-serving nonprofits, including CAA, receive funding from the city might also explain why they prefer to maintain amicable relations with city administrators. This, however, was not a factor that nonprofit respondents themselves offered as an explanation for their collaborative advocacy style.

Advocacy with the Immigrant Rights Commission and the Mayor's Office

Immigrant-serving nonprofits also worked directly with the Immigrant Rights Commission (IRC) and the Cultural Competency Task Force created by Mayor Newsom in 2005. CAA and the Chinese Community Development Center helped the IRC develop a five-year status report on EASO. "We worked closely with the commission to research and draft this report that looks at compliance plans that [city departments] had submitted," one CAA employee commented. "That kind of community involvement in doing research and writing is a fairly specific form of advocacy that shouldn't be confused with lobbying. It's advocacy looking at departments' language ability, seeking effective monitoring and review, and then looking to amend [the ordinance] to address some of the problems we identified."[44] In discussing their work with the IRC, the CAA employee was quick to point out that this kind of administrative advocacy was distinct from lobbying legislative officials, which is limited by federal law.

The status report, published in 2006, showed that almost all of the fourteen covered city departments had failed to comply with a substantial number of the law's provisions (San Francisco 2006a). It recommended ways to strengthen EASO's enforcement mechanisms and underscored the need for additional resources to implement the ordinance successfully. The IRC forwarded the noncompliance findings to the Board of Supervisors and the mayor, prompting the Board to hold public hearings in May 2006 where department heads were asked to explain why they had neglected their obligations. The report also interested Aaron Peskin, then supervisor for the district including Chinatown, in amending EASO and codifying the report's recommendations. Peskin's interest was idle, however, and EASO was only amended in August 2009 when he was succeeded by Supervisor David Chiu. Using their expertise to help the IRC thus gave immigrant-serving nonprofits another way to pressure city departments into improving their language access.

As nonprofit advocates were working with the IRC to document EASO's implementation woes, Mayor Newsom created the Cultural Competency Task Force to fix translation mistakes on the city's websites. A local editor of *Sing Tao Daily*, the dominant Chinese-language newspaper in San Francisco, had complained to the Mayor's Office that the Cantonese translations of city websites were inaccurate (Murphy 2006). For years, the city had relied on machine translations for its websites, producing garbled information and even information contrary to what was intended. Even poor communities and the nonprofits that serve them make heavy use of the internet to access city information and services, as evidenced by the more than twenty thousand page hits that the city's fifty thousand web pages receive daily (Sabatini 2006). Newsom, who made internet access a key theme of his mayoralty, saw the task force as a way to bolster his image as a tech-savvy mayor.

The Cultural Competency Task Force brought together language access experts from the public, private, and nonprofit sectors. It included a representative from CAA and the IRC and was chaired by Assessor-Recorder Phil Ting, who is of Chinese descent. Although the mayor charged the task force with improving website translations, task force deliberations expanded to include improving language access and cultural competency in city government more generally. Over six months, the task force collected and reviewed best practices from the public and private sectors and explored ways to make city services more accessible to limited English proficient individuals.

The 2006 task force recommendations prominently cited CAA's research, reemphasized EASO's objectives, and echoed many of the findings from the five-year status report published by the IRC earlier that year (San Francisco 2006b). Most importantly, it recommended creating a centralized office for language services to provide technical assistance and infrastructure to city departments. City Administrator Ed Lee helped to realize the Office of Language Services in 2007. In 2009, this office became part of the Office of Civic Engagement and Immigrant Affairs, which is housed in the city's General Services Agency and at the time was under Lee's direct supervision. The mayor's Cultural Competency Task Force thus gave CAA yet another opportunity to leverage their issue expertise to advocate EASO's full implementation.

Blurring the Public-Private Divide

By the end of 2006, immigrant-serving nonprofits had language access allies in both the legislative and executive branches of San Francisco government.

Supervisor Aaron Peskin, Mayor Gavin Newsom, Assessor-Recorder Phil Ting, and City Administrator Ed Lee had all developed, in one way or another, a commitment to improving language accessibility in city government.[45] This made it easier for immigrant-serving nonprofits to advocate improvements in language access implementation. Yet the widespread support for language access, which nonprofit advocates had helped to create by sharing their issue expertise with public officials over an extended period of time, also introduced the risk of government cooptation.

City Administrator Lee and Assessor-Recorder Ting both talked about deepening their collaboration with immigrant-serving nonprofits to further improve the city's provision of linguistically accessible services. Lee discussed the creation of a Quality Assurance Panel:

> Now that they know they have people [in city government] who want to accomplish the same goals, I think the role of nonprofits is beginning to change, or it has to change, from pure advocacy to more working with us administratively, identifying how best to set this up, how best to run good government programs that are language accessible. . . . What I would like to have is groups of nonprofits that serve immigrant rights, for them to be part of a Quality Assurance Panel, so that we can always test how well we're doing and which departments are providing the most critical services and whether they're actually providing those in a linguistically accessible and culturally competent manner.[46]

Ting similarly talked about nonprofits taking on the role of "personal trainers" of city departments:

> I'd like immigrant rights groups to be involved with the next generation of this [Cultural Competency] Task Force and help us set up a system, and I kind of joke about this, that allows us to become the personal trainers of [city departments that need to carry out EASO], where we're going to work to set realistic goals, concrete goals toward implementation, and we're going to work with [departments] to help them achieve their goals.[47]

Lee's and Ting's proposals did not ask immigrant-serving nonprofits to do anything they had not already been doing. By 2006, immigrant advocates were already providing assistance to city departments, the Immigrant Rights Commission, and the mayor's Cultural Competency Task Force. Their proposals, however, were asking nonprofits to help these city officials reach their goals on city officials' terms. If realized, immigrant-serving nonprofits would be fully coopted into the city's administrative apparatus.

Lee's Quality Assurance Panel, however, never materialized. At the time, CAA was not interested in formalizing their relationship with city government in the way that Lee had envisioned:

> City folks, I think, now finally get the importance of language services, and I think even the mayor gets it. This doesn't mean that we can lighten up because there are still reasons for why we need to advocate for better language services. . . . We want more than just translated documents, we want more than just what the ordinance requires. We'll continue to work closely with the Immigrant Rights Commission and [city] departments to make that happen as well as other individuals who want to eliminate this issue. . . . And, yes, it's true that sometimes that line between them and us is blurry, but we don't forget that our primary duty is to fight for the rights of our community's most marginalized. . . . If that helps city officials with political agendas who want to be known as advocates for these communities, so be it, but that's not what drives us.[48]

The Asian Law Caucus and the Interfaith Coalition for Immigrant Rights also did not formalize their partnerships with city government. They explained that doing so would compromise their ability to be a critical outside voice for their immigrant communities. They also worried that such formalized partnerships would undermine their relationships with their immigrant clients, who turn to them for help and confide in them exactly because they see nonprofits as distinct from government entities.[49]

Since 2007, immigrant-serving nonprofits have continued to deploy their issue expertise on behalf of expanding EASO. To this end, they have collaborated with Supervisor David Chiu, who replaced Aaron Peskin in 2008 in the district that includes Chinatown. With Chiu's sponsorship, CAA, Mujeres Unidas y Activas (United and Active Women), and their nonprofit allies successfully amended EASO in August 2009. The Board unanimously adopted the new ordinance, renamed Language Access Ordinance. It requires thirteen additional Tier 1 Departments to provide language access consistent with EASO as of July 2010.[50] It also requires city boards, commissions, and departments to offer interpretation services at public meetings and translate meeting minutes if requested. The ordinance gives the Office of Civic Engagement and Immigrant Affairs (OCEIA) new responsibilities in providing technical assistance for language services to city departments. However, it still does not allow aggrieved individuals to bring a lawsuit against the city for noncompliance with the ordinance. In April 2014, when city officials determined that more than ten thousand limited English proficient Filipinos resided in San Francisco, Tagalog became the third certified foreign language to be covered under EASO.

Ongoing advocacy from immigrant-serving nonprofits pushed the Board of Supervisors to amend EASO for a second time in February 2015. Adopted with unanimous support, the amended ordinance seeks to address remaining gaps in language access consistency, quality, budgeting, and implementation across city departments. It expands the scope of the 2009 Language Access Ordinance to apply to *all* city departments that provide information and services to the public. It also revises the complaint procedure for alleged violations of the ordinance and enhances the requirement for departments' annual language access compliance reports.

The growing role of OCEIA and the continued support of the Board of Supervisors have translated into new resources for the implementation and enforcement of the Language Access Ordinance since 2012. In fiscal year 2013–2014, about $1 million of OCEIA's budget of $3.6 million was dedicated to language access, including four full-time staff positions and $570,000 in Language Access Community Grants for nonprofits to conduct outreach and education as well as to assess and evaluate language access needs in the community (Budget and Legislative Analyst 2014). Immigrant-serving nonprofits have been able to maintain a degree of autonomy in this new public-private partnership for language access by creating the San Francisco Language Access Network, a coalition of eight nonprofits headed by CAA. CAA was the lead recipient of a large collaborative language access grant from OCEIA and subsequently subcontracted with the other network organizations. This arrangement has given nonprofits control over grant money spending as well as decision-making and the division of labor within the coalition, while minimizing overhead and oversight from OCEIA.

Nonprofit-Government Collaborations Reassessed

Immigrant-serving nonprofits were able to bring about the enactment and implementation of EASO by leveraging their language access expertise with legislative and administrative city officials. These government officials did not challenge these groups but in fact benefited from their work. Nonprofit advocates helped legislative officials develop a strong EASO bill and convinced a veto-proof majority of supervisors to support it in 2001 and amend it in 2009 and 2015. They also helped administrative officials to improve the implementation and enforcement of the ordinance, thereby institutionalizing language accessibility into the daily practices of city departments. By advocating in this collaborative style, immigrant-serving nonprofits significantly eased the work of city officials. City officials do not have ready access to immigrant communities, making it more difficult for them to develop the required policies and procedures. The collaborative style of advocacy also made city officials less likely to question whether advocates had exceeded their legal lobbying limits, thereby helping immigrant-serving nonprofits to navigate the lobbying constraints inherent in their status as 501(c)(3) organizations.

The case of EASO invites us to look at nonprofit advocacy in a different light. Civil society scholars recognize that nonprofits interact with government in myriad ways (Najam 2000). Yet they tend to equate nonprofit public policy advocacy with conflict, where nonprofits adopt a confrontational posture toward government and where nonprofit advocates and government officials disagree on both policy goals and the preferred strategies to accomplish them (Bass et al. 2007; Berry and Arons 2003; Cordero-Guzmán et al. 2008; Pallares and Flores-González 2010; Voss and Bloemraad 2011). Most of the research also assumes that government, through its power of the purse, defines both the space and nature of nonprofit advocacy. The EASO case shows, to the contrary, that nonprofit advocacy can be done in a nonconflictual manner. It illustrates the ways in which nonprofits—including those that receive government funding—can use their community and issue expertise as an independent source of power in local policymaking.

The EASO case also shows the importance of considering not only the nonprofit influence on policy enactment—as most civil society scholars do—but also on policy implementation and enforcement. Some scholars downplay the importance of nonprofit advocacy with city departments and agencies, arguing that it is a poor substitute for the legislative lobbying in which other types of advocacy organizations can engage more freely (Berry and Arons 2003). Others dismiss nonprofits' advocacy with the local bureaucracy as government cooptation of nonprofit organizations (Wolch 1990). In this case, we see that nonprofit advocacy with local administrative officials complements other types of advocacy, including advocacy directed at local legislators, the courts, and the media as well as advocacy involving local ballot measures. Immigrant rights and integration policies, after all, are only as good as their implementation. Had nonprofits not worked closely with city administrative personnel, San Francisco immigrants would not enjoy the language access they enjoy today.

Collaborations with government officials are one strategy that immigrant-serving nonprofits can use to influence the policymaking process on behalf of disadvantaged immigrants. They can also join with other types of advocacy organizations, like labor unions, to promote immigrant rights and integration policies. Such cross-organizational collaborations, like the cross-sectoral collaborations discussed here, allow immigrant-serving nonprofits to overcome some of the constraints on them. Because labor unions have more advocacy freedoms, more political resources, and more clout than nonprofits, working with unions can put immigrant-serving nonprofits in a stronger position to influence local policymakers. However, these same asymmetries can frustrate immigrant-serving nonprofits that collaborate with labor unions. The disparity in resources can lead to a power imbalance within cross-organizational coalitions and enable unions to crowd immigrant-serving nonprofits out of the policymaking process.

CHAPTER 4

Raising Minimum Wages through Nonprofit-Union Collaborations

Relations between San Francisco labor unions and nonprofit organizations brimmed with hostility during the 1990s. The Service Employees International Union (SEIU), which represents city workers and is San Francisco's largest union, was laying siege to nonprofits with city contracts in the name of better job conditions and higher wages for their members ("City Hall and Labor Gang Up on Nonprofits" 1998). In 1998, SEIU won a concession from Mayor Willie Brown giving unions veto power over any nonprofit work that could be done by unionized city employees. That same year, unions successfully lobbied the Board of Supervisors to enact the Nonprofit Public Access Ordinance, requiring open board meetings and financial disclosures of nonprofits with city contracts over $250,000. Nonprofits have strongly criticized this transparency mandate for the additional administrative responsibilities it created for them. The campaign for a Living Wage Ordinance, which would require nonprofits with city contracts to pay a minimum wage above the federal and state minimums, raised the prospect of another divisive union-nonprofit battle.

Instead, unions and nonprofits started working together in campaigns to raise labor standards for San Francisco's low-wage workers, collaborations that have since endured. Such cross-organizational collaborations, which have become common also in other U.S. cities, reflect unions' realization that they need to work in coalition with community nonprofits to revitalize the long-declining U.S. labor movement (Applegate 2007; Fine 2006;

Luce 2004; Needleman 1998). An extensive literature analyzes how such collaborations have benefited unions, such as in their fights to prevent plant closures, to establish or renew union contracts, to organize the unorganized, and to pass living wage policies (for an overview, see Nissen 2004). But what do they mean for immigrant-serving nonprofits seeking to improve working conditions for disadvantaged immigrants?

The San Francisco experience suggests that collaborating with labor unions is another way immigrant-serving nonprofits overcome constraints on their advocacy. Unions have more political resources, more clout, and more freedom to engage in politics than nonprofits. Collaborating with them can put nonprofits in a stronger position to pursue their goals. Since the disparity in resources between nonprofits and unions is larger in the enactment phase of policymaking than in policy implementation and enforcement, collaborating with unions is especially helpful at that juncture. However, the same things that make unions attractive coalition partners in campaigns to enact new labor protections can also frustrate immigrant-serving nonprofits. The disparity in legislative and electoral resources can give unions the means to overshadow nonprofits in the legislative and initiative processes but not in policy implementation and enforcement.

Immigrant advocates in San Francisco collaborated with labor unions around the enactment, implementation, and enforcement of three ordinances that together have substantially improved the lives of San Francisco's lowest-paid workers, many of whom are immigrants. After a bruising and protracted campaign, the San Francisco Board of Supervisors enacted the Minimum Compensation Ordinance (popularly known as the Living Wage Ordinance) in 2000 to raise the wages of an estimated twenty-two thousand low-wage workers employed in businesses with city service contracts (Reynolds 2004). The Minimum Wage Ordinance, enacted via the ballot box in 2003, mandated that *all* low-wage workers in the city be paid at least $8.50, an hourly wage higher than the federal and state minimums. This ordinance boosted pay for an estimated fifty-four thousand workers (Reich and Laitinen 2003). Finally, in 2006, the city's legislators adopted the Minimum Wage Implementation and Enforcement Ordinance to strengthen enforcement of the Minimum Wage Ordinance against noncompliant private-sector employers. These interrelated ordinances each involved a distinct advocacy campaign in which immigrant-serving nonprofits played central roles.

Mending Fences and Building Bridges

Tensions between unions and nonprofits in San Francisco date to the 1960s and 1970s, when unions and nonprofits clashed over land use issues. While unions backed city hall plans to expand the downtown business district, non-profits advocated that the land slated for redevelopment be used to build more affordable public housing for the poor (Castells 1983; DeLeon 2003). After the redevelopment frenzy subsided in the 1980s, the increased priva-tization of city services became another point of contention (Hirsch 2005). Many immigrant-serving nonprofits welcomed local government contracts to help them serve the city's growing immigrant and poor populations, but public-sector unions fought them, fearing that they would reduce the num-ber of public-sector jobs and lower public-sector wages ("City Hall and Labor Gang Up on Nonprofits" 1998). Since the late 1990s, however, unions and immigrant-serving nonprofits have worked together in common cause, largely as a result of increased pressures on unions to become more inclusive of immigrants and to seek support from community organizations for labor's re-empowerment at the city level (Applegate 2007).

Echoing national trends, Bay Area unions have suffered a steep decline since the 1970s. In 1955, around the time that union density levels in the United States peaked, 51 percent of the Bay Area labor force was unionized (Milkman and Rooks 2003). By 1998, when the Minimum Compensa-tion Ordinance campaign began, that number had dropped to 18 percent (Hirsch and Macpherson 2010). Meanwhile, the demography of the San Francisco workforce shifted toward immigrant workers, whose share of the city's expanding service sector increased from 18 percent in 1970 to 55 per-cent in 1990 (Wells 2000).

Recruiting the growing numbers of immigrant service workers into union ranks was therefore a precondition for rebuilding the San Francisco labor movement. Some labor unions, however, were quicker to realize this than others. The hotel and restaurant union HERE started organizing immi-grant workers in San Francisco as early as the late 1970s (Lee 1988; Wells 2000), and SEIU and the United Food and Commercial Workers (UFCW) followed suit in the 1980s and 1990s (Voss and Sherman 2000). Yet only in 2006 did the San Francisco Labor Council (SFLC)—the countywide federation of local AFL-CIO unions—publicly acknowledge its common interests with immigrant workers (SFLC 2006).

The unions seeking to organize immigrant workers benefit from working with immigrant-serving nonprofits. These nonprofits can help unions gain access to immigrant communities. While many immigrants are receptive to unionism (Milkman 2006), they can shy away from organizing that puts them in the spotlight because of their immigration status or limited English language skills (Fine 2006). Immigrants also tend to work in industries that are difficult to unionize due to the small size of the workplace, the decentralized nature of the industry, or the isolated nature of work. In this context, nonprofits provide safe havens for immigrants to address a variety of labor issues, and they can help unify disparate workers within a community and provide legitimacy for grassroots organizing campaigns (Martin 2012; Ness 2005).

Nonprofits also can help rally support for unions among immigrants by expanding the union agenda to include issues especially salient to immigrants, such as immigration reform, affordable housing, and ESL classes (Lee 1988; Wells 2000). They can also help unions win recognition outside the traditional National Labor Relations Board elections process, for example, by pressuring employers to recognize neutrality agreements (Sherman and Voss 2000). Finally, nonprofits legitimate union power in local policymaking and community relations. While unions continue to be associated with strong-arm tactics to further their goals, nonprofits wield moral capital due to their association with charitable causes and social justice initiatives (de Graauw 2008).

Nonprofits committed to promoting immigrant labor rights have their own reasons for wanting to build ties with unions. Nonprofit advocates understand well the power of a union contract in shoring up worker protections and setting industry standards in wages, benefits, and workplace safety and health (Luce 2004). Lacking union representation, immigrant workers must rely on the weak and under-enforced labor protections encoded in state and federal laws (Gleeson 2012). Nonprofits allied with unions can also borrow strength from the larger membership, staff, and other politically relevant resources that unions enjoy. Unlike unions, immigrant-serving nonprofits are typically not membership organizations, and even those that are rarely collect membership dues and have much smaller memberships they can mobilize in the political process. Nonprofits cannot use government funding for policy advocacy, and private foundations are leery of funding nonprofit advocacy and organizing. Furthermore, as discussed in chapter 1, federal restrictions limit the amount and the types of political work that nonprofits can legally undertake.

Cross-organizational collaborations can reward immigrant-serving nonprofits, unions, and the workers whose interests they have at heart. Yet it is challenging to build them, and their costs and benefits are not always equally distributed. The resource asymmetry between unions and nonprofits can generate stresses within coalitions (Luce 2005). Although unions and nonprofits are both committed to economic justice, they differ in their tactics and approaches to strengthening worker rights. Unions tend to be managed in a hierarchical fashion and face significant pressure from their members to deliver short-term results in wages and working conditions (Nissen 2004). Immigrant-serving nonprofits, in contrast, operate in a more bottom-up manner and have at least a rhetorical commitment to the slow and labor-intensive process of cultivating immigrant empowerment (Wong 2006).

The emphasis in this chapter is on the nonprofit experience in working with unions that have an edge in political and policy advocacy. The coalitional dynamics around campaigning for higher wages in San Francisco show that immigrant-serving nonprofits needed help from unions to enact new labor rights protections benefiting immigrant workers. In the enactment phase of the policymaking process, unions were able to overshadow immigrant-serving nonprofits. Nonprofit advocates, however, were able to assert themselves effectively in policy implementation and enforcement.

The Living Wage Campaign

By adopting the Minimum Compensation Ordinance (MCO) in 2000, San Francisco joined a long list of municipalities that had passed laws requiring employers with city or county government contracts to pay their workers wages that would sustain a decent living standard. Baltimore first enacted a Living Wage Ordinance in 1994, and more than 140 municipalities nationwide had such laws on the books by 2006 (Dean and Reynolds 2009). Coalitions of labor unions, churches, and community organizations waged similar campaigns around the country, and their collective victories have added up to a living wage movement (Reynolds 2004). Motivated by the conviction that no full-time worker should live in poverty, this movement reacted forcefully to the declining value of the federal minimum wage, the outsourcing of municipal services, and rising income inequality (Luce 2004). Living wage campaigns emerged primarily as grassroots impulses targeting municipal politics because business opposition to raising wages was weaker at the local level than at the federal and state levels and because poverty and the problems of low-wage employment are more severe in cities (Pollin and Luce 1998).

When MCO took effect in October 2000, it required businesses leasing city property and for-profit businesses and nonprofit organizations with city service contracts to provide covered employees an hourly wage of $9 as well as twelve paid days and ten unpaid days off per year. Exempted were contractors supplying goods to the city, contractors with twenty or fewer employees, for-profit businesses with service contracts of less than $25,000, nonprofit service providers with contracts of less than $50,000, and nonprofit contractors that could prove that compliance with the ordinance would cause them economic hardship. These provisions remain, but as of January 2016, the hourly wage is $13.34 for new and amended contracts in the case of for-profits and, as of May 2015, $12.25 in the case of nonprofits (OLSE 2015). MCO covers an estimated three hundred nonprofit organizations. An estimated twenty-two thousand workers have received pay raises directly attributable to the ordinance, and additional workers have received wage increases indirectly,

as a result of vertical and horizontal wage push. The majority of these beneficiaries are ethnoracial minorities, including many immigrants (Alunan et al.
2000; Reich, Hall, and Hsu 1999).[1]

The Living Wage Coalition

The Living Wage Coalition, a broad constellation of labor, religious, and community groups, came together in 1998 to lobby the Board of Supervisors to
enact the ordinance. More than twenty labor organizations, twenty-eight religious leaders, forty-five community organizations, and ten immigrant-serving
nonprofits supported the work of the Living Wage Coalition, but a core group
of ten organizations formed the coalition's Steering Committee and made
decisions about the goals and execution of the living wage campaign. Unions
controlled five of the ten votes on the Steering Committee. The remaining five votes were distributed among religious organizations and nonprofits
representing the city's poor, African Americans, and immigrants (see table 9).

Table 9 Member organizations of the Living Wage Coalition's Steering Committee

Name	Type	Description
Bay Area Organizing Committee	Coalition of 501(c)(3) nonprofits	A coalition of interfaith congregations that engage in community organizing around health care, employment, redevelopment, housing, and immigration issues
Chinese Progressive Association	501(c)(3)/nonprofit	Provides services/advocacy to low-wage Chinese immigrants
Coalition for Ethical Welfare Reform	Coalition of 501(c)(3) nonprofits	A Bay Area coalition of more than seventy labor, religious, homeless, legal, and immigrant organizations that advocate for welfare reform and economic justice
HERE Local 2	501(c)(5)/union	Represents hotel and restaurant employees in San Francisco and San Mateo; in 2004, HERE merged with UNITE, the textile and laundry workers union, to form UNITE-HERE Local 2
Northern California Coalition for Immigrant Rights	Coalition of 501(c)(3) nonprofits	A coalition of 129 immigrant-serving nonprofits in the Bay Area; it disbanded in 2001 as a result of budget issues and internal leadership conflicts
OPEIU Local 3	501(c)(5)/union	Represents clerical, university, and nonprofit employees in the Bay Area
People Organized to Win Employment Rights	501(c)(3)/nonprofit	Serves low-income African Americans and advocates for economic, racial, and gender justice
San Francisco Labor Council	501(c)(5)/union	The San Francisco federation of local AFL-CIO unions
SEIU Local 250	501(c)(5)/union	Represents health care workers in northern California
SEIU Local 790	501(c)(5)/union	Represents public employees in local government, schools, and hospitals as well as nonprofit employees in the Bay Area

These organizations were all committed to raising wages for the city's lowest-paid workers, but each had its own motivation for getting involved. For unions, MCO would strengthen the position of unionized municipal workers. They also thought that the ordinance would help them organize new workers, particularly at San Francisco International Airport and in the homecare industry. "The living wage provided a useful context for organizing," an organizer with OPEIU Local 3 commented, "especially among airport baggage screeners, retail workers, and security guards."[2] Unions also were excited about opportunities to educate workers about their rights and get them activated in the labor movement. "About 80 to 90 percent [of homecare workers] are immigrants, and many were skeptical of this whole living wage thing and didn't understand what social responsibility was or government accountability," an organizer with SEIU Local 250 explained.[3] "We wanted them to come on board so they could learn to better advocate for themselves."[4] Finally, unions welcomed the opportunity to build ties with community organizations, especially those serving immigrants. An organizer with HERE Local 2 mentioned that the minimum wage campaign "allowed us to forge bonds with immigrant rights groups and stand in solidarity with *all* working people."[5]

Religious leaders viewed MCO as a campaign for basic morality and human dignity. Father Peter Sammon, a member of the Bay Area Organizing Committee, felt it was a disgrace that "poverty-level wages" were paid to "thousands of workers in a wealthy city" like San Francisco. He urged city officials to adopt an ordinance to help people "to survive on what they earn and support their families without relying on public welfare for emergency health care and food stamps and other public assistance" (Sammon 2000). Reverend Kay Jorgensen, a member of a committee within the Living Wage Coalition called Clergy for a Just Living Wage, quipped that "poverty in the midst of affluence is morally unconscionable. A living wage ordinance will empower employees to better their lives and thereby the lives of everyone else as well."[6] San Francisco's archbishop, William Levada, who rarely spoke up for social justice, even published his plea for living wages as an editorial in the *San Francisco Chronicle*. He emphasized that people who work for a living should not have to rely on church-run soup kitchens to survive and that "poverty-level wages create a situation in which individual respect and human dignity are diminished" (Levada 1999).

The MCO campaign provided immigrant-serving nonprofits opportunities to educate San Francisco officials about the difficult economic situation of immigrants. "We always had a sense that the lowest-paid workers in the city were immigrant workers," an advocate with the Northern California

Coalition for Immigrant Rights (NCCIR) commented. "In fact, [immigrants] often work more than one job and they're *still* having a hard time surviving. . . . We wanted [city officials] to see that there's something very wrong with that picture."[7] A colleague added that the campaign could catalyze future legislation that would be even more meaningful for immigrants. "We realized that [MCO] would not directly impact a large number of our immigrant base, but we hoped that it could grow into something larger beyond this one particular initiative," he said. "We really hoped [MCO] would have spillover effects and result in a citywide pay raise for all workers, including the immigrants served by our member organizations."[8]

Finding Common Ground

Early on, the Living Wage Coalition had to address the question of whether MCO should cover the nonprofit sector, a divisive issue among immigrant-serving nonprofits. NCCIR, the lead organization representing immigrant-serving nonprofits in the Living Wage Coalition, strongly believed that they should be included and made a point of paying its own employees a $13 minimum wage. The NCCIR director at the time argued that this had contributed to lower staff turnover and higher worker productivity (Mar 1999; Nishioka and Ni 1999). Before the Board of Supervisors, he testified that "we have no choice but to pay our workers a living wage. In working to eliminate poverty in our community, how could we not pay a living wage to our staff?"[9] The La Raza Centro Legal (the Community's Legal Center) director echoed these remarks. Drawing on her experience as an employer who paid her employees a living wage, she testified that better-paid workers are less likely to rely on city-funded services, thereby saving the city money in the long run.[10]

However, immigrant-serving nonprofits with large city service contracts supported the concept of living wages but did not want to be covered by MCO for fear that having to pay higher wages would result in staff layoffs and service cuts to the poor and low-income communities whom the ordinance was designed to help. The director of Self-Help for the Elderly, a nonprofit that was receiving city contracts worth as much as $3 million to provide services to senior Chinese immigrants, estimated that MCO would increase her organization's labor cost by $1.5 million annually and result in service cuts by as much as 40 percent (Chen 1999). A staff member with On Lok, another government-dependent nonprofit provider of services to elderly Chinese, opposed MCO for similar reasons (Chen 1999). The Living Wage Coalition pushed back on these and other nonprofit critics and organized community events in an effort to dispel statements printed in the Chinese ethnic press about MCO's negative budgetary impact.[11]

Nonprofit critics also received pushback from unions, which wanted MCO to cover nonprofit contractors. SEIU Local 790 felt strongly about this and blamed the loss of public-sector jobs and the depression of public-sector wages on nonprofits with city service contracts. An important shift occurred, though, when unions learned that a significant percentage of nonprofit workers actually were union members.[12] A co-director of the Living Wage Coalition remembers the key moment when unions learned of their common interests with nonprofits:

> Unions and nonprofits realized that having funds in the city budget was important to both of them, and unions realized [that in demanding nonprofits to pay living wages] they couldn't squeeze blood from a turnip and that the issue was the city. . . . That if union workers and nonprofits get a raise, then the city needs to provide that, and so they ended up working together on budget issues. . . . That's how unions and nonprofits were able to reforge their relationship and how the Living Wage Coalition was able to move beyond that very sticky point of nonprofit coverage.[13]

Instead of fighting each other, unions and nonprofits now both pointed the finger at city officials, arguing that their longtime practice of shifting work to nonprofit providers had undercut San Francisco's wage structure. While several large nonprofits outside the Living Wage Coalition remained skeptical of and even opposed to MCO, the unions and nonprofits inside the coalition agreed that they could only expect nonprofit service contractors to raise their wages if they could pass the cost on to city government.

Opposition from City Hall and the Business Community

In 1998, when the federal minimum wage was $5.15 and the California minimum wage was $5.75, the Living Wage Coalition developed at $14.50 living wage proposal. In deciding on this figure, the coalition relied on a study by the California Budget Project that showed that a single parent with one child living in San Francisco needed to earn an hourly minimum wage of $14.50 to be self-sufficient and maintain a basic standard of living (CBP 1998). The author of this wage proposal—a temp agency owner and co-chair and benefactor of the Living Wage Coalition—commented that $14.50 was "pie in the sky" and intended for "shock value."[14] Unions saw

$14.50 as unobtainable. The Living Wage Coalition nonetheless chose that figure to make a normative statement to city legislators about what a living wage should be in the high-cost city of San Francisco during times when city coffers were flush and the city was giving tax breaks to local businesses.

The proposal created an anxious buzz around city hall. Within a week of its release, Mayor Willie Brown called a meeting with various business and union leaders to discuss it. The Board of Supervisors acted on the proposal as well. Supervisor Tom Ammiano, at the time the Board's foremost advocate for economic and social justice, supported the proposal and was already working with the Living Wage Coalition. Many of his colleagues, however, were concerned about the economic impact of a high living wage. The Board's Finance Committee, which in 1998 consisted of business-friendly supervisors Barbara Kaufman, Mabel Teng, and Gavin Newsom, proposed to create a task force to study the costs of various living wage proposals before the Board could vote on any specific proposal. The San Francisco Chamber of Commerce and the Golden Gate Restaurant Association—business groups that opposed MCO—strongly endorsed the task force idea. The Living Wage Coalition, however, viewed the task force as a ploy to "study the issue to death" and as an attempt by Kaufman to hijack the living wage plan from her political rival Ammiano (Johnson 1998).

During hearings in the Finance Committee, immigrant-serving nonprofits and unions both testified that the fifteen-member task force would overrepresent business interests and lack representation from low-wage workers intended to benefit from the pay raise (Isaacs 1998a; Johnson 1998). As a result, the Finance Committee altered the composition of the task force to include four appointees from business, labor, low-wage workers, and the nonprofit sector, in addition to the eleven appointees selected by the Board of Supervisors (Isaacs 1998b). Nonprofits and unions also testified that the mandate for the task force was too narrow. They successfully advocated that the task force also study the benefits of living wage proposals, not only the costs, and address implementation and enforcement issues, which they knew had been the weak link in living wage ordinances enacted in other cities (Reynolds 2001). With these amendments, the Board of Supervisors unanimously passed the resolution establishing the Living Wage Task Force in November 1998. Ammiano, however, gave his support only reluctantly (Gordon 1998).

Immigrant-serving nonprofits and unions in the Living Wage Coalition remained skeptical of the task force. They called it a "task farce" and said that it would limit public debate and recommend to city legislators a watered-down version of their $14.50 proposal (Babcock 1999). The task force started work in March 1999. In May, Kaufman proposed to extend its work for six months, and Teng requested an independent economic analysis of the $11 living wage that Ammiano had proposed earlier that month. Citing endless delays and foot-dragging, three task force members representing low-wage workers and organized labor angrily resigned in May 1999, leaving task force deliberations in the hands of twelve individuals representing businesses and nonprofits opposed to living wage legislation (Lewis 1999a). After nine months and forty meetings, the task force published its findings in December 1999. It recommended that the Board of Supervisors enact a living wage ordinance with an hourly wage of only $7.50 and exemptions for nonprofits with service contracts of less than $100,000 (Clark and O'Hara 1999).

Though living wage advocates had failed to get the task force to support their goals, they continued to work with Ammiano to build public support for their $14.50 wage proposal. Because Ammiano had gotten the most votes in the 1998 Board of Supervisors election, he became Board president and controlled committee assignments. He assigned himself, along with Leland Yee and Sue Bierman, to serve on the powerful Finance Committee. These supervisors—termed the "Gang of Three" in the media—supported living wage legislation and had frequently voted against other Board colleagues who had supported the mayor and his business-friendly policies (Epstein 1998). Because he too was skeptical that the Living Wage Task Force would adequately represent the interests of low-wage workers, Ammiano had organized two Finance Committee hearings in March 1999 to solicit public testimony on the $14.50 proposal.

Members of the Living Wage Coalition and other nonprofit and union representatives filled the seats reserved for the public and provided statement after statement supporting a living wage of $14.50. More than four hundred people attended the hearings, which resembled pep rallies rather than objective public meetings. They made it clear, though, that the living wage campaign was about survival, not just calculating abstract numbers about the cost of local wage increases. Nonprofits and unions both recruited low-wage immigrant workers to testify to the travails of minimum-wage jobs, lending urgency to the proposed living wage. These testimonies allowed local papers, including *AsianWeek* (Nishioka 1999), the *San Francisco Bay Guardian* (Thompson 1999), the *San Francisco Chronicle* (DeBare 1999), and the *San Francisco Examiner* (Brazil 1999), to run stories on the human dimension of living wages, underscoring the point that low-wage immigrant workers had not shared in the city's dot-com boom.

Because Ammiano was unwilling to wait for the Living Wage Task Force to complete its work before the Board of Supervisors could resume discussions about living wages, he introduced his own living wage proposal to the Board on May 3, 1999. His proposal was weaker than that of the Living Wage Coalition but stronger than what the task force ultimately recommended. It called for an $11 hourly wage and benefits, including health coverage and compensated time off. It applied to both for-profit and nonprofit service contractors. The ordinance, however, would phase in nonprofits over a three-year period, enable them to qualify for a hardship waiver, and exempt them if they had city contracts of less than $50,000. Supervisor Teng, however, put Ammiano's proposal on hold in late May 1999 with a motion requiring the Board to delay action on the proposal until after the Living Wage Task Force had completed its independent study and the Board had reviewed its findings (Epstein 1999a). As a result, the Board would only resume hearings on Ammiano's wage proposal in May 2000, a full year after its introduction.

Despite the long hiatus, immigrant-serving nonprofits continued to keep the living wage proposal on the public agenda through other channels. NCCIR relied heavily on the ethnic press to publicize the issue and to conduct outreach to immigrant communities:

> Our main responsibility [within the Living Wage Coalition] was to bring as many immigrants as possible to hearings, rallies, and to do media work related to the ordinance . . . specifically the Latino media, the Vietnamese, and Chinese media. . . . We had a very close relationship with a TV station, Univision, which is Channel 14, and so we were in the news almost two or three times per week, talking about the living wage and also other immigrant issues. . . . That partnership with Channel 14 was tremendously helpful. That's how we were able to bring the message to the immigrant community. . . . That's also how we mobilized the immigrant community when we wanted them to attend a rally or a hearing.[15]

In addition, they got the Immigrant Rights Commission to hold a hearing in May 1999 on how the living wage issue was particularly relevant to immigrants. They also organized a meeting in the heavily Hispanic Mission district in September 1999 to educate concerned nonprofit staff about the need for a strong living wage policy that included nonprofit contractors.

The issue also played out in the 1999 mayoral election, which pitted challenger Ammiano against Mayor Brown. Brown had taken a back seat in the early stages of the living wage campaign due to a deal he had struck with labor unions. In exchange for an early reelection endorsement from them in January 1999, Brown had promised to sign "whatever living wage measure" would reach his desk (Finnie 1999). But when a union-funded survey showed that 60 percent of voters supported Ammiano's $11 wage proposal, Brown capitalized on the living wage issue to build his candidacy (Lewis 1999b; Wilson 1999).

Brown was opposed to mandatory living wages, which he believed would unduly burden the city budget. Instead he proceeded to raise wages for low-wage workers in a piecemeal fashion, as the city could afford them. In an attempt to take the wind out of Ammiano's sails, Brown raised the wages from $7 to $9 for 6,500 homecare workers in July 1999 and for 2,100 airport workers in November 1999. Tensions burst into the open when Ammiano decided to run for mayor through a last-minute write-in campaign (Epstein 1999b). He placed second in the November election and lost to Brown in the December run-off. Commenting on the mayoral race, Ammiano quipped that Brown's pay raises constituted "an exotic marriage" between his living wage proposal and Brown's electoral strategy (Epstein 1999c).

Unions Overshadow Nonprofits in the Legislative Process

Thus far in the campaign, immigrant-serving nonprofits and unions worked together well, each deploying their respective resources to build support for the living wage proposal. When the Board of Supervisors resumed deliberations on Ammiano's $11 wage proposal in May 2000, however, it raised the stakes in a way that nonprofits could not directly influence. They continued to have a clear presence in the front-room public hearings, but unions and business interests dominated the back-room negotiations orchestrated by Mayor Brown. In reflecting on the final stages of the campaign, NCCIR and other immigrant advocates complained that they did not know exactly what was going on in these negotiations and that they had little input in formulating the compromises that brought the campaign to a successful conclusion. Instead, the unions in the Living Wage Coalition—masters at negotiating contracts and using their electoral clout and organizational resources to exert pressure on the mayor—resuscitated the living wage legislation after it was pronounced dead. They negotiated the compromise ordinance that would be enacted as the Minimum Compensation Ordinance in August 2000.

In May 2000, Ammiano's $11 wage proposal received two hearings in the Finance Committee, which revealed the large gap between the positions of living wage supporters and opponents. The Living Wage Coalition continued to press for a strong and broad living wage and testified to the benefits that the legislation would bring to low-wage workers, the city, and businesses alike. The opponents, including the San Francisco Chamber of Commerce, the Golden Gate Restaurant Association, and several large nonprofit service providers, countered by saying that Ammiano's $11 proposal would result in cuts in low-wage jobs and nonprofit services and create a hostile business climate in the city.

The Living Wage Coalition asked Mayor Brown to referee the living wage negotiations in the hopes of bringing the two sides together and hammering out an agreement acceptable to all. Brown, however, was hardly an impartial voice in these negotiations. While a long-time ally of organized labor, he did not want to support the $11 wage as long as unions supported his political opponent Ammiano. Making his position clear during negotiations on Ammiano's wage proposal, Brown asked union advocates, "Why would I date you when you're still married to your husband?" (Epstein 2000). At the same time, Brown did not want to fund nonprofits' pay raises since he was unhappy about the quality of their services (Epstein 2000). Brown's opposition to Ammiano's proposal swayed many members of the Board of Supervisors on the issue. Though Ammiano and Bierman strongly supported the legislation, an internal Living Wage Coalition memo indicated that the remaining nine supervisors were on the fence, noncommittal, or outright opposed to the $11 wage proposal.[16]

Upon learning that the Board lacked a majority for the $11 wage proposal and seeing that the mayor's negotiations were slow and unproductive, the Living Wage Coalition mounted a signature campaign to qualify the proposal for the November 2000 ballot. They chose this tactic, according to a flyer the coalition circulated in June 2000, "to put pressure on the Mayor and the Board of Supervisors to act on the Living Wage" and use the ballot "as a back-up in case they don't act." In just two weeks, union-financed signature gatherers collected twenty thousand signatures, more than double the number needed to put the proposal on the ballot (Lelchuk 2000). The large number of signatures, along with a union-funded poll in July 1999 that showed that 60 percent of San Francisco voters supported the $11 living wage, encouraged the Living Wage Coalition about succeeding at the ballot box (Lewis 1999b; Wilson 1999).

Although unions had spent significant resources on the signature campaign and survey, they preferred to resolve the living wage issue through legislative, rather than electoral, channels. One co-director of the Living Wage Coalition explained that a ballot campaign "would have been tremendously costly for unions as their business opponents were ready to spend millions of dollars" to prevent the measure from passing.[17] Going with the ballot, a

HERE Local 2 organizer added, also "would've created a split in the [Living Wage] Coalition" just when unions had committed themselves to building more unity among low-wage workers and union members.[18] Union leaders also understood that it would be difficult to communicate the intricacies of the living wage law via a simple ballot measure. Mayor Brown, in turn, also wanted to avoid a living wage ballot fight because it would have pitted his staunchest allies—business and labor—against each other, putting him in an awkward position (Brannon 2000).

Unlike unions, immigrant advocates wanted to take the issue directly to voters, believing that the initiative process would produce a stronger and more comprehensive wage policy. The same Living Wage Coalition co-director remembers well the tensions the ballot issue created within the coalition:

> There were real strategy differences between unions and some of the immigrant rights groups that didn't have bases the size of unions and that saw the living wage campaign as a way to build those bases. There were strategy differences over targeting the mayor versus working with the mayor, because labor had those relations. There were strategy differences over negotiating compromises versus how far you're willing to go to get a deal or not get a deal. . . . A union like SEIU Local 250 had ten thousand members who would be affected by this. They were very practical, because it was about getting their members real raises. Compare that to the immigrant groups: they publicly continued to call for a $14.50 living wage and they felt more comfortable targeting the mayor in a ballot campaign.[19]

Limited resources meant that nonprofit advocates ultimately had little influence over final campaign decisions. "None of these immigrant rights groups had the kind of money it would take to finance a ballot campaign," the same co-director said. "The nonprofit activists would say, 'Let's hold out.' And I'm like, 'Okay, but are you writing the check?'"[20]

This power imbalance within the Living Wage Coalition makes clear that exerting influence in San Francisco politics requires a large membership base and money, and immigrant-serving nonprofits do not have either. Unions have large memberships and can use their membership dues and affiliated political action committees (PACs) to finance their political advocacy.[21] This enables them to influence coalitional dynamics and have the final say over campaign strategies and decisions.

In deciding to keep the living wage issue off the ballot, union leaders worked with Mayor Brown to develop a new, scaled-back proposal—the

Minimum Compensation Ordinance (MCO)—which was introduced to the Board of Supervisors in July 2000. This version of the ordinance called for a $9 hourly wage, provisions for paid and unpaid time off, and applied to both for-profit and nonprofit service contractors as well as tenants at the airport. Unlike Ammiano's $11 living wage proposal, it did not include health benefits, which would be provided separately through the Health Care Accountability Ordinance of 2001. Brown and a small team of union leaders and business representatives negotiated the final compromise, which the Board of Supervisors adopted with a unanimous vote on August 28.

As a compromise to business interests, the final MCO exempted restaurants operating on Fisherman's Wharf, which is city property, and would not adjust the wage level to reflect cost of living changes after three years.[22] As a compromise to nonprofits, Mayor Brown agreed to provide more city funds to help nonprofit contractors cover the cost of increased wages for a limited transitional period. In the end, all sides claimed victory, and Brown signed MCO into law on September 8, 2000. During a press conference announcing MCO, a Living Wage Coalition staff member commented that the ordinance was a "good first step," providing an early hint that the fight for higher wages in San Francisco was not yet over (Gordon 2000).

The Minimum Wage Campaign

In a second breakthrough movement, 60 percent of San Francisco voters approved Proposition L, the Minimum Wage Ordinance (MWO), in November 2003, making San Francisco one of a growing number of municipalities that have adopted local minimum wage ordinances (NELP 2015). MWO requires *all* employers to pay at least the city minimum wage to *all* employees, regardless of citizenship and documentation status, who work two or more hours per week in San Francisco. It adjusts the city's minimum wage annually based on the previous year's Consumer Price Index for urban wage earners in the San Francisco–Oakland–San Jose metro area. When the ordinance took effect in 2004, the San Francisco minimum wage was $8.50 per hour, $1.75 above the California minimum wage and $3.35 above the federal minimum wage. As of May 2015, the San Francisco minimum wage is $12.25, compared with $9 at the state level and $7.25 at the federal level.[23] The ordinance initially exempted small businesses and nonprofit organizations but phased them in over a two-year period starting in 2005. A study commissioned by the Board of Supervisors estimated that MWO would increase pay for more than fifty-four thousand workers, amounting to 11 percent of the city's workforce. It also estimated that the city's minimum wage would disproportionately benefit immigrants, native-born minorities, and workers under the age of twenty-five (Reich and Laitinen 2003).

The San Francisco Office of Labor Standards Enforcement, the agency responsible for enforcing labor laws adopted by the Board of Supervisors and San Francisco voters, is responsible for enforcing MWO.[24] The ordinance allows aggrieved workers to file claims against employers who fail to pay the mandated minimum wage. It also allows unions and community organizations to file wage claims on behalf of aggrieved workers. MWO requires every workplace to post bulletins announcing the current San Francisco minimum wage in English, Chinese, Spanish, and any additional language spoken by more than 5 percent of the workforce. Finally, MWO prohibits employers from discriminating against workers who exercise their rights under the ordinance. In comparison to MCO, MWO contains more provisions aimed at protecting vulnerable immigrant workers who—due to unfamiliarity with government agencies, undocumented status, or limited English proficiency—are less likely to contest labor law violations or speak up against unscrupulous employers (Gleeson 2012). Immigrant-serving nonprofits had an influential role in formulating the language of MWO and insisted on writing these protections for immigrant workers into the ordinance.

The Minimum Wage Coalition

The pressures of negotiating a deal with Mayor Brown in 2000 had divided the Living Wage Coalition. However, the cross-organizational partnership endured, and immigrant-serving nonprofits and labor unions were able to reconstitute their relationship around the Minimum Wage Coalition, the main force advocating for MWO. Like the Living Wage Coalition, the Minimum Wage Coalition included a cross-section of labor and community organizations (table 10 lists the twelve most active).

Unions initially hesitated to get involved with the minimum wage campaign. While they recognized that it might help them organize new workers and strengthen their community ties, the policy would bring few direct benefits to union members, most of whom were already earning over $8.50 per hour. Many in the labor community also thought that 2003 was a bad year to launch a new campaign. It was a mayoral election year, and Mike Casey, the president of HERE Local 2 and SFLC, doubted that unions could add fundraising for an effective wage campaign, likely costing more than $250,000, to what they would already spend on the mayor's race.[25] The San Francisco economy was in a downturn following the collapse of the dot-com bubble in 2001. And unions anticipated strong opposition from businesses, which

Table 10   The twelve most active organizations in the Minimum Wage Coalition

Name	Type	Description
Association of Community Organizations for Reform Now	501(c)(3)/ nonprofit	Advocates for low- and moderate-income families, with a focus on neighborhood safety, voter registration, health care, living wages, and affordable housing
Central City SRO Collaborative	501(c)(3)/ nonprofit	Provides services/advocacy to low-income tenants in single room occupancy hotels in the Tenderloin and South of Market districts
Chinese Progressive Association	501(c)(3)/ nonprofit	Provides services/advocacy to low-wage Chinese immigrants
Day Labor Program	501(c)(3)/ nonprofit	A program of Dolores Street Community Services; provides services/advocacy to immigrant day laborers
HERE Local 2	501(c)(5)/ union	Represents hotel and restaurant employees in San Francisco and San Mateo; in 2004, HERE merged with UNITE, the textile and laundry workers union, to form UNITE-HERE Local 2
Mission Agenda	501(c)(3)/ nonprofit	Provided services/advocacy to low-income tenants in single room occupancy hotels in the Mission district; the organization no longer exists
Mission Anti-Displacement Coalition	Coalition of 501(c)(3) nonprofits	A coalition of nonprofits fighting gentrification in the Mission district
People Organized to Win Employment Rights	501(c)(3)/ nonprofit	Serves low-income African Americans in San Francisco and advocates for economic, racial, and gender justice
San Francisco Labor Council	501(c)(5)/ union	The San Francisco federation of local AFL-CIO unions
SEIU Local 250	501(c)(5)/ union	Represents health care workers in northern California
SEIU Local 790	501(c)(5)/ union	Represents public employees in local government, schools, and hospitals as well as nonprofit employees in the Bay Area
Young Workers United	501(c)(3)/ nonprofit	A worker center catering to young and immigrant workers in San Francisco's low-wage service sector

would view a higher citywide minimum wage as an additional burden during tough economic times. Nonetheless, they ultimately joined the fight for MWO. As an SEIU Local 250 organizer explained, they wanted "to create a strong minimum wage policy that included indexing and that excluded a tip credit."[26] He added that "standing in solidarity with working people and our community partners" also influenced unions' decision to campaign in support of MWO.[27]

Six of the twelve most active organizations in the Minimum Wage Coalition were nonprofits representing immigrants. They included the Chinese Progressive Association (CPA) and the Day Labor Program, which work with low-income Chinese and Latino immigrants, respectively; Mission Agenda and Central City SRO Collaborative, which advocated for low-income tenants in single room occupancy hotels in the heavily immigrant Mission, Tenderloin, and South of Market districts; the Mission Anti-Displacement Coalition, a group of organizations that fight the eviction and displacement of working-class Latino immigrants in the Mission district; and Young Workers United (YWU), a worker center serving young and immigrant workers in San Francisco's low-wage service sector.

These immigrant-serving nonprofits supported higher wages for immigrant workers, but they also got involved in the campaign to organize marginalized immigrant communities and to develop immigrant leadership skills. "The minimum wage campaign," an advocate with Mission Agenda commented, "was a good tool for us to train single room occupancy hotel tenants [in] the skills for how to conduct a campaign."[28] A Day Labor Program staff member similarly explained that "organizing workers is the only way we're going to make systemic change, especially if the laws are meant to benefit them. That's why we got our day laborers involved with the campaign."[29]

Going for the Ballot

The Minimum Wage Coalition opted for the initiative process rather than work through the Board of Supervisors and allow dialogue on the issue between supporters and opponents. According to a Mission Agenda advocate, they decided to short-circuit the legislative process because they wanted "exclusive control over the content of the ordinance" and because they wanted the fate of the ordinance "to rest in the hands of San Francisco voters, not policymakers and the business community."[30]

The Minimum Wage Coalition also hoped that putting an ordinance on the ballot would ease the strains between unions and immigrant-serving nonprofits. In commenting on the final stages of the living wage campaign, Mike Casey, president of HERE Local 2 and SFLC, expressed regret over the tensions within the Living Wage Coalition created by negotiating a compromise ordinance with Mayor Brown and the business lobby.[31] Casey and others in the Minimum Wage Coalition believed that a ballot initiative would make it easier to maintain coalitional unity.

Supervisor Matt Gonzalez, the strongest MWO supporter on the Board of Supervisors, also preferred to enact a citywide minimum wage through the ballot box. Gonzalez had been elected to the Board in 2000 as part of a slate of candidates who sought to change the direction of city policy and minimize the influence of Mayor Brown. Legislating MWO via initiative, he explained, was a way to circumvent the mayor in the policymaking process.

Gonzalez did, however, organize a public hearing on the minimum wage issue to gauge how fellow supervisors and members of the public thought about it before going to the ballot. He explained:

> You put the measure out there. You can tweak it as you hear criticism. You give the public a chance to dialogue on it. You give your critics a chance to dialogue on it. You gauge what kind of support you have. And when it's all finished, you just say, "Okay, forget this process; we're going to the ballot." You get all the benefits of the legislative process, but none of the negatives and none of the stuff that went down with the living wage ordinance.[32]

Gonzalez felt that following the hearing with a ballot campaign was "an incredibly crafty way" of dealing with the wage issue given the economic downturn and strong business opposition.[33]

Held by the Finance Committee in February 2002, the hearing produced predictable results: Members of the Board were noncommittal; immigrant-serving nonprofits, unions, and low-wage workers testified in support of a wage hike; and the business community opposed it and argued for the need of an impartial study to determine the cost of a municipal minimum wage to the city's restaurant industry in particular. To placate the business lobby but also to help determine what minimum wage amount would achieve strong support at the polls, Gonzalez asked UC Berkeley economist Michael Reich to study the economic impact of a municipal minimum wage.[34] A hearing in the Finance Committee in May 2003 on Reich's study concluded that a minimum wage of $8.50 would bring benefits to thousands of low-wage workers and only minor costs to a very small percentage of city businesses (Reich and Laitinen 2003).

In April 2003, the Minimum Wage Coalition finalized the text of the ordinance and decided to put the measure on the ballot via a signature campaign. Members of the Board of Supervisors and leaders of the business community both strongly criticized this decision, arguing that a ballot proposition stifled democracy and deprived them of the opportunity to weigh in on the discussion of a policy with such far-reaching economic consequences. In an attempt to subject the ordinance to the deliberative process, pro-business supervisors Fiona Ma, Bevan Dufty, and Gavin Newsom proposed a resolution in June 2003 to create a Minimum Wage Task Force. The task force would have responsibilities similar to those of the Living Wage Task Force.

Gonzalez and minimum wage advocates opposed creating such a task force. During a May meeting of the Minimum Wage Coalition, Gonzalez had questioned the utility of a task force as the ordinance was already on its way to the ballot, and he called the task force idea an attempt to delay action. During a Rules Committee hearing in the Board of Supervisors in June 2003, he added that creating a task force gave the false impression that there was room for negotiation on MWO. Whether or not to include a tip credit, he said, was the primary concern, and neither side felt the issue was negotiable. A tip credit would allow employers to pay tipped workers, such as restaurant servers and bar tenders, a lower hourly rate than that mandated by MWO so long as employees' total wages equaled at least the city minimum wage. The business lobby insisted that MWO include a tip credit, while the Minimum Wage Coalition insisted on its exclusion.

After the Minimum Wage Coalition had submitted more than double the number of needed signatures to the city's Department of Elections to qualify MWO for the ballot, the Board tabled the task force idea.[35] The Minimum Wage Coalition next went ahead with the ballot campaign.

Unions Overshadow Nonprofits in the Initiative Campaign

The ballot campaign to enact MWO broke with convention. Rather than targeting middle-class liberal and progressive voters in high-turnout neighborhoods such as Noe Valley and Bernal Heights, the Minimum Wage Coalition focused on lower-turnout neighborhoods of working-class people, immigrants, and people of color, who would benefit most from MWO, including Chinatown, the Mission, and Bayview. This strategy gave immigrant-serving nonprofits the opportunity to mount a field campaign in the communities they served. CPA, the Day Labor Program, and Mission Agenda all mobilized immigrants to participate in phone-banking and precinct walks to get out the vote on Election Day. They placed paid arguments in support of MWO in the city's official voter guide and used the local mainstream and ethnic media to advertise the ballot measure. The director of the Day Labor Program, for example, wrote an article in *El Tecolote*—a bilingual English-Spanish newspaper circulating in the Mission district—right before the November election urging readers to vote yes on Proposition L (Saucedo 2003).

Their efforts did not compare with those of unions, however. Some nonprofit advocates explained that they held back in the ballot campaign because of their tax-exempt status and electioneering restrictions for nonprofits. They saw MWO as the pet issue of Gonzalez, who was running for mayor when MWO was on the ballot. Because of this close connection, some nonprofit advocates feared that their efforts to mobilize voters would be mistaken for illegal campaigning on behalf of a candidate for elective office. While the ballot campaign and Gonzalez's mayoral campaign were separate undertakings, it is easy to see why they would be concerned. Gonzalez had initiated the public debate on a citywide minimum wage, wanted MWO to be on the ballot, and participated in meetings of the Minimum Wage Coalition. He also identified low-wage worker rights as a key issue in his mayoral platform and contributed $1,000 to the ballot campaign fund. Unions, in contrast, were less concerned about the legal limits on their electoral participation. They are subject to campaign finance laws but are otherwise free to endorse and campaign in support of and opposition to ballot measures and candidates for elective office.

Nonprofit advocates also lacked the large memberships needed to pull off the ballot campaign. CPA, the Day Labor Program, and YWU all mobilized immigrants as campaign field workers, but the unions fielded many more. "We had about twenty of our people working on the field campaign," an YWU advocate commented, "but unions were able to bring out hundreds and hundreds of people. They have the ability to get out massive numbers. . . . It just dwarfs what we can do."[36] The same advocate added that "unions are very experienced at doing precinct operations" and had the advantage of being able "to fold Prop. L into their larger slate of issues and candidates" for the November election.[37] Also, few immigrant-serving nonprofits had the financial means to contribute to the campaign, although CPA made a one-time contribution of $500.[38] Labor unions and key donors largely paid for the MWO campaign.

As in the earlier living wage campaign, the nonprofit-union collaboration in the minimum wage campaign demonstrated the imbalance of political resources between the two types of organizations. This frustrated nonprofit advocates. A Mission Agenda leader commented that "there were tensions between unions and community organizations because folks felt that unions asserted their presence and unions were coopting the work that CBOs had been doing in immigrant communities and communities of color for many years."[39] Similarly, a Day Labor Program organizer mentioned that "unions are so much more powerful than us and throughout the [MWO] campaign there had been difficulties between unions and community-based nonprofits. The nonprofits felt disrespected in the campaign, as if their voices weren't as important."[40] An important reason why unions had a stronger presence in the ballot campaign and were able to overshadow immigrant-serving nonprofits in the initiative process was because of nonprofits' relative resource disadvantage.

At the end of the day, the Minimum Wage Coalition conducted a strong field campaign, and 60 percent of San Francisco voters approved the ballot measure in November 2003. The forceful business opposition feared by the Minimum Wage Coalition never materialized. The San Francisco Chamber of Commerce and the Golden Gate Restaurant Association did campaign against the ordinance, but not as strongly as they had done three years previously against MCO. "We realized that the ballot measure was popular among voters," the Golden Gate Restaurant Association director explained, "and we knew that the unions and the Minimum Wage Coalition had launched a strong campaign."[41] He added that the business lobby was in the difficult position of trying "to educate 780,000 San Francisco residents about the intricacies of a tip credit" and explain why the restaurant industry wanted a citywide minimum wage that included it.[42] The weakness of business opposition, according to a staff member of the Minimum Wage Coalition, is also explained by the fact that mayoral candidate Gavin Newsom advised his allies in the business community not to waste their resources on a ballot measure that was very likely to pass.[43]

Implementing and Enforcing the Minimum Wage Ordinance

Despite its popularity, it was not easy to implement MWO. Minimum wage violations have been common among immigrants who speak little English, who work in restaurants and the garment industry, or who work as domestic workers or day laborers. The employers who mistreat immigrant workers are often themselves immigrants or native-born co-ethnics, which complicates enforcement (CPA 2010). Additionally, the San Francisco Office of Labor Standards Enforcement (OLSE), the agency responsible for enforcing MWO, has been understaffed. Since enforcement is entirely complaint-driven, the reluctance of aggrieved immigrant workers to report wage violations, especially against co-ethnic employers, has further hampered enforcement.

Immigrant-serving nonprofits have helped OLSE in getting low-wage immigrant workers the wages to which they are legally entitled. Just as civil society organizations have improved the enforcement of local, state, and federal labor laws elsewhere in the country (Gleeson 2012; Luce 2005), immigrant-serving nonprofits have brought wage violations to OLSE's attention. With input from nonprofits, OLSE has recovered $6.5 million in back wages for immigrants and other low-wage workers between 2004 and 2013 (OLSE 2013). Though they helped enact the law, unions have been notably absent from this wave of administrative advocacy. Not only do they seem to lack interest in enforcing MWO, but they also lack nonprofits' community expertise and their ability to bridge the gaps between immigrant communities and city administrative agencies.

Educating Immigrant Workers and Finding Wage Violations

Immigrant-serving nonprofits have a keen understanding of the importance of good enforcement, distilled from years of seeking action from state and federal labor enforcement agencies, including the California Division of Labor Standards Enforcement (DLSE) and the Wage and Hour Division of the U.S. Department of Labor. "Like so many," an advocate with the Day Labor Program commented, "we have so much experience with state labor laws and how easy it is for employers to skirt the system because of the lack of enforcement at the statewide level. We didn't want this to happen in San Francisco."[44] Similarly, a CPA advocate explained that "we understood that the Minimum Wage Ordinance would only be as good as its enforcement. . . . We've dealt with DLSE enough to know that non-enforced labor rights often equal no rights at all."[45] When MWO took effect in February 2004, a group of mostly immigrant-serving nonprofits—including the Asian Law Caucus, CPA, the Day Labor Program, the Filipino Community Center, People Organized to Win Employment Rights (POWER), and YWU—began meeting to strategize about what they could do to prevent MWO from becoming a symbolic measure.

They decided that first they needed to educate low-wage workers about their rights under the ordinance and what they should do when they are not paid the city's minimum wage. "We planned this huge blitz of the city where we targeted low-wage immigrant workers in areas of the city with high densities of restaurants," commented an YWU advocate. "We handed out flyers to tons of workers, formally surveyed nearly two hundred of them, and talked to about a thousand more in a period of two months."[46] CPA conducted similar outreach among Chinese workers, as did the Day Labor Program among Latino workers and POWER among low-wage African American workers. These outreach campaigns focused on educating especially noncitizens and undocumented workers, who were also entitled to the local minimum wage (as well as state and federal labor protections).

The Chinese community was particularly in need of outreach and education. Chinese restaurant and garment workers frequently did not receive the state minimum wage, an advocate with CPA commented, making them skeptical that they would receive the higher municipal minimum wage even if they filed a complaint with OLSE:

> There wasn't total unity in the Chinese community around raising the minimum wage because most of the workers weren't getting the old minimum wage. And they'd ask, "What's the point of raising [the

minimum wage] if we're not even getting the old minimum wage?" They thought it would be better to enforce the state minimum wage instead of the more progressive city minimum wage. . . . A lot of Chinese garment workers get piece rates, and they're maybe getting $2 or $3 per hour. These workers had low expectations of their worth and a very poor understanding of [the pay] they're entitled to. So it was important for us to educate them on the merits of the Minimum Wage Ordinance and make them understand the importance of good enforcement.[47]

These outreach efforts enabled nonprofit advocates to find the first cases of minimum wage violations involving immigrant workers. They collected information on these workers' employment conditions and brought these cases to OLSE for administrative review and investigation.

It was perhaps understandable that unions did not undertake such efforts. They do not represent sub-minimum wage workers, and there is low union density among the industries that commonly employ immigrant workers and violate minimum wage requirements. Labor unions also experienced pressures from their members to move on after winning MWO and push for other policy issues, including universal health care and paid sick leave. It is harder for unions to focus on a single issue for a long time compared with immigrant-serving nonprofits, and they consequently lack the follow-up attention necessary to monitor the implementation and enforcement of MWO.

Most significantly, unions lack the close access to immigrant communities that nonprofits have developed and, according to a Day Labor Program organizer, they have little experience using government agencies to enforce wage issues:

> Unions aren't filing these [wage] claims. It's organizations like us that are filing the claims. They don't even know OLSE and how it works. They go like, "Oh! This is how it works?" They don't know the ins and outs of the system, and they don't know where the system is failing. . . . They're not as involved with enforcing the ordinance because it's less connected to their members. But immigrant workers come to us with wage complaints all the time.[48]

Similarly, an advocate with YWU flatly stated that "unions just don't do public enforcement," explaining that they do not rely on administrative agencies like OLSE to correct the behavior of noncompliant employers.[49] Unions can enforce wage standards directly through collective bargaining and contracts, the grievance process, and litigation. This has meant that nonprofits, especially those serving disadvantaged immigrants, have been the only organizations advocating with OLSE for better minimum wage enforcement.

With ready access to immigrant communities and on-the-ground knowledge of what is happening at the worksite, immigrant-serving nonprofits have emerged as important intermediaries between immigrant workers and OLSE. They register workers' wage complaints, collect information on their employment conditions, and relay that information to city officials, enabling OLSE to investigate these cases further and possibly start administrative procedures against noncompliant employers. Immigrants feel more comfortable seeking help from nonprofit organizations instead of OLSE, even though MWO includes various protections for immigrant workers and OLSE has multilingual staff to assist immigrants. Some immigrants have had bad experiences with government in their native countries. Others are undocumented and do not want to interact with public officials for fear of alerting them to their whereabouts. Still others do not have the English proficiency to navigate the OLSE bureaucracy and the claims-making process on their own.

Given their ability to provide linguistically and culturally appropriate education and outreach in immigrant communities, immigrant-serving nonprofits have the unique ability to build trust and case-manage immigrant workers in a way that government agencies cannot. An OLSE compliance officer conceded to the shortcomings of his office and commented on the important role of immigrant-serving nonprofits with regard to Asian immigrant workers:

> In the Asian community, we know there are many labor violations. But it's such a big hurdle for [workers] to come over to our office and it takes an extraordinary skill to coach people and encourage them to come forward. It's a real challenge for us to do that kind of education and outreach. Organizations like the Chinese Progressive Association are so important in empowering workers to go forward with complaints and steering the complainants to our office so we can do our share of the work.[50]

Immigrant-serving nonprofits have a symbiotic relationship with OLSE. Immigrants trust nonprofits and feel more comfortable exercising their labor rights through nonprofit advocates. When nonprofit advocates notify OLSE of immigrants' wage concerns, OLSE can then use the force of government to investigate and demand back wages for aggrieved immigrant workers.

Amending the Minimum Wage Ordinance

From the beginning, OLSE has struggled with funding and staff shortages. "A persistent theme," the OLSE manager commented with some bitterness, "is that our city passes great laws, but there's consistently not enough thought given to the enforcement and the staffing and funding of enforcement. That's always an afterthought."[51] Though MWO designated OLSE as the enforcement agency, it did not stipulate a funding or staff level that would permit OLSE to do its time-consuming investigative work. Initially, existing OLSE staff monitored employers' compliance with MWO. After OLSE successfully resolved some wage claims, word of these successes caused more wage claims—and more complicated wage claims—to flow into the office. OLSE could not keep up with the increased workload. With time, an OLSE compliance officer commented, nonprofit advocates grew "frustrated with the backlog" and "the lack of resources to investigate the claims that they helped generate," and they complained that MWO amounted to an "unfulfilled voter mandate."[52]

This frustration caused nonprofit advocates to initiate conversations in 2005 with OLSE staff, the city attorney, and Supervisor Sophie Maxwell about amending the legislation to ensure comprehensive employer compliance. CPA and the Day Labor Program helped to formulate the text of the ordinance, and their staff and clients testified in support of it during public hearings in the Board of Supervisors. Despite opposition from the restaurant industry and Mayor Gavin Newsom's concern about the proposed funding mechanisms, the Board of Supervisors voted unanimously to pass the Minimum Wage Implementation and Enforcement Ordinance (MWIEO) in July 2006. As a result, OLSE added three minimum wage compliance officers to its staff of eleven, all paid for through the city's General Fund. MWIEO has also allowed OLSE to enforce state labor laws in the course of their minimum wage investigations and provided OLSE with additional enforcement tools, including the issuance of hefty administrative penalties and citations.

MWIEO underscores how nonprofits enhance OLSE's enforcement work. The text of the ordinance characterizes immigrant-serving nonprofits as valuable watchdogs of MWO, stating that they "report that violations of the City's minimum wage and other labor laws are still widespread in San Francisco. For example, based on worker surveys and labor market research, CPA estimates that approximately 9,000 Chinese restaurant and garment workers in San Francisco are currently being paid wages below the City's established minimum wage."[53] The ordinance explicitly seeks to integrate immigrant-serving nonprofits into OLSE's monitoring and enforcement process. In a move to institutionalize "community-driven regulation" (O'Rourke 2002), MWIEO mandates that OLSE contract with nonprofits to launch a community-based outreach program to educate the city's most exploited and marginalized workers about their labor rights and inform them of how OLSE can recover their unpaid wages.

This partnership got off the ground in 2008. Since then, OLSE has issued yearly contracts to immigrant-serving nonprofits—including CPA, the Filipino Community Center, and La Raza Centro Legal—and Pride at Work, an AFL-CIO constituency group that supports lesbian, gay, bisexual, and transgender workers. The funding for the partnership has been a political hot potato, however. Mayor Newsom allocated $195,000 for the partnership in fiscal year 2008–2009 but cut funding from his budget in subsequent years, leading the Board of Supervisors to restore the money, with contracts totaling about $192,000 in fiscal year 2010–2011.[54] In fiscal year 2012–2013, the Board of Supervisors approved a budget of $482,000 for OLSE's education and outreach program, which benefited six community-based nonprofits that serve immigrants and other low-wage workers (OLSE 2013).

The increased funding notwithstanding, the partnership has been challenging because OLSE and nonprofit advocates have discovered some drawbacks in their collaboration. Each has sought to maintain some distinct spheres of work. In a memorable 2006 minimum wage case, the close collaboration between YWU and OLSE was so confusing that the restaurant owners under investigation contacted OLSE when they wanted to follow up with the nonprofit that was helping an undocumented, pregnant worker from Mexico with her wage complaint. The owners of Si Señor Taqueria fired Sonia Cano just days after she filed a wage claim with OLSE, beginning what appeared to be a retaliation campaign that left both Cano and her undocumented husband facing deportation. An OLSE compliance officer believed that the disastrous outcome stemmed from the inability of the restaurant owner to distinguish OLSE staff from the YWU advocates.[55]

To prevent the public-private partnership from hurting those it intends to benefit, nonprofits have had to retain some distance so as to maintain trust with their immigrant clients while simultaneously helping OLSE build successful cases against noncompliant employers. This dilemma was similar to that faced by nonprofits advocating for better implementation and enforcement of the language access policy discussed in chapter 3. Some organizations, including CPA and La Raza Centro Legal, like the idea of receiving government funding for the labor rights education they have been doing in immigrant communities for years. Others, including YWU, have chosen not to formalize their relationship with OLSE with a contract. They fear that doing so will demobilize their organization and undermine their ability to provide an outside perspective on the policymaking process and serve as a safe haven for vulnerable immigrant workers who need help.

The partnership has proven challenging also for OLSE. OLSE staff want to take advantage of nonprofits' expertise and access to immigrant communities, but they are not sure whether the MWIEO-mandated partnership is the best way to do that. One OLSE compliance officer preferred to institutionalize nonprofits' community expertise in a fundamentally different way:

> For us to be more effective, we need the face of the immigrant community here [in the OLSE office]. I think internally we need to have people who come with the background and the life's experience of the advocates who come out of those communities. I don't entirely disagree with the collaborative effort, but my preference would be to have people like Alex Tom [from CPA] working on staff here . . . that they bring that deep belief and empathy and that experience into working for our agency and that they don't lose touch with that. The real key to change is that we have to intrinsically change the environment here in government. It's not what you do on the outside; it's internally here.[56]

Instead of collaborating with immigrant-serving nonprofits, OLSE would rather hire nonprofit advocates to join their staff.

OLSE also has had reservations about funding nonprofit advocates. The same compliance officer commented that OLSE needs to remain neutral in minimum wage investigations and does not want to create the impression that it is "funding street protests."[57] Another OLSE staff member added that since immigrant-serving nonprofits are also "focused on building their own organization," it was hard for OLSE to hold its nonprofit partners accountable for specific outcomes, such as the number of referrals. OLSE and immigrant-serving nonprofits thus need one another to monitor and enforce MWO effectively. Yet they also understand the importance of remaining autonomous and separate as they work together to improve the rights of vulnerable immigrant workers in San Francisco. This tension means that the current public-private partnership to enforce MWO likely remains in flux.

The Challenges and Opportunities of Cross-Organizational Collaborations

The literature on labor-community coalitions teaches us that cross-organizational collaborations are more viable when they build on shared ideologies and aligned interests, mutual trust among union and nonprofit leaders, and a shared pool of resources to support the coalition (Tattersall 2005; Tattersall and Reynolds 2007). The Living and Minimum Wage Coalitions active in San Francisco during the late 1990s and early 2000s had all three ingredients. Immigrant-serving nonprofits and labor unions both shared a progressive ideology and were interested in economic justice for all low-wage workers in the city. They have gone to bat for one another and moved from circling in the ring between the 1960s and 1980s to working together since the 1990s to upend the pro-business economic policies supported by the mayor and his allies in the business community. Finally, both nonprofits and unions committed staff time and other resources to coalition meetings and actions.

Yet differences in tax-exempt status and a disparity in organizational resources made it challenging for immigrant-serving nonprofits and labor unions to work together. Compared with immigrant-serving nonprofits, unions have more members, more money, and greater freedom to lobby legislators and engage in electoral politics. This enabled unions to take the upper hand in the final stages of the campaigns to enact MCO and MWO. By contrast, immigrant-serving nonprofits have been the dominant advocates in getting MWO implemented and enforced. Unions had little interest and little expertise in policy implementation and enforcement, allowing nonprofit advocates to take advantage of their commitment, expertise, and freedom to engage in this kind of administrative advocacy. Any examination of cross-organizational collaborations thus needs to consider not only ideology, interests, and leadership but also broader questions of organizational structure, resources, and status.

The nonprofit-union collaborations analyzed here have spilled over into a number of other advocacy campaigns in San Francisco. After MCO was enacted in 2000, immigrant-serving nonprofits and unions teamed up to fight the firing of Filipino immigrants at San Francisco International Airport when airport screeners, previously employees of the city, were federalized under the Transportation Security Administration in the aftermath of the 2001 terrorist attacks. Immigrant-serving nonprofits and unions have also collaborated on other policies concerning San Francisco's low-wage labor market, including the Health Care Accountability Ordinance of 2001, the Health Care Security Ordinance of 2006, the Paid Sick Leave Ordinance of 2006, the Wage Theft Prevention Ordinance of 2011, and the Minimum Wage Increase Ballot Measure (Proposition J) of 2014.[58] They also collaborated in the campaign to enact the Municipal ID Ordinance discussed in the following chapter.

Immigrant-serving nonprofits have also helped to implement and enforce these more recent ordinances, thereby cementing their relationship with unions. One YWU advocate commented on this development:

Our organization, CPA, and the Day Laborers have long struggled with implementing the Minimum Wage Ordinance. . . . It's given us a real expertise that's put us in an interesting position with the Health Care Access Coalition, which is very driven by unions. We were in it from the beginning, but we pulled in CPA because unions were like, "Well, how are you going to do the enforcement for this?" We're like, "Well, we're actually the experts. We know OLSE [also responsible for enforcing the Health Care Security Ordinance], how they function, and we know the structure." So we got pulled into the Enforcement Committee of the Health Care Access Coalition. . . . Unions were appalled to learn that enforcement of the health ordinance was complaint-driven. They just didn't understand how difficult public enforcement is, how under-funded it is, and how the system is not that great. Our expertise with OLSE has raised the visibility of our type of organization and OLSE with labor, which is good.[59]

Nonprofits' expertise in policy implementation shows that they have a lot to offer unions with similar bases in disadvantaged communities in achieving their mutual goals. Nonprofits and unions each have unique resources; only when they work together in recognition of each other's strengths and weaknesses can they form an advocacy coalition that can continue to strengthen the labor rights of immigrants and other low-wage workers in San Francisco.

Collaborations between nonprofits and government and collaborations between nonprofits and unions are strategies that have enabled immigrant-serving nonprofits to overcome constraints on their advocacy and influence the enactment and implementation of immigrant rights and integration policies in San Francisco. A final strategy, discussed in the next chapter, is nonprofits' use of strategic issue framing and administrative advocacy to enact and implement the Municipal ID Ordinance, a controversial law that allows San Francisco to issue identification cards to undocumented immigrants.

CHAPTER 5

Strategic Framing and Municipal ID Cards

"They don't call it the Wild West for nothing." This is how Cinnamon Stillwell (2008), a political columnist for the *San Francisco Chronicle*, satirized San Francisco's welcoming treatment of undocumented immigrants at a time when federal policies and practices increasingly focused on immigration controls. According to Stillwell, San Francisco officials were flouting federal immigration laws by inappropriately using the city's sanctuary policy to shield juvenile undocumented lawbreakers from federal immigration officials. Fed up with the city's "insistence on emphasizing ideology over public safety," she commented that the sanctuary policy "has resulted in an untenable and anarchic situation that is taking its toll on city residents and surrounding counties alike. Providing sanctuary for law-breakers at the expense of law-abiding citizens is neither a compassionate nor a moral approach. . . . The local government is absconding its duties" (Stillwell 2008).

Stillwell's colleagues at the *Chronicle*, San Francisco's largest newspaper, provided similar coverage of undocumented immigrants and city officials' treatment of them. Debra Saunders, another political columnist, wrote that "San Francisco's 'sanctuary city' policy . . . put the welfare of juvenile gang-bangers and drug dealers, who also were illegal immigrants, before the safety of law-abiding residents who are victimized by gangs and thugs" (Saunders 2008a). Crime reporter Jaxon Van Derbeken (2008a–n) penned a series of scathing articles on San Francisco's undocumented immigrants and city officials' defiance of federal immigration laws, earning him a journalism award from the Center for Immigration Studies, an anti-immigrant research group based in Washington, D.C. By the end of 2008, stories in the local mainstream press overwhelmingly portrayed immigration, especially undocumented immigration, as a major problem and key policy concern. They pressured city officials to toughen their stance on immigration.

In this environment, immigrant rights advocates have struggled to develop sympathetic counter-rhetorical frames to portray immigrants as deserving of government help. Issue framing was a particular challenge when nonprofit advocates sought to promote rights for undocumented immigrants, as they did in the municipal ID card campaign. Public opinion continues to oppose helping undocumented immigrants because they violated the country's immigration laws to live in the United States. Immigration opponents criticize local policies that promote the rights of undocumented immigrants on the ground that they challenge the federal government's exclusive power to regulate immigration and citizenship (Bonanno 2009). Because municipal ID card programs help undocumented immigrants to conduct their daily lives, explicitly condone their presence, and facilitate their access to city services, these critics argue that they unconstitutionally usurp federal law. To minimize the potential for attacks, nonprofit advocates thus had to convince city officials and the larger public that a municipal ID card program would address widely acknowledged public problems affecting *all* city residents and that it could legally coexist with federal immigration enforcement laws.

Immigrant advocates succeeded in doing this in San Francisco. Their framing strategies played a key role in proposing, enacting, and implementing the Municipal ID Ordinance, which allows San Francisco to issue its own ID cards. The Board of Supervisors adopted the ordinance in November 2007 to improve the welfare of undocumented immigrants as well as that of other city residents who have difficulty obtaining identification documents, including transgender individuals, the homeless, elderly, and youth. While nonprofit advocates sought specifically to help undocumented immigrants, their messaging to city officials and the media downplayed that undocumented immigrants were among the policy's primary beneficiaries. Instead, they framed municipal ID cards as a public safety and civic integration initiative benefiting all city residents and formulated the ordinance so that it was silent on the issue of immigration. This strategic framing failed to resonate fully with the media, mayor, and police chief. However, it does help explain why city legislators adopted the policy despite concerns over cost and why a court challenge ultimately failed to block implementation of the ordinance.

The Identification Challenges of Undocumented Immigrants

Undocumented immigrants live under difficult circumstances, to say the least. Since the 1980s, federal, state, and local laws and practices—all reflecting the public distaste for illegal immigration—have curtailed the rights and freedoms of undocumented immigrants. The 1986 Immigration Reform and Control Act aimed to remove undocumented immigrants from the labor market, though it also created a path to legalization for 2.7 million undocumented immigrants (Jones-Correa and de Graauw 2013). The more severe Illegal Immigration Reform and Immigrant Responsibility Act and the Welfare Reform Act of 1996 denied both recent legal and all illegal immigrants access to a range of public benefits, as did initiatives adopted by voters in California and Arizona in 1994 and 2004, respectively.[1] Alabama, Georgia, Indiana, South Carolina, and Utah all enacted laws in 2011 modeled after Arizona's controversial 2010 law that made it a state crime for undocumented immigrants to seek work or hold a job and that gave local police broad powers to stop and verify the immigration status of anyone they suspect of being undocumented.[2] Finally, following the 2006 enactment of the Illegal Immigration Relief Act in Hazleton (Penn.), more than 130 cities nationwide have passed or considered similar ordinances that bar undocumented immigrants from working and renting homes in their cities (Varsanyi 2010a).[3]

An added difficulty is that undocumented immigrants can no longer obtain government-issued identification documents at a time when these are increasingly necessary to enter facilities or receive services. In the aftermath of the 2001 terrorist attacks, the U.S. Congress enacted the REAL ID Act of 2005, which imposes national security standards for state-issued photo IDs. To get them, immigrants must provide proof of lawful immigration status, thereby making it impossible for undocumented immigrants to get state-issued photo IDs that federal agencies will accept for official purposes. In 2002, state-issued driver's licenses were still available to undocumented immigrants in most states (NILC 2002), but in 2011 that was the case only in New Mexico, Utah, and Washington, whose licensing laws then did not require proof of citizenship or legal residency.[4] Inability to present a government-issued ID prevents undocumented immigrants from availing themselves of the few public and private services for which they still qualify, limits their physical mobility, and intensifies their fear of contacting police and other government institutions (Matos 2008; Varsanyi 2007).

In this context, various local governments and businesses started accepting consular registration cards as a valid form of identification. Foreign governments, through their consulate offices, issue these photo IDs to their nationals living abroad. Since the largest population of undocumented immigrants hail from Mexico, the Mexican "matrícula consular" is the most common example of this form of identification.[5] The Mexican government has issued these cards since 1871, but they have only been accepted as valid identification in the United States after 9/11. With a matrícula consular, undocumented immigrants can open bank accounts and identify themselves to local police and other local government agencies that require identification before public services can be delivered. In early 2015, there were nearly 4.3 million valid matrículas in use by Mexican nationals living in the United States. By August 2013, 371 counties, 1,036 police departments, and 356 financial and other public and private institutions nationwide accepted them.[6] By early 2015, nine states, Washington, D.C., and Puerto Rico also allowed their use in obtaining a driver's license.[7] This has made many undocumented immigrants feel more secure and more included in local civic life.

San Francisco was among the first cities to adopt the matrícula consular for identification purposes (GAO 2004). Pressure from immigrant-serving nonprofits led the Board of Supervisors to adopt a resolution "urging the police, sheriff, and other local agencies to recognize the matrícula consular as official identification in the City and County of San Francisco" in November 2001.[8] In February 2002, the Board strengthened that statement by requiring all city departments to accept as valid identification the Mexican matrícula and similar consular registration cards issued by other countries.[9] In December 2002, the San Francisco Federal Building was the first in the nation to pilot the acceptance of the matrícula consular. After a dozen members of the U.S. Congress protested this action, however, the U.S. General Services Administration, which manages federal buildings, suspended it in January 2003 (Egelko 2003). Today, the federal government does not recognize the matrícula as valid identification, and the card cannot be used to enter federal buildings or to go through airport security.

Organizing to get municipal governments and financial institutions to recognize matrículas as a valid form of identification laid the groundwork for the push for municipal ID cards. Hartford (Conn.), New Haven, San Francisco, Oakland, Richmond (Calif.), Los Angeles, and New York City adopted municipal ID programs between 2007 and 2015.[10] Having a municipal ID card minimizes the risk that undocumented immigrants interacting with local law enforcement officials will be flagged for deportation. Undocumented immigrants can use the card to check out books at local libraries, access health services at city-run clinics, and enroll their kids in local public schools but not to access public services that are restricted to American citizens and legal permanent residents. They can also use the card to open bank accounts, which makes it easier for them to buy a home, start a business, or pay for their children's education. Municipal ID cards, however, have no currency outside the city that issued them. They also do not confer legal status, give authorization to work or permission to drive, prove legal age to purchase alcohol or tobacco, or increase cardholders' eligibility for public services.

Municipal ID cards, like consular registration cards, have real benefits for undocumented immigrants who do not have access to state-issued photo IDs. Unlike consular registration cards, however, municipal ID cards are available to *all* city residents. They can therefore bypass the stigma that continues to attach to consular registration cards because only undocumented immigrants need them. Local governments also control the security features of municipal ID cards. Amid concerns that consular registration cards are unreliable and insecure (Varsanyi 2007), city-issued municipal IDs can, for example, reassure banks that cardholders are who they say they are. A final advantage of municipal ID cards is that they can serve purposes other than identification. The New Haven and San Francisco cards also function as library cards and discount cards for local businesses, and both cities are considering having their IDs serve as public transportation cards as well. The Hartford (Conn., once implemented), New Haven, Oakland, Richmond (Calif.), and Los Angeles (once implemented) cards serve also as prepaid debit cards to improve local commercial participation. In sum, municipal ID cards are far more promising than consular registration cards in promoting the civic integration of undocumented immigrants.

Envisioning an ID Card for Undocumented Immigrants

Nonprofit advocates proposed the creation of a San Francisco ID card with the city's estimated 30,000 to 45,000 undocumented immigrants in mind (Hill and Johnson 2011; MPI 2014). The Alianza Latinoamericana por los Derechos de los Inmigrantes (ALDI, Latin American Alliance for Immigrant Rights) first advocated a "certificate of county residence" in response to immigration raids that took place in the Bay Area in 2006 and 2007. Upon its founding in 2006, ALDI established a hot line where immigrants could report raids and learn about their rights when dealing with local police and federal immigration officials. "We received more than 100 calls a month," an ALDI staff member commented, "and we realized that immigrants who weren't high-priority targets were also swept up in the raids because they couldn't show identification. Lots of people were calling these numbers saying 'the police pulled me over and they impounded my car because I didn't have a license' or 'they arrested my cousin for not having a license.' . . . There were all these collateral arrests."[11] Advocates with ALDI believed that a "certificate of county residence" would minimize the risk that local police or federal immigration officials would detain undocumented immigrants not targeted in the raids.

Soon other immigrant-serving nonprofits—including Chinese for Affirmative Action (CAA), the Central American Resource Center, La Raza Centro Legal (the Community's Legal Center), St. Peter's Housing Committee, and Young Workers United—also came forward to support a local ID card. Despite differences in organizational structure and size, the immigrant communities they serve, the services they provide, and the policy issues they advocate, these nonprofits joined ALDI in a loose coalition in support of local ID cards for undocumented immigrants. They all had quite a bit of experience with the difficulties faced by their undocumented clients, and advocating for ID cards would extend their earlier campaign against the federal "no-match letters" and immigration raids in the Bay Area.[12] They supported local ID cards as part of a larger campaign aimed at empowering undocumented immigrants against the national onslaught of immigrant rights restrictions. The idea of immigrant empowerment resonated widely and helped to unify and mobilize a diverse group of immigrant-serving nonprofits into a Municipal ID Card Coalition.

In discussing why the ordinance was important, these advocates emphasized that the cards would promote the rights and integration of undocumented immigrants in San Francisco. They often invoked cosmopolitan (Carens 1989) and postnational (Soysal 1994) ideals of membership to explain why they believed that San Francisco's undocumented residents should have access to a local ID card. An ALDI staff member commented, "It's a basic human right that someone has an identity they can prove. Nobody should have to walk around without papers and be excluded from the community because they're undocumented."[13] A CAA advocate added, "Our advocacy around the city ID card is informed by our belief that because immigrants live and work here, that that creates grounds for claims-making."[14] Nonprofit advocates envisioned San Francisco as the space where the cosmopolitan and postnational ideals for a more inclusive society, which includes undocumented immigrants, could be realized.

Nonprofit advocates also linked the Municipal ID Ordinance to the city's sanctuary policy. The City of Refuge Ordinance of 1989 forbids the city from using its resources to assist in the enforcement of federal immigration laws and prohibits city employees, including local police, from soliciting or disseminating information about individuals' immigration status unless legally required to do so (Bau 1994; Ridgley 2008).[15] The ordinance was prompted by the need to offer shelter to thousands of Salvadoran and Guatemalan war refugees who were unable to gain political asylum in the United States when the Reagan administration supported repressive military dictatorships in Central America. Over time, it evolved into administrative practices aimed at protecting all undocumented immigrants living in San Francisco. Many nonprofit advocates, including those at ALDI, St. Peter's Housing Committee, and CAA, emphasized that the Municipal ID Ordinance was important because it provided San Francisco the opportunity to "live up to" and "materialize and strengthen" its sanctuary status.[16]

While a variety of immigrant-serving organizations joined the campaign, there were clear tensions among them. ALDI, a relatively young organization led by two men, aroused tensions with more established immigrant-serving nonprofits with women leaders. ALDI staff members criticized the Central American Resource Center, La Raza Centro Legal, and St. Peter's Housing Committee for "selling out to city hall" and "serving as gatekeepers of issues" as well as for not wanting to "share their turf" and "give credit to us for initiating the ID card proposal."[17] Others in turn criticized ALDI for not having "organizational discipline" or a "real membership base" and for being "very sexist" and "not at all strategic about their advocacy."[18] These tensions lasted throughout the campaign and prompted ALDI to act unilaterally at times. Against the wishes of its coalition partners, for example, ALDI staged protests on the steps of city hall and talked directly to the media to increase the public visibility of the ID card proposal.

Enacting an ID Card for all San Franciscans

While nonprofit advocates wanted San Francisco to create a local ID card to help undocumented immigrants, they understood that this was not the best way to sell their idea. Their public relations effort with the Board of Supervisors downplayed undocumented immigrants as the policy's primary beneficiaries. Chris Daly and Tom Ammiano, both supervisors with progressive political views, were receptive toward ALDI's idea for a "certificate of county residence." They encouraged ALDI to research what other cities and counties had done around residency cards and submit a formal proposal for the Board's consideration. ALDI shared their proposal, which called for a "city ID card," with the two legislators in May 2007. In the summer, one of Ammiano's legislative aides held several meetings with the coalition of immigrant rights advocates to develop the idea. The aide described this coalition, which also included several labor unions, as a "down and dirty strategic coalition" that sought to secure broad-based support for the policy among local community groups before Ammiano would go public with the ID card proposal.[19]

These coalition meetings focused on crafting a strategic message. Ammiano's aide noted that since the federal government was cracking down on illegal immigration in the Bay Area, it would be difficult to enact a local ID card program because it would "draw strong public criticism due to the benefits it offered to specifically illegal immigrants."[20] Similarly, a St. Peter's Housing Committee staffer noted, "We didn't want this card to be couched as something for just illegal immigrants because we knew that could burn us."[21] Nonprofit advocates also feared that an ID card oriented solely toward the undocumented might actually make matters worse. "We didn't want the ID card to be a scarlet letter for the city's undocumented community," the same staffer explained. "We wanted the card to be carried by all city residents."[22] The coalition's goal, in the words of a CAA advocate, was to make the ID card "appealing to as many city residents as possible."[23]

One way to expand the ID card's beneficiaries was for immigrant-serving nonprofits to forge common cause with community organizations that work with transgender and homeless individuals as well as the elderly and youth. Like undocumented immigrants, these populations have difficulty obtaining government-issued identification. Transgender individuals face barriers obtaining documents that match their gender identity. The homeless have trouble applying for state-issued IDs because they cannot provide a home address or prove state residency. Many elderly no longer drive and do not want to go to the Department of Motor Vehicles, described in one interview as "hell's waiting room," to renew a license they will not use.[24] And youth under sixteen are ineligible to drive and often only have their school IDs, which are not accepted as valid identification outside the school.

To make the municipal ID card appealing to these different constituencies, St. Peter's Housing Committee proposed to make the card gender-neutral. There also was a proposal to allow homeless shelters and other social service agencies with city contracts to confirm the San Francisco residency of homeless individuals so that they could get the card. Finally, immigrant rights advocates proposed that the municipal ID card include medical information to appeal to the elderly and emergency contact information to appeal to youth's parents. As a result of these discussions about how to expand the beneficiary populations, the Municipal ID Card Coalition grew from a handful of immigrant-serving nonprofits and local unions to a broader coalition of twenty-two organizations (see table 11), including the Coalition on Homelessness, the Transgender Law Center, and the elderly-serving Bernal Heights Neighborhood Center.

Table 11 Municipal ID Card Coalition

Name	Type	Description
Alianza Latinoamericana por los Derechos de los Inmigrantes★	Unincorporated organization	Advocates for immigrant rights
American Civil Liberties Union of Northern California	501(c)(4)/social welfare organization	Provides legal advocacy on civil liberties
Association of Community Organizations for Reform Now	501(c)(3)/nonprofit	Advocates for low- and moderate-income families
Bay Area Immigrant Rights Coalition★	Coalition of 501(c)(3) nonprofits	A coalition of over fifty immigrant-serving nonprofits; the coalition is no longer active
Bernal Heights Neighborhood Center	501(c)(3)/nonprofit	Provides services/advocacy to seniors
Central American Resource Center★	501(c)(3)/nonprofit	Provides services/advocacy to Central American immigrants
Chinese for Affirmative Action★	501(c)(3)/nonprofit	Provides services/advocacy to low-wage Chinese immigrants
Coalition on Homelessness	Coalition of 501(c)(3) nonprofits	Provides services/advocacy to homeless individuals
Immigrant Legal Resource Center★	501(c)(3)/nonprofit	Advocates for immigrant rights
La Raza Centro Legal★	501(c)(3)/nonprofit	Provides services/advocacy to low-wage Hispanic immigrants
Lawyers' Committee for Civil Rights of the San Francisco Bay Area	501(c)(3)/nonprofit	Advocates for the rights of disadvantaged populations, including immigrants
Mission Neighborhood Resource Center★	501(c)(3)/nonprofit	Provides information services to Hispanic immigrants
People Organizing to Demand Environmental and Economic Justice★	501(c)(3)/nonprofit	Advocates for environmental rights and social justice in the Hispanic community
Pride at Work	501(c)(5)/union	Part of AFL-CIO; advocates for the labor rights of lesbian, gay, bisexual, and transgender workers
San Francisco Immigrant Legal and Education Network★	Coalition of 501(c)(3) nonprofits	A coalition of thirteen immigrant-serving nonprofits
San Francisco Labor Council	501(c)(5)/union	The San Francisco federation of local AFL-CIO unions
SEIU Local 87	501(c)(5)/union	Represents property service workers in San Francisco
SEIU-UHW	501(c)(5)/union	Represents health care workers in California
St. Peter's Housing Committee★	501(c)(3)/nonprofit	Provides services/advocacy to low-income Hispanic tenants; in 2010, St. Peter's Housing Committee and Just Cause Oakland merged to form Causa Justa (Just Cause)
Transgender Law Center	501(c)(3)/nonprofit	Provides services/advocacy to transgender individuals

Name	Type	Description
UNITE-HERE Local 2	501(c)(5)/union	Represents garment and hospitality workers in San Francisco and San Mateo
Young Workers United*	501(c)(3)/nonprofit	A worker center catering to young and immigrant workers in San Francisco's low-wage service sector

* Immigrant-serving organizations.

The coalition also emphasized that the cards would address the broader issues of public safety and civic integration for the benefit of all city residents. "We put public safety and civic engagement front and center to our argument," a CAA advocate explained, "because we recognized that that would resonate with most people in the city, because everybody wants safer communities . . . everybody thinks it's good when people actively participate in community affairs."[25] On several occasions, nonprofit advocates testified in Board hearings and other public venues that people will be more willing to cooperate with police to report crimes or come forward as witnesses when they have an ID, thereby making the city safer for everyone. They also explained that when more people, and especially vulnerable and marginalized populations, feel welcome to participate in community affairs, this will help the city thrive and grow stronger. While it was implied that undocumented immigrants would also benefit from more public safety and civic engagement, nonprofit advocates strategically focused on the broader issues, not the specific beneficiary populations.

When promoting the Municipal ID Ordinance in public settings, nonprofit advocates testified how the card's multiple uses would make life easier for city residents. During a Board of Supervisors hearing, an advocate with La Raza Centro Legal mentioned that the municipal ID card would facilitate access to bank accounts for the city's unbanked populations, thus helping people to keep their earnings safe and build their wealth.[26] Other nonprofit advocates emphasized that the municipal ID card would double as a library card and possibly as a public transportation card and that the card would provide access to city-run health clinics and the programs of the Recreation and Park Department, including the city's zoo and six public golf courses. Finally, they explained how the ID could serve as a discount card at local stores and stimulate local commercial participation. These multiple uses led an ALDI staffer to conclude that a municipal ID card would "help integrate segments of the city that heretofore had not been integrated."[27]

Nonprofit advocates and their allies also wanted the text of the Municipal ID Ordinance to be silent on immigration or undocumented immigrants. "For us," an advocate with St. Peter's Housing Committee commented, "the point was precisely that immigration and citizenship status shouldn't matter for how city government treats city residents. . . . Why then would we want to raise red flags by including those very words in the ordinance?"[28] The aide to Ammiano, who worked closely with advocates to develop the ordinance, noted that the text of the ordinance was specifically designed to minimize media, political, and legal scrutiny. "It isn't an accident that the word 'immigrant' isn't in the ordinance or anything about illegal immigrants," she explained. "You can read the entire ordinance and not know that immigrants benefit from this policy."[29] With its emphasis on public safety, local services, and improved communications between city officials and all city residents, the ordinance reads like a policy developed to facilitate the workings of local government for the benefit of all city residents, not one narrowly tailored to help undocumented immigrants.

Skeptics of the Non-Immigrant Frame

Despite these efforts, the coalition's strategic framing of the Municipal ID Ordinance never fully resonated with the media, the mayor, and the police. The media and Mayor Gavin Newsom were only hesitantly supportive of a municipal ID card program, which they overwhelmingly portrayed as designed for undocumented immigrants. Police Chief Heather Fong was even less convinced by the public safety frame, and she never publicly endorsed the card as a form of identification that officers would recognize or accept for official police business.

In early September 2007, the idea for a municipal ID card was leaked, and a local Spanish-language TV station broke the story before Ammiano was ready to go public.[30] The story soon percolated to the local mainstream media, and the *San Francisco Chronicle* first reported the story on September 7 with a headline reading, "City Has a Plan for Immigrant ID Card" (Buchanan 2007a). That same day, the front-page headline of the *San Francisco Examiner*, the city's second-largest newspaper, ran "Immigrants May Be Given City ID Cards" (Eslinger 2007). The *Chronicle*'s second story on September 19, published the day after Ammiano officially introduced the Municipal ID Ordinance to the Board of Supervisors, read, "ID Card Plan Would Help Immigrants Get Basic Services" (Buchanan 2007b).

These and similar stories did not necessarily portray the proposed ordinance negatively, but they did stir a national debate and put the Municipal ID Card

Coalition on the defensive. "The frustration we had," Ammiano's aide reflected, "was that we weren't in control of the message. We wanted to break it and be in control of it, but instead we were put in this reactionary position and the local media had already framed it as a card for illegal immigrants."[31] The aide also reflected on how these local news reports reverberated nationally. "As soon as it became public, the story was hitting the right-wing news stations and was national news," she said. Ammiano was "getting called by Fox, CNN. . . . All these stations that wanted to interview him. We were getting hate calls from all over the country. So, we knew when it was on the news, because we'd start getting 50 million phone calls. . . . They were really hateful."[32]

Mayor Newsom also did not see the municipal ID as a card for all city residents. Given his earlier support for the city's sanctuary policy, Newsom's initial backing of the municipal ID card program was not surprising. In his mind, as in the minds of many others, sanctuary and municipal ID cards were closely related policies, both benefiting undocumented immigrants. When asked at a news conference, however, whether he himself planned to get a municipal ID card to promote the program, Newsom responded, "I've got more IDs than I need. This is for other people. This is not for the mayor of San Francisco. . . . I appreciate some city employees getting it, but I wish it was going to the people it was intended for" (Knight 2009a). Much to the frustration of nonprofit advocates, Newsom failed to understand, embrace, and communicate their framing of the municipal ID card program as something that would fully work only when all city residents, and not just undocumented immigrants, carried and used the card.

Finally, Police Chief Heather Fong, who has been described as "press-shy" and is known "to balk at community policing initiatives," never endorsed the Municipal ID Ordinance (Garcia 2009; Knight 2009b). Given nonprofit advocates' emphasis on public safety and their argument that it would be easier for the police to do their work if everyone carried an ID, they found Fong's lack of public support for the ordinance surprising and disappointing. "We thought the police would be excited about the card," an advocate with the Asian Law Caucus commented. "Chief Fong, I think, was supportive of the ordinance, but she was in the process of leaving the force, and she might not have had the support of other officers or the Mayor's Office. . . . We were surprised that she didn't do more around [the ordinance.]"[33] Fong, a daughter of Chinese immigrants, reasserted the police department's commitment to San Francisco's sanctuary policy on several occasions. Yet when she and other San Francisco police officials spoke publicly about the Municipal ID Ordinance, they focused primarily on the card's security features and expressed concern about the need to make the card fraud-resistant.

The skepticism to the non-immigrant frame in San Francisco contrasts sharply with advocates' experience in New Haven, which in June 2007 became the first city to adopt a municipal ID program. The New Haven Resident Card program was also advocated by grassroots organizations, notably Junta for Progressive Action, New Haven's oldest Latino nonprofit dating from 1969, as well as Unidad Latina en Acción (ULA, Latinos United in Action), an unincorporated immigrant rights organization founded in 2003 (Matos 2008). These organizations also talked about municipal IDs as a means to improve public safety and integrate all residents into New Haven civic life. Both Mayor John DeStefano and Police Chief Francisco Ortiz publicly endorsed the program using that language. "This is an opportunity that will benefit all segments of our city," Mayor DeStefano testified during a rare appearance before the New Haven Board of Aldermen. "The debit component of the card will support wealth creation. The card will assist with the public's access to city services such as libraries and parks . . . and a common and broadly used card will ensure greater public safety for all our residents."[34] Police Chief Ortiz, a Latino, similarly praised the ID card program as a "useful public safety tool" that would make it easier for the police to do their job (O'Leary 2007, 2008). As a strong supporter and practitioner of community policing, he added that adopting a municipal ID program was a "common sense approach to strengthen community-police relations."[35]

Supporters of the Non-Immigrant Frame

Even though advocates' framing of the Municipal ID Ordinance never fully resonated with the media, mayor, and police chief, it nonetheless helped to convince a veto-proof majority of city legislators to adopt the policy, despite cost concerns. During public hearings before the Board of Supervisors in October and November 2007, Ammiano honed in on the card's public safety and civic engagement benefits. He emphasized the different groups of city residents that would benefit as well as the card's multiple uses. Staff and clients from more than a dozen immigrant-serving nonprofits testified in support of the ordinance, highlighting the importance of a municipal ID card to immigrants and other city residents. Various city departments, including the Recreation and Park Department, the Office of the Treasurer and Tax Collector, and the San Francisco Public Library, expressed their support for the ID card program and identified the different ways in which the card could be used to access their programs and services.

There was little public opposition to the Municipal ID Ordinance during Board hearings, but several supervisors expressed concern over implementation cost, which was difficult to estimate.[36] Given the challenges of counting undocumented immigrants and unsheltered homeless individuals—likely the main beneficiary populations—potential demand was hard to calculate. At the same time, there was little precedent on which to base San Francisco's policy. New Haven was the only other city with an ID card program in place at the time, but that city's experience was not very informative for San Francisco.

New Haven (124,001 residents in 2006) is one-sixth the size of San Francisco (744,041 residents in 2006) and includes relatively more Latinos (21% vs. 14%) and many fewer Asians (4% vs. 32%). Such demographic differences made New Haven a poor baseline for San Francisco. Additionally, New Haven's Resident Card Program developed as an administrative rather than legislative initiative and was funded through a private grant, in the amount of $250,359, from a local community development bank (Bailey 2007; Matos 2008). This enabled New Haven's aldermen to avoid difficult discussions about committing taxpayer dollars to a program also benefiting the city's undocumented residents.

For lack of alternatives, supervisors nonetheless based their demand and cost estimates on those of New Haven. The county clerk, who would be responsible for issuing the cards, expected to receive 93,208 card applications annually and testified that the costs of issuing them would be significant, ranging from $423,293 to $1,110,641 in year one, from $324,346 to $868,144 in year two, and from $329,325 to $882,813 in year three of implementation. However, she qualified her estimate by noting, "There is no factual basis for the assumption that any of New Haven's statistics or numbers on demand-volume would apply to San Francisco."[37] Supervisor Sean Elsbernd echoed those concerns and commented, "New Haven is not San Francisco. . . . It was just faulty to base how we're going to run a program on how New Haven did it."[38] Various supervisors and the Board's budget analyst zeroed in on the uncertainty of the program's cost during public hearings. They questioned the ID card's fiscal impact at a time when Mayor Newsom announced that the city was facing a $229 million deficit, which would require a hefty 13 percent budget cut across city departments (Vega 2007).

In the end, supervisors' concerns over cost had little influence on their vote: All supervisors except Elsbernd voted to adopt the Municipal ID Ordinance. Honoring San Francisco's reputation as a vanguard city figured into their decision. San Francisco prides itself on being at the leading edge of social and political change (DeLeon 1992, 2008). During public hearings on the ordinance, Supervisor Gerardo Sandoval stated that he would be "proud" if San Francisco became "the first major American city to issue ID cards to its residents."[39] Additionally, Elsbernd observed that national criticism of how the city's action would help undocumented immigrants "only emboldened some supervisors further in their pursuit of the Municipal ID Ordinance."[40] Eagerness to be the policy frontrunner in all-inclusive ID card legislation and to develop a policy that other cities could replicate helped to push the supervisors toward a veto-proof majority despite concerns over cost.

The supervisors, however, were also influenced by how nonprofit advocates framed the ordinance. "Based on how my colleagues voted," Elsbernd commented, "I think immigrant rights groups and other community groups and also Supervisor Ammiano did a commendable job in promoting this ordinance as a public safety and civic participation measure. . . . They tried to get my support, particularly the different groups in the Mission [district] that do very good work with the day laborers . . . but I voted against it for budgetary reasons."[41] The aide to Supervisor Ammiano, the lead sponsor of the ordinance, agreed. "The various community groups had an effective message . . . that this ordinance was about public safety, bringing people out of the shadows, participating in civic life," she said. "Most supervisors support immigrant rights, like you said, but this way of talking about municipal IDs made it easier for them to support the ordinance . . . made it easier to talk to their constituents" about it.[42]

Implementing the Municipal ID Ordinance

Immigrant-serving nonprofits continued to use the broad, non-immigrant issue frame during the implementation of the Municipal ID Ordinance. When San Francisco's sanctuary policy became the subject of harsh media scrutiny and a federal investigation in the summer of 2008, the Municipal ID Ordinance was similarly criticized for benefiting undocumented immigrants. The controversy caused Mayor Newsom, who continued to see the municipal ID as a card for primarily undocumented immigrants, to postpone the policy's implementation. It also encouraged the anti-immigrant Immigration Reform Law Institute based in Washington, D.C.[43] to file a lawsuit in California Superior Court on behalf of four San Francisco residents who sought to strike down the Municipal ID Ordinance. While nonprofit advocates were not able to change the critical media coverage on undocumented immigrants, their broad framing helps explain why the court challenge ultimately failed to block the implementation of the ordinance.

Mounting Criticism of San Francisco's Sanctuary Policy

On June 22, 2008, Edwin Ramos, an undocumented immigrant from El Salvador and an alleged member of the Mara Salvatrucha (MS-13) street gang, committed a triple homicide in San Francisco. Ramos, who was twenty-one years of age at the time of the murders, had been convicted for two felonies as a teen but was never surrendered to federal immigration officials for possible deportation. After the murders, the *San Francisco Chronicle* ran a series of scathing articles accusing the city's sanctuary policy of shielding juvenile criminal offenders from federal immigration officials (Knight 2008a, d; Saunders 2008a–b; Stillwell 2008; Van Derbeken 2008a–n). Reports that city funding enabled more than a dozen undocumented juvenile offenders to fly back home to be reunited with their families drew especially sharp criticism, as did stories that undocumented youth had escaped from southern California group homes where the San Francisco Juvenile Probation Department had sent them for rehabilitation (Van Derbeken 2008a–b).

The *Chronicle* coverage galvanized nationwide sentiment against San Francisco's sanctuary policy and subjected Mayor Newsom to fallout from the city's perceived kid-glove treatment of undocumented lawbreakers.[44] Anti-immigrant firebrand Lou Dobbs, for example, targeted Newsom on his popular CNN television show. The media hype also energized the anti-immigration blogosphere and encouraged the Minuteman Project, a group of private individuals who patrol the U.S.-Mexico border to keep undocumented immigrants out, to launch a protest in San Francisco and demand Newsom's resignation (Gardner 2011; Knight 2008c). In the wake of the *Chronicle* reports, ICE assistant secretary Julie Myers wrote a letter to Newsom in which she publicly admonished him for compromising the safety of San Francisco residents and demanded that he give federal immigration officials greater access to city jails (La Ganga 2008). Finally, U.S. Attorney Joseph Russoniello convened a federal grand jury to investigate whether city officials had violated federal immigration law by harboring and transporting undocumented immigrants (Egelko 2008).[45]

Chronicle headlines attacking the City of Refuge Ordinance depicted immigrant youths as "illegals," "crack dealers," "drug suspects," and "teen felons" (Van Derbeken 2008b, d, i, j, m). In so doing, the *Chronicle* ignited a discourse of immigrant threat and challenged nonprofit advocates' contention that public safety could best be achieved through immigrant inclusion rather than aggressive removal tactics. As a result, Mayor Newsom changed the city's sanctuary policy regarding undocumented youth (Gardner 2011; Johansen 2011). The new Policy 8.12, implemented in August 2008, instructed Juvenile Probation Department officers to report undocumented juveniles to federal immigration officials when they were arrested for a felony, before an attorney had been appointed for them and before they had gone to trial. By treating detained undocumented youth as a new criminal class, San Francisco morphed from being a model of immigrant integration on this issue into a city that affords undocumented youth few due-process rights and few protections from federal detention and deportation.

Tensions over sanctuary soon spilled over to the Municipal ID Ordinance, as the media emphasized the link between sanctuary and municipal IDs. Many *Chronicle* reports mentioned that the supporters of the city's sanctuary policy also supported municipal ID cards. They implied that ID card legislation was simply an extension of the city's sanctuary policy and would enable undocumented immigrants to fly under the radar of federal immigration officials. The sanctuary and ID card policies were linked in Mayor Newsom's mind as well, leading him to suspend implementation of the Municipal ID Ordinance in August 2008 (Coté 2008). Concerned that the controversy could be his Achilles' heel in the 2010 gubernatorial race, Newsom aligned his approach on ID cards with his hardened position on sanctuary for undocumented youth. He said that he would only move ahead with the ID card program when he received confirmation that it complied with state and federal laws and when he was sure that the ID card could not easily be tampered with, counterfeited, or duplicated fraudulently (Coté 2008).

Nonprofits' Use of Non-Immigrant Framing to Secure Policy Implementation

This environment made it hard for immigrant-serving nonprofits to maintain their framing of the Municipal ID Ordinance as promoting public safety and providing civic integration benefits for all city residents. The advocates tried four different ways to downplay the centrality of undocumented immigrants as the primary beneficiaries. First, some tried to convince the mayor and local news reporters that the Municipal ID Ordinance was unrelated to the City of Refuge Ordinance and was thus not an immigrant rights policy. "We wanted to separate the two policies because the sanctuary ordinance had been marred by the whole juvenile justice debate," a CAA advocate commented. "For the ID card to be truly viable, it must benefit many different people . . . it cannot be perceived as something just for the undocumented."[46] This strategy proved unsuccessful. The mayor, who needed the most convincing of this argument, was difficult to access for community groups, and his views did not change. Also, the reporting of local mainstream newspapers such as the *Chronicle* remained one-sided and continued to link municipal ID cards with the city's ill-fated sanctuary policy.

Second, immigrant-serving nonprofits helped to build out the card's different uses to make it attractive to U.S. citizens and legal immigrants who would likely already have passports and state-issued driver's licenses for identification purposes. The immigrant rights administrator, the position created by Mayor Newsom in 2008 to oversee departmental compliance with the city's sanctuary policy, had responsibility for developing uses for the municipal ID card. But because she was given few resources to do so, nonprofit advocates stepped in to develop the card's discount function. "Immigrant rights groups went around to different parts of the city getting small businesses to agree to give discounts to cardholders," the immigrant rights administrator noted.[47] They succeeded in enlisting more than thirty businesses citywide—including restaurants, bakeries, nail and beauty salons, pharmacies, shoe stores, gyms, and even a cosmetic dental office—to offer discounts to cardholders. "The stores that offer discounts aren't stores that only undocumented immigrants use," a CAA advocate commented. "We tried really hard to involve small businesses, local businesses with customers from many walks of life."[48]

Third, nonprofit advocates filed an amicus curiae (friend of the court) brief and served as intervening defendants in the court case *Langfeld v. City and County of San Francisco* (2008), filed by the Immigration Reform Law Institute on behalf of four San Francisco residents who sought to strike down the Municipal ID Ordinance. In addition to the charge that the ordinance was an illegal expenditure of city funds and a violation of state environmental laws, the plaintiffs alleged that the ordinance aided and abetted illegal immigration and treated undocumented immigrants like U.S. citizens. In their court petition, the plaintiffs stated that by issuing ID cards to undocumented immigrants, San Francisco officials "encourage, induce and aid illegal aliens to reside in the United States" and offer them "all benefits available to citizens and legal residents of San Francisco, as if the cardholder were a lawful citizen or resident of the City."[49] They argued that city officials had overstepped their bounds and asked the court to declare the Municipal ID Ordinance null and void on state and federal preemption grounds.

In his demurrer to the plaintiffs' allegations, the city attorney used language that echoed the broad, non-immigrant framing that immigrant-serving nonprofits had used since they started advocating for the policy in 2007. He stated that the ordinance has only a "purely speculative and indirect impact on immigration" and is a policy of "modest utility" that "merely creates an administrative process that would provide an easy way for San Francisco residents to prove identity and residency to police officers, other city officials, and third parties who choose to accept the card."[50] The city attorney also pointed out that "immigration status is not considered at all under the Ordinance" and that city officials at no point make a determination about the immigration status of ID card applicants.[51] Finally, he emphasized that just because undocumented immigrants are among the policy's beneficiaries, that does not render the ordinance a regulation of immigration or an encouragement for undocumented immigrants to settle in San Francisco.

Nonprofit advocates similarly argued that the Municipal ID Ordinance could not be considered an impermissible regulation of immigration if its text was silent on the issue of immigration. In their amicus brief, St. Peter's Housing Committee and advocates representing the homeless and LGBT communities pointed out that the Municipal ID Ordinance is "immigration status–neutral" and "contains no reference to immigration status."[52] A St. Peter's Housing Committee advocate explained that it was a "déjà vu type thing" because "the plaintiffs were framing [the Municipal ID Ordinance] as only an immigrant thing" just like the media, the mayor, and the police chief had done earlier in the campaign to enact the ordinance.[53] "We stuck with our initial strategy," she added, of framing the ordinance as a policy with public safety and civic integration benefits for all city residents.[54] By pushing the supervisors to adopt an ordinance that makes no reference of undocumented immigrants, advocates now helped to defeat the court challenge and secure the policy's implementation.

In the end, the California Superior Court sustained the city attorney. Judge Peter Busch, believing that the plaintiffs had no cause of action, dismissed *Langfeld* and entered judgment in favor of the city. The court thereby sustained a program that does not explicitly identify undocumented immigrants as beneficiaries, yet still benefits them. It created a path by which San Francisco officials could promote the integration of undocumented immigrants as long as they framed their actions in terms of public safety and civic benefits to all San Franciscans. It also provided Mayor Newsom with assurances he wanted about the legality of the Municipal ID Ordinance.

Lastly, nonprofit advocates developed amendments to the ordinance that addressed Mayor Newsom's lingering security concerns. Supervisor Ammiano proposed ways to tighten the documentation requirements for card applicants to prove identity and city residency, but this might make it harder for people to obtain the ID card. In response, immigrant-serving nonprofits successfully suggested alternative documents that city residents, including the undocumented, could show to qualify for the municipal ID card. "Immigrant rights groups reminded us to make the card as widely available as possible. . . . [They] helped us think through what are some other documents that would pass a higher line of muster," the immigrant rights administrator reflected. "They suggested things like court orders, restraining orders, and rulings from the Rent Stabilization and Arbitration Board. Some of these are negative documents, but they're valid documents that have come through a legal process. . . . We expanded the list to include those in the amendments."[55]

Mayor Newsom signed the amendments into law on November 25, 2008, thereby removing the last major hurdle to launching the municipal ID card program.[56] The city issued the first municipal ID cards on January 15, 2009, five months later than originally planned. By January 1, 2015, the county clerk had issued 22,417 cards, though 44,590 people had scheduled appointments to get a card.[57] While the county clerk did not keep data on the card recipients, she reported that the majority of the people booking an appointment had Hispanic last names.[58] While not conclusive, this suggests that immigrants are especially interested in getting a municipal ID card.

Ongoing Support for the Municipal ID Ordinance

Since its launch, nonprofit advocates have remained involved with the ID card program. They have partnered with the Office of Civic Engagement and Immigrant Affairs (OCEIA)[59] to organize workshops to inform immigrants and other city residents about the purposes of the card and to educate them about the documents that would permit them to apply for one. Given that OCEIA initially had few resources, it welcomed this partnership. "The only way we're going to get the right information out to the public," OCEIA's executive director commented, "is really to work through our network of community-based organizations . . . getting education out there on what the purpose of the card is, in addition to what the process is."[60] The San Francisco Immigrant Legal and Education Network, a collaborative of thirteen immigrant-serving nonprofits that was part of the Municipal ID Card Coalition, organized the first outreach workshop in the heavily Hispanic Mission district in February 2009, and others have followed since.

Nonprofit advocates also have provided city officials with community feedback on the program. At a May 2009 hearing of the Public Safety Committee of the Board of Supervisors, staff of the Asian Law Caucus, the Central American Resource Center, Young Workers United, and Mujeres Unidas y Activas (United and Active Women) testified that immigrants who obtained the card reported feeling safer and more included in the civic life of the city. They also highlighted several problem areas, including the cumbersome process and long waiting list to get the card. More alarmingly, nonprofit advocates reported several incidents where San Francisco police officers had not recognized or accepted the card, and they subsequently requested that officers receive additional training to familiarize them with the program.

Immigrant-serving nonprofits continue to monitor the program and suggest further improvements as it unfolds.

The media spotlight on the Municipal ID Ordinance has faded since 2009, but the city's sanctuary policy has remained controversial. San Francisco has faced three legal challenges involving the City of Refuge Ordinance, including one initiated by the federal government.[61] The June 2009 activation of Secure Communities—a federal program requiring San Francisco to share the fingerprints of anyone booked into its jails with federal immigration officials—created yet another setback for the city's sanctuary policy (Gordon 2010a).[62] Then in November 2009, an alliance of twenty immigrant-serving nonprofits successfully pressured the Board of Supervisors to override Newsom's veto of an ordinance barring probation officers from turning juveniles over to the federal government until they are convicted of a felony, not when charged, the practice Newsom instituted with his Policy 8.12 in August 2008 (La Ganga 2009). Saying that it violates federal law, Newsom subsequently refused to implement the ordinance and instructed probation officers to ignore it (Knight 2009c).

Mayor Ed Lee, who succeeded Newsom when he became lieutenant governor of California in January 2011, announced in May 2011 that the city would no longer report undocumented juveniles arrested for a felony to federal authorities if they had family in the Bay Area, were enrolled in school, and were first-time offenders (Gordon 2011). In October 2013, Lee signed the Due Process for All Ordinance into law, barring San Francisco law enforcement officials from honoring most federal immigration hold requests issued through the Secure Communities program (McMenamin 2013).[63] The killing of Kate Steinle on a San Francisco pier in July 2015 by an undocumented immigrant who had been deported to Mexico five times has ignited a new political firestorm over the city's sanctuary policy and practices. A barrage of angry media has targeted San Francisco and California officials, prompting congressional officials to draft legislation to strip federal funding from San Francisco and other sanctuary cities.

The Pros and Cons of Non-Immigrant Issue Framing

In the face of media and political opposition to helping undocumented immigrants, immigrant-serving nonprofits sought to use a neutral issue frame in their quest to enact and implement the Municipal ID Ordinance. They constructed an advocacy logic that downplayed undocumented immigrants as the policy's primary beneficiaries and emphasized the policy's public safety and civic integration benefits for all city residents. While this strategy did not fully resonate with the media and certain San Francisco officials, it did play an important role in getting the ordinance enacted and implemented.

Advocates in other cities have used similar non-immigrant framing for policies that address the rights of undocumented immigrants. The evolution of New York City's sanctuary policy from one specifically designed to protect undocumented immigrants into a general privacy policy benefiting all city residents between 1989 and 2003 is one example (Firestone 1997; Murthy 2007; Rodríguez 2008). Ironically, immigration *opponents* in several new immigrant destinations have also used non-immigrant issue framing to push policies that *restrict* the rights of undocumented immigrants. They have, for example, advocated housing, zoning, and anti-loitering laws that appear neutral and innocuous but in practice drive away undocumented immigrants (Jonsson 2006; Romero 2008; Varsanyi 2008). They too have been framed as public safety measures that serve the interests of the larger community. Pro- and anti-immigrant advocates have thus both used non-immigrant issue framing to try to minimize media and political scrutiny and maximize public support for what in reality are controversial pro- and anti-undocumented immigrant policies.

The use of non-immigrant issue frames has enabled immigrant rights advocates to realize important benefits for undocumented immigrants who lack the political clout to win changes on their own. In San Francisco, undocumented immigrants now have access to a government ID that they can use to identify themselves to police and other local government officials, access basic city services, and open a bank account. Advocates' use of the non-immigrant frame also encouraged some undocumented immigrants to participate in the political process. By linking the policy interests of undocumented immigrants with those of other city residents, advocates signaled that municipal ID cards constitute a legitimate issue for government attention. Some undocumented immigrants responded by testifying about the benefits of ID cards, for themselves and others, before the Board of Supervisors.

Nonprofit advocates also embraced the non-immigrant issue framing to try to give greater visibility to a new discourse on undocumented immigrants. In contrast to immigration opponents who talk about undocumented immigrants as pariahs needing to be excluded from mainstream society, nonprofit advocates sought to promote the idea that society is better off when it integrates undocumented immigrants and emphasizes the interests and concerns they have in common with others. This required them to talk about undocumented immigrants as one of many beneficiary groups without drawing too much attention to that fact. But it was challenging for advocates to make policymakers and the larger public understand the plight of undocumented immigrants without making that the prime focus of the debates about municipal ID cards. This dilemma about how to frame a policy benefiting undocumented immigrants is reminiscent of debates about how best to promote policies that help other marginalized and politically controversial groups, including the poor and ethnoracial minorities.

Skocpol (1991) argues that poverty is best addressed through programs that serve a range of income classes, such as the Social Security program. Wilson (1987) makes the case that race-neutral programs can best address the problems of racial minorities. Their viewpoints rest on the belief that adopting more universal framing and policy prescriptions will increase the political support for, and viability of, programs that target the needs of the poor and racial minorities, especially in climates of budgetary constraint and class or racial antagonism. They essentially advocate that the best strategy to help the poor and racial minorities is not to talk about them, just as immigrant-serving nonprofits in San Francisco sought to help undocumented immigrants by not talking about them. In the context of the United States, where the poor, racial minorities, and undocumented immigrants are politically weak and negatively constructed populations (Schneider and Ingram 1993), their advocates need to make strategic framing and policy choices to be able to improve their situation.

There are possible drawbacks, however, to using neutral or universal frames to advocate policies that target the problems of marginalized and politically unpopular groups such as undocumented immigrants. When such policies fall short of providing the broader outcomes or benefits, it can cast a shadow over the integrity of the policymaking process and can lead constituents to question advocates' true motivations for wanting the policy enacted. In the case of the Municipal ID Ordinance, only a small number (22,417 out of nearly 800,000) of San Franciscans have opted to get the card despite advocates' claims about the card's wide appeal. The city invested $538,000 just to purchase the equipment to print the cards, initial sunk costs that have not yet been recovered with the collected fees of cards that cost $15 for adults and $5 for seniors, low-income individuals, and children under the age of fourteen. Although this has not yet been publicly raised as an issue, the policy's critics could validly do so.

The San Francisco experience also raises the question of what type of policy better serves the interests of undocumented immigrants. Is it a policy that addresses head-on their unique problems and needs? Such a targeted policy, while politically more controversial, may advance the debate about undocumented immigration and educate the larger public about the plight of these individuals. Or is it instead a policy that is silent on the fact that undocumented immigrants are among the key beneficiaries? Such a universal policy, while politically less controversial, may sweep the problems of undocumented immigrants under the rug and keep them perpetually under the radar. Thus far, avoiding the issue has produced a confused and contradictory patchwork of policies. Depending on where they live, undocumented immigrants can be treated quite differently by local governments. This serves to remind us that only the federal government, by adopting a large-scale legalization program, can set a uniform policy that will ensure the equal and fair treatment of undocumented immigrants nationwide.

Conclusion
Making Immigrant Rights Real

This book has identified and explored three ways that immigrant-serving nonprofits have sought to influence local government policies toward immigrant rights and immigrant integration in San Francisco. Much of the literature on nonprofits suggests that they are in a poor position to shape local policymaking because of government restrictions on their lobbying and limited organizational resources (e.g., Andrews and Edwards 2004; Bass et al. 2007; Berry and Arons 2003). Yet immigrant-serving nonprofits in San Francisco were able to overcome these and other constraints and drive some of the most important progressive integration policies and practices anywhere in the nation.

How did they do it? The three policy cases in this book illuminate a tripartite model of strategies—focused on (a) administrative advocacy, (b) cross-sectoral and cross-organizational collaborations, and (c) strategic issue framing—that these seemingly limited organizations used to propose, enact, and implement immigrant-friendly policies. First, as the language access case shows, while federal lobbying restrictions limit nonprofits' ability to interact with legislative officials, they can certainly interact at length with agency administrators around program development and implementation. Indeed, they have unique advantages in this domain. They deeply understand the communities that public agencies are trying to engage and serve. Their extensive contracts with city agencies have taught them the ins and outs of program management and connected them with the key implementers. This makes them valued partners and creates a symbiotic relationship that, though not without some negative aspects, serves both parties well.

Second, San Francisco's immigrant-serving nonprofits have collaborated with other kinds of organizations that have fewer express limits on their political activities and more resources, particularly labor unions. The kinds of jobs immigrants get and the conditions under which they work are central to the trajectory of immigrant integration. The service-sector workforces of cities like San Francisco are increasingly dominated by immigrants. The service sector is also the area in which the U.S. labor movement will have to grow if it is to reverse its downward trend in membership. As a result, labor unions have much in common with nonprofits serving and advocating for immigrant interests, despite their many and real differences. Here too, as with public agency administrators, the different strengths and weaknesses characterizing nonprofits and labor unions can lead to a division of labor that draws on the strengths of both, while requiring them also to find ways to manage their differences in organizational structure, resources, and status. The ordinances concerning living and minimum wages and working conditions they achieved in San Francisco can serve as models for other cities.

Finally, immigrant-serving nonprofits have become careful students of shaping the content of public discourse in ways that serve their ends to counterbalance the negative public constructions of immigrants, particularly undocumented immigrants. Many immigration opponents have characterized undocumented immigrants in highly negative ways to try to sway public opinion and policymakers against them. San Francisco's immigrant-serving nonprofits were able to frame the debate about municipal ID cards so as to minimize this danger while building alliances with disadvantaged non-immigrant groups and making the case that integrating the undocumented can serve the broader public good. The campaign to create a municipal ID card program in San Francisco, while building on the New Haven experience, carried forward the argument that helping immigrants benefits the whole in ways that carried the day not just in that city but also other cities such as Oakland, Los Angeles, and New York City.

As a result of their advocacy using these strategies, immigrant-serving nonprofits in San Francisco played a central role in enacting new rights for disadvantaged immigrants, including language access provisions for limited English proficient immigrants, stronger labor protections for low-wage immigrant workers, and municipal ID cards for undocumented immigrants. More importantly, they also have consistently aided the implementation of these new rights in ways that built them into the daily practices of San

Francisco government. The gap between rights on the books and rights in practice is often wide, and new rights will remain hollow absent effective implementation and enforcement (Epp 2010; Gleeson 2012; McCann 1994). Nonprofit advocates in San Francisco were instrumental in bridging this gap. They pushed local government to be accountable to the city's disadvantaged immigrants even though elected and appointed city officials generally are not likely to pay attention to them (Schneider and Ingram 1993).

These findings have important implications for how we theorize and conceptualize the political integration of immigrants, particularly disadvantaged immigrants. They also shed new light on the important role of nonprofit organizations in urban politics, especially in terms of the enduring debate about who has (what kinds of) power and who governs. The book's findings also hold valuable lessons for scholars and practitioners of coalition building by emphasizing the need to pay more attention to questions of organizational structure, resources, and status. Finally, the experiences related here suggest that we need to reevaluate the efficacy and impact of nonprofit advocacy and the factors shaping bureaucratic responsiveness to marginalized city residents.

Nonprofits and Immigrant Political Integration

A range of behaviors captures immigrants' integration into the American political system, including the acquisition of U.S. citizenship, participation in the electoral process, and participation in more informal political acts such as petition-signing campaigns, demonstrations, and other activities of civic organizations. Immigrants' political integration can also be measured by their participation in political institutions through both ethnic (or demographic) representation and policy (or substantive) representation (de Graauw 2013). Yet political scientists tend to view the electoral arena as the primary locus of political integration, with scholarship largely focusing on immigrants' participation in electoral politics and their fit with existing frameworks of American racial politics (e.g., Ramakrishnan 2005; Schmidt, Sr. et al. 2010). Electoral participation, while emblematic of a democracy, provides an incomplete picture of political integration dynamics, particularly for disadvantaged immigrants who tend to lack the resources or legal right to participate in the electoral process.

Policy representation and implementation are other key dimensions of immigrants' political integration that merit more study. In particular, this book has made the case that nonprofit advocates can play and have played a critical role in helping San Francisco officials to make rights real for disadvantaged immigrants, many of whom do not have the right to vote. It thereby challenges the assumption, implicit in much of the literature, that policy representation only can follow when immigrants have naturalized, exercised their right to vote, and then elected co-ethnic representatives who advance their interests in the policymaking process (Dahl 1961). Indeed, policy representation can precede electoral participation, and there are different pathways toward immigrants' inclusion in the American political system. Even immigrants who are politically marginalized and economically disadvantaged can have their interests addressed in the policymaking process.

This book also has highlighted a different set of variables that drive political integration dynamics. Scholars often rely on *microlevel* determinants, such as immigrants' resources, skills, and interests (Bass and Casper 2001; Cain, Kiewiet, and Uhlaner 1991; Ramakrishnan and Espenshade 2001; Yang 1994), and *macrolevel* variables, including a range of policy, institutional, and contextual factors (Jones-Correa 2001; North 1987; Portes and Curtis 1987), to explain the occurrence or absence of immigrant integration into the American political system. This book instead has underscored the vital role of *mesolevel* structures—namely, local nonprofit organizations that can mediate between immigrant individuals and larger political communities—in the political integration process.

Other scholars have explored the political and civic significance of immigrant-serving nonprofits by studying their involvement in street protests and their role in mobilizing immigrants and other community members to action (Bloemraad 2006; Cordero-Guzmán et al. 2008; Voss and Bloemraad 2011; Wong 2006). This work misses another very important aspect of nonprofits' work, namely their advocacy to secure and make real immigrant rights. When we take a long time frame and analyze nonprofits' involvement in the policymaking process from beginning to end, we see that immigrant-serving nonprofits can set the agenda on immigrant rights issues, push for the adoption of immigrant-friendly policies, and shape policy implementation. Protest tactics did not figure prominently in the action repertoire of immigrant-serving nonprofits in San Francisco. Instead, they effected policy change by using administrative advocacy, cross-sectoral and cross-organizational collaborations, and strategic issue framing in local campaigns for stronger immigrant language access and labor rights and municipal ID cards.

Nonprofits and Urban Politics

Political science has always asked who has power, who governs, and to what extent groups and individuals outside of government have influence over elected and appointed government officials. Most scholars who ask these questions about urban politics do not consider nonprofits to be influential actors in the ecology of local decision-making. They are missing something important. The federal, state, and local push to privatize public services since the 1970s has quadrupled the number of 501(c)(3) nonprofits, from about 265,000 in 1982 to over 1 million in 2013 (Heuchan 1985–1986; IRS 2014; Smith and Lipsky 1993). These nonprofits are increasingly reliant on government funding, often channeled through local governments, making local politics increasingly important to them. Also, in this age of retrenchment of government spending, nonprofits have become urgently interested in advocating for funding, programs, and policies benefiting their clients (Marwell 2004; Mosley and Ros 2011). As nonprofits have increasing opportunities and motivations to engage in local politics, scholars clearly need to incorporate them into their theorizing about power dynamics in cities.

In the 1950s and 1960s, the community power debate pitted "elitist" sociologists against "pluralist" political scientists. Hunter's (1953) famous study of Atlanta used reputational analysis to show that local power was concentrated in the hands of a small socioeconomic elite, with elected and appointed government officials in a decidedly subordinate role. Using three case studies of decision-making in New Haven, Dahl (1961) countered that local power was diffused across a multiplicity of groups that mobilized resources to influence different kinds of policy decisions. In his pluralist conception of community power, Dahl found that elected officials—particularly the mayor—played a critical role in important local government decisions. He found that interest groups outside of government—including business and labor—also exercised power, but not consistently over all issues. Largely because they predate the ascent of the nonprofit sector, neither elitist nor pluralist explanations of urban political power explicitly account for how nonprofit organizations influence local decision-making.

The racial unrest of the 1960s and the fiscal crisis of the 1970s led "structuralist" sociologists and political scientists—ranging from those on the left like Friedland and Palmer (1984) and Logan and Molotch (1987) to public choice theorists on the right like Peterson (1981)—to criticize pluralists for not taking into account how the economic and socio-structural context influences urban decision-making. By situating urban power relations in the larger political economy, structuralists argued that city officials are motivated to pursue business development policies to foster urban economic growth, thereby systematically privileging business groups over those representing disadvantaged city residents. "Regime theorists" like Stone (1989, 1993) subsequently synthesized the pluralist and structuralist perspectives. They acknowledge that the economic environment constrains city officials but emphasize that city officials are not merely controlled by business groups and have to consider other interest groups as well. City officials and business groups, however, have a mutual interest in building stable and dominant coalitions, or "regimes," which can persistently sideline disadvantaged city residents in policy decisions across issues. Some structuralists and regime theorists thus recognize nonprofits as actors in local politics but still do not credit them with much policy influence.

The evidence provided in this book reinforces the idea that urban decision-making comes about through collaboration and cooperation between governmental and nongovernmental actors. Nonprofit advocates in San Francisco played an instrumental role in bringing city officials together with leaders of various community organizations in a loose public-private partnership concerning immigrant policy issues that has endured for over a decade. Nonprofit advocates brought to the table a strong commitment to immigrant rights and an unrivaled community expertise essential to developing, enacting, and implementing immigrant integration policies. City officials in turn marshaled the fiscal and regulatory resources to fund immigrant rights and integration initiatives and the enforcement power to give these initiatives real substance. In a city with a large foreign-born population like San Francisco, city officials and nonprofit advocates have both come to understand the need and the benefits of working together to ensure that local policymaking does not overlook the interests of disadvantaged immigrants.

By placing community-based nonprofits at the center of analysis, this book provides a different perspective on urban governance and urban power. The relationships that immigrant-serving nonprofits developed with San Francisco officials differed from those maintained by labor unions and business groups. That is largely because immigrant-serving nonprofits had to use their unique issue expertise and access to disadvantaged immigrant communities to work with city officials to get things done. Unions and business groups instead relied more on their electoral and financial clout to influence local politics and policymaking. While weaker in some ways, nonprofits still managed to secure several important new immigrant rights policies. Power to effect urban policy change thus can take different forms and does not flow only from electoral power or from organizations with more advocacy freedoms, deep coffers, and large bases of voting members.

Much more work needs to be done to understand the circumstances under which nonprofits can foster productive relationships with public officials in other cities and can effect change in other policy arenas. The now-common contracting practice of local government has brought nonprofits more fully into the public service production process (Salamon 1981; Wolch 1990) and probably also into the process of urban governance. In examining this development, scholars should focus on public–private partnerships not only to enact policy but to implement and enforce it as well. Federal lobbying restrictions on 501(c)(3) tax-exempt organizations may make some non-profits shy about pursuing new policy development work, but they may feel more comfortable implementing and enforcing existing policies. Nonprof-its' willingness and ability to work in partnership with city officials therefore may be more readily observed in policy implementation and enforcement rather than in the policy enactment process.

Nonprofits and Coalition Building

Collaborations are integral to the ability of immigrant-serving nonprofits to advocate for immigrant rights and integration policies. Limited orga-nizational resources and restrictions on lobbying compel them to work in coalitions during the policymaking process. In so doing, they interact with elected and appointed city officials, who control funding allocations to them and who have the authority to enact, implement, and enforce the policies they are seeking. They also work in larger coalitions with other immigrant-serving nonprofits to pool resources, multiply advocacy voices, and camouflage their political activities from individuals critical of or opposed to nonprofit advocacy. And nonprofit advocates have collaborated with labor unions because they have more resources, more clout, and fewer restrictions on their lobbying than nonprofits.

The power relationships between nonprofits and local government officials and labor unions are clearly asymmetric, but this does not mean that nonprofit advocates have no influence. Rather, their power is some-what hidden and indirect, lodged in the relationships nonprofit organiza-tions have with their clients and the communities in which their clients live. Cross-sectoral and cross-organizational collaborations have allowed immigrant-serving nonprofits to leverage this community expertise to over-come their resource limitations and the advocacy restrictions resulting from their 501(c)(3) tax-exempt status. In San Francisco, government officials and union organizers in turn have welcomed collaborations with nonprofit advocates to help them navigate language, culture, and trust barriers with immigrant communities.

We can best characterize the resulting coalitions as policy-specific rather than comprehensive governing coalitions. Certainly, immigrant-serving non-profits provided much of the impetus for the language access, labor rights, and municipal ID card policies analyzed here. They strategically sought out partners—local legislators and administrators, other immigrant-serving nonprofits, labor unions, and other community allies—to get these policies enacted. Some immigrant-serving nonprofits were active in multiple policy coalitions, but overall each specific coalition had different participants. Each also had distinct internal dynamics, partly because power relations among coalition participants differed and partly because each policy issue encountered particular challenges in the legislative (or initiative) process. After the language access, labor rights, and municipal ID card ordinances had been on the books for several years, the initial cross-sectoral and cross-organizational coalitions slowly dissolved. Individual immigrant-serving nonprofits, however, have continued to work on carrying out these policies.

The nonprofit experience of building coalitions around immigrant rights in San Francisco adds to the literature on coalition building. A range of scholars, including those who study coalitions between ethnoracial minorities and whites (e.g., Browning, Marshall, and Tabb 1984; Sonenshein 1993) and coalitions between labor unions and other community organizations (e.g., Tattersall 2005; Tattersall and Reynolds 2007), have argued that coalitions are more likely to form, cohere, and succeed when coalition partners share common interests and ideologies, trust one another, and invest time and resources to realize coalition goals. These conditions prevailed in San Francisco during the late 1990s and 2000s, and nonprofit advocates there succeeded in building successful policy coalitions to advance immigrant rights in part because they and their partners among city officials and union leaders came to share a political belief that immigrant interests should be included and advanced, they decided to act together to realize them, and each dedicated organizational and staff resources to realizing coalition goals.

This sounds simple, but it was in fact quite complex. Even in the best of circumstances, where disparate groups and individuals shared beliefs, interests, and trust with one another, working together was still challenging on an organizational level, especially for nonprofits. Their unique organizational characteristics made it difficult for them to operate on a level playing field with their collaborators. In particular, federal lobbying restrictions and nonprofits' financial ties to city hall limited their range of action, while unions had more financial and staff resources as well as legal scope to devote to political advocacy. Even collaborations among immigrant-serving nonprofits were challenging when smaller and newer nonprofits worked with larger and more established ones.

The dominant accounts of coalition building tend to miss this organizational perspective on collaborations. Race and ethnic politics scholars (e.g.,

Browning, Marshall, and Tabb 1984; Sonenshein 1993) examine how African American and Hispanic leaders and activists collaborated with white power brokers to advance minority interests in the electoral and policymaking processes. While making many important points, this research does not address how the different types of organizations that provide the base for these leaders and activists shape their coalitional undertakings. Immigration scholars (e.g., Ramakrishan and Bloemraad 2008; Wong 2006) do focus on the role of individual unions, nonprofits, churches, and hometown associations in mobilizing immigrant constituencies but do not examine how they collaborate among and across organizations to cumulate their individual strengths. And labor scholars (e.g., Tattersall 2005; Tattersall and Reynolds 2007) tend to examine the benefits that labor-community coalitions bring to unions, thereby giving little consideration to the characteristics and experiences of nonprofit organizations. Scholars and practitioners will learn more about both the challenges and opportunities of collaborations to promote immigrant rights and other policy changes as they give more consideration to broader questions of organizational structure, resources, and status.

Nonprofits and Policy Implementation

The long policy campaigns described in this book show that nonprofit advocates can be particularly influential through sustained interactions with officials in city departments and agencies as they work to realize policy benefits for disadvantaged immigrants. Policy implementation is not automatic in San Francisco or anywhere else, and it can be as hard to achieve as policy enactment in the first place. Because their tax-exempt status does not restrict this form of advocacy, immigrant-serving nonprofits have been able to cultivate effective and long-lasting relationships with the city administrative officials responsible for carrying out policy. Indeed, because they often receive contracts from city government, they have ready access to these individuals and a deep understanding of what they are trying to do. As we have seen, they also have unrivaled expertise in the communities that city administrative officials are trying to reach and serve.

Research examining nonprofits' political advocacy habitually considers only their legislative and electoral activities. With such a narrow scope, scholars often find that nonprofits are unwilling or unable to effect policy change because their tax-exempt status limits their legislative advocacy and bars their partisan electioneering (Bass et al. 2007; Berry and Arons 2003; Schneider and Lester 2001). As other scholars (Majic 2011; Mosley 2010) have also noted recently, it is important to adopt a broader definition of advocacy to be able to assess nonprofits' public policy efficacy and impact. We need to consider also how nonprofits interact with political institutions *beyond* the legislature and the ballot box, including executive and judicial officials, other advocacy organizations, and the media.

Highlighted here is the critical role that nonprofit advocates play with city administrative officials. Previous research has either downplayed the importance of advocacy that targets local bureaucracies (Berry and Arons 2003: 40) or has dismissed it as government cooptation (Wolch 1990). The experiences recounted and analyzed here show to the contrary that nonprofit advocacy with local administrative officials is an important and necessary complement to lobbying local legislators or advocating local ballot measures. After all, immigrant rights and integration policies are only as good as their implementation. It would also be incorrect simply to label nonprofits' administrative advocacy as government cooptation. Immigrant-serving nonprofits, including those that received city contracts, were not at the mercy of San Francisco officials. Instead, they found ways to cultivate dynamic relationships with administrative officials, which ultimately served their purposes and helped them to represent their constituencies in the city bureaucracy.

Indeed, we should explore further what some have called "immigrant bureaucratic incorporation." While local administrative officials are reputed for their unresponsiveness to the less privileged sections of society (Etzioni-Halevy 1983; Lineberry 1977; Lipsky 1980; Schattschneider 1960), they have in fact moved to accommodate newcomers' needs, including those of undocumented immigrants. Various scholars make the case that this bureaucratic responsiveness to immigrants cannot be explained by variation in types of city departments or differences in partisan control of local government. It can be seen within municipal agencies dealing with education (Gonzales 2010; Jones-Correa 2008; Marrow 2009), law enforcement (Lewis and Ramakrishnan 2007), health care and social services (Marrow 2009, 2011), and employment and workplace rights (de Graauw 2015a; Gleeson 2012), as well as in liberal and more conservative municipal settings (Gleeson 2012; Jones-Correa 2008). To find its source, they argue, we must look instead to how strong professional norms and inclusive agency missions—factors internal to the bureaucracy—may drive bureaucrats to apply particular rights and services to disadvantaged immigrants.

The evidence presented in this book illustrates the central importance of nonprofits in pressuring and helping city agencies to become more inclusive toward immigrants. Professional norms and agency missions are certainly important in this respect, but they are not always sufficient. External pressure is needed to overcome urban bureaucracies' inherent inertia against serving immigrants and other disadvantaged populations. The high-level bureau-cratic appointees and street-level civil servants I interviewed in San Fran-cisco all had a cosmopolitan outlook and shared a commitment to serve immigrants, including noncitizens and undocumented immigrants. Yet it still took constant pressure from nonprofit advocates to make city departments and agencies *substantively* inclusive by making sure they adopt the practices and procedures needed to accommodate the unique needs and circumstances of disadvantaged immigrants. Outside advocacy pressure also made city departments and agencies more *procedurally* inclusive by granting nonprofits a role in making the bureaucratic decisions and monitoring the bureaucratic actions that affect immigrants' daily lives.

In short, immigrant-serving nonprofits in San Francisco became embed-ded in the policy implementation process. Even though many of them relied on local government funding, this did not prevent them from pursuing their own policy agendas and criticizing existing city policies and practices. We must therefore challenge the conventional wisdom that nonprofits can effectively advocate for social change only when they are independent from government. The findings here also question the assumption in the social movement literature that nonprofits can best achieve social change by using protest tactics and disruptive non-institutionalized actions (Andrew 2010; Andrews and Edwards 2004; Piven and Cloward 1977; Tarrow 1996, 2011). In a day and time when nonprofits and local governments are increasingly intertwined and codependent, nonprofits can successfully push city admin-istrative officials to hear their concerns, prioritize their interests, and allocate resources toward their preferred policy goals.

Beyond San Francisco?

How widely can the strategies that nonprofit advocates deployed success-fully on behalf of disadvantaged immigrants in San Francisco be applied elsewhere? San Francisco is one of the most liberal cities in the country, and its status as a city-county consolidation means that it bears more responsibil-ity for social welfare functions than most large U.S. cities. It has an infra-structure of politically sophisticated and active nonprofits, which enjoy easy access to San Francisco's fragmented government. Also, the city's immigrants are disproportionately Asian, who tend to be more positively constructed than Latinos (Bender 2003; Hsu 2015). These factors likely made it eas-ier for immigrant-serving nonprofits to influence the local governance of immigrant rights by using the tripartite strategy of administrative advocacy, cross-sectoral and cross-organizational collaborations, and strategic issue framing. Yet the policy cases discussed in the book make clear that nonprofit advocacy still was very challenging in San Francisco. Therefore, successful immigrant rights advocacy using these strategies may well be even more difficult in other, less progressive cities and in cities with a less developed infrastructure of nonprofit organizations and a more diverse (and more Latino) immigrant population.

On the other hand, immigrant-serving nonprofits elsewhere still can draw valuable lessons from the advocacy strategies that nonprofits adopted in San Francisco. Immigrants and the nonprofits that serve them now can be found all across the country as immigration has diffused to new destinations since the 1990s (Andersen 2010; de Leon et al. 2009; Hung 2007; Modares and Kitson 2008; Wong 2006). In the absence of a national integration program, local government is the locus for responding to these new populations, so immigrant-serving nonprofits, regardless of location, are increasingly turning their focus to this level (Jones-Correa 2011). Nonprofit advocates operating in less favorable local contexts can learn from the strategies deployed in San Francisco about how to overcome constraints flowing from their 501(c)(3) tax-exempt status, limited organizational resources, and local consequences of federal immigration enforcement. Each in its own way can use administrative advocacy, cross-sectoral and cross-organizational collaborations, and strategic issue framing to enact and implement immigrant rights and integration policies.

And there is evidence suggesting that they are doing this. Immigrant-serving nonprofits in Philadelphia, New York City, and Washington, D.C., have won enactment and implementation of local language access policies by collaborating with other immigrant-serving nonprofits, labor unions, and elected and appointed city officials (Bernstein et al. 2014; NYIC 2010; Wilson 2013).[1] They too framed language access strategically as a civil rights issue rather than an immigrant rights issue and used federal civil rights legislation to push city officials to adopt local legislation that brings city practices in compliance with federal language access mandates. Also, nonprofit advocates in all three cities have directed much of their advocacy at administrative officials in city departments and agencies—including those in the Managing Director's Office and the Office of Multicultural Affairs in Philadelphia, the Mayor's Offices of Operations and Immigrant Affairs in New York City, and the Office of Human Rights in Washington, D.C.—to strengthen and improve the implementation of local language access policies.

Immigrant-serving nonprofits in New Haven, Oakland, and New York City broke new ground by securing the enactment and implementation of municipal ID card programs (CPD 2013; de Graauw 2014; Matos 2008).

New Haven launched the Elm City Resident Card Program in 2007, and Oakland and New York City enacted their ID card programs in 2009 and 2014, respectively. Nonprofit advocates provided the genesis for the ID card programs in these cities, and they too framed the programs as public safety and civic integration initiatives benefiting all city residents, not just undocumented immigrants. Immigrant-serving nonprofits subsequently collaborated with nonprofits serving African Americans and homeless individuals, churches, and labor unions to pressure city officials into adopting the ID card programs. Finally, immigrant-serving nonprofits in all three cities have collaborated with administrative officials in the Community Services Administration and the Office of New Haven Residents in New Haven, the Offices of the Mayor and City Administrator in Oakland, and the Mayor's Offices of Operations and Immigrant Affairs in New York City to develop multiple community, arts, and business uses for the cards and to ensure that local police recognize and honor the cards carried by undocumented immigrants.

Philadelphia, New York City, Washington, D.C., New Haven, and Oakland are majority-Democratic cities with mayor-council forms of government, similar to San Francisco. However, compared with San Francisco, they have quite different migration histories, demographic compositions, city size, and power configurations among local politicians and interest groups. They also differ in the size, maturity, and level of political sophistication of their nonprofit sectors. Thus, while the three advocacy strategies deployed in San Francisco may not work the same way everywhere, the experiences of these other cities suggest that they nonetheless have great promise. Additional comparative analysis of nonprofit immigrant rights advocacy would shed further light on the opportunities for and barriers to deploying these advocacy strategies to advance immigrant rights and integration in other U.S. municipalities.

Looking Forward

Immigrant rights and the challenge of fostering immigrant integration will remain highly salient issues in years to come. The United States admits over 1 million legal immigrants per year (DHS 2014a). The federal government continues to take a laissez-faire approach to immigrant integration, and the United States has no real national policy tools to promote immigrants' social, economic, civic, and political advancement. Undocumented status keeps an estimated 11.3 million immigrants on the margins of U.S. society (Passel et al. 2014). As the U.S. Congress remains gridlocked over whether to offer these immigrants an earned path to legalization, the Obama administration, through the Deferred Action for Childhood Arrivals (DACA) program, started offering qualified young undocumented immigrants a two-year (renewable) stay of deportation and the ability to apply for a legal work permit in 2012. In 2014, the Obama administration sought to offer deferred action to a larger group of undocumented individuals with the expanded DACA and Deferred Action for Parents of Americans and Lawful Permanent Residents (DAPA) programs. Although federal court has temporarily suspended these 2014 programs and no federal funding has been allocated to support their implementation, they could affect more than 3.8 million more undocumented immigrants around the country (MPI 2014). Should these executive initiatives proceed, the burden of immigrant integration will fall mainly on immigrants themselves, as well as the community-based organizations that cater to them.

While the ecology of organizations serving and advocating for immigrants is longstanding and richly elaborated, at least in the major immigrant-receiving cities, they should not be the only promoters of immigrant rights and integration. Labor unions, religious institutions, grant-making institutions, and immigrants themselves have worked with or parallel to immigrant-serving nonprofits and will doubtless continue to do so. As in other cities, however, San Francisco's Democratic Party has largely shirked its responsibility to help immigrants integrate (Jones-Correa 1998; Rogers 2006; Wong 2006). Local businesses—especially new technology companies—have contributed to debates about comprehensive immigration reform, but they are less visible in debates about immigrant integration. Before we can expect the needed policy changes to happen, political parties and business groups will have to engage these debates more actively. Immigrant integration initiatives are more likely to succeed when they draw active support from all sectors of society, including government, nonprofits, business, labor, faith, and philanthropy (DHS/Task Force on New Americans 2008).

While the burden of integrating immigrants falls most heavily on the places where they have established new communities, making cities and increasingly suburbs the logical level for action by immigrant advocates, it behooves the states and federal government to be more proactive as well. Immigrant integration would be faster, easier, and more successful if all levels of government shared in the responsibility (Jiménez 2007). Some states have recently taken initiatives in this direction (Laglagaron et al. 2008), and in Illinois, through the New Americans Integration Initiative, the state has become an important partner for local immigrant-serving nonprofits (Jiménez 2011). More of this needs to happen. State and federal integration policies should focus on language training and job training as well as on promoting civic and political participation so that immigrants can enjoy the same opportunities and life chances as mainstream Americans (White House Task Force on New Americans 2015). Because cities have launched the most innovative integration practices to date, their initiatives can be scaled up to the state and national levels. As this happens, input from immigrant-serving nonprofits and other advocacy organizations can help ensure successful and effective policy development, implementation, and monitoring.

States and the federal government need to make immigrant integration a higher priority because the gains of the local case studies described above are place-bound and limited. Municipal ID cards in San Francisco, New Haven, Oakland, and New York City, for example, can be used only in those cities. Only workers (including immigrant workers) in San Francisco are entitled to that city's minimum wage. And city officials in San Francisco, Philadelphia, New York City, and Washington, D.C., are not allowed to translate state and federal documents originally published in English. Thus, local-level policies that help or empower disadvantaged immigrants generally stop at the city border. Only state and federal action can rectify this situation.

Because undocumented status remains the single most potent barrier to integration, the federal government must move beyond immigration enforcement toward broader immigrant inclusion. Only the federal government can authorize a legalization program that can give undocumented immigrants the greater personal security, economic mobility, and political voice that their contributions to American society warrant. The DACA and DAPA programs are steps in the right direction, but (if and when all have been launched) they provide only temporary deportation relief and work authorization to a segment of the undocumented population. Lest we continue down the path toward reinforcing undocumented immigrants as a permanent underclass, we must give them an opportunity to become legal residents of the United States. If and when this happens, immigrant-serving nonprofits will play a crucial role in helping millions of undocumented immigrants fulfill complicated procedures to change their status. Federal, state, and local government assistance should help them do so. The pathbreaking gains in San Francisco, which nonprofit advocates achieved without federal and state support, suggest just how profound such a contribution from all levels of government would be.

APPENDIX

Immigrant-Serving Nonprofits in San Francisco, 2006

Nonprofit	Website	Surveyed	Interviewed
Acción Latina	http://accionlatina.org	•	
Aegean Friends	http://web.itu.edu.tr/~altilar/AegeanFriends		
African Immigrant and Refugee Resource Center (now: African Advocacy Network)	http://aansf.org	•	•
Agape Community Center		•	
Alianza Latina Americana			
American Maoming Association			
Arab Cultural and Community Center	www.arabculturalcenter.org	•	
Arab Women's Solidarity Association			
Arab-American Media Center			
Ararat Armenian Society			
Arriba Juntos	www.arribajuntos.org	•	•
Asian American Arts Foundation			
Asian American Dance Performers			
Asian American Journalists Association	www.aaja.org		
Asian American Recovery Services	www.aars.org	•	
Asian American Voter Project		•	

(Continued)

Nonprofit	Website	Surveyed	Interviewed
Asian Americans/Pacific Islanders in Philanthropy	http://aapip.org/who-we-are/chapters/san-francisco-bay-area		
Asian and Pacific Islander American Health Forum	www.apiahf.org		
Asian and Pacific Islander Wellness Center	www.apiwellness.org	•	•
Asian Business Association			
Asian Business League of San Francisco	www.ablsf.org		
Asian Improv Arts	www.asianimprov.org		
Asian Law Caucus	www.advancingjustice-alc.org	•	•
Asian Neighborhood Design	www.andnet.org	•	
Asian Pacific American Community Center		•	
Asian Pacific American Internal Revenue Employees			
Asian Pacific American Leadership Project			
Asian Pacific Islander Cultural Center	www.apiculturalcenter.org	•	
Asian Pacific Islander Legal Outreach	www.apilegaloutreach.org	•	•
Asian Perinatal Advocates	www.apafss.org	•	•
Asian Society for Education Research Technology		•	
Asian Women United	www.asianwomenunited.org		
Asian Women's Shelter	www.sfaws.org	•	
Asian, Inc.	www.asianinc.org		
AsianWeek Foundation	www.asianweekfoundation.org		
Asociación de Damas Bolivianas			
Asociación Gay Unida Impactando Latinos/Latinas A Superarse	www.sfaguilas.org	•	
Asociacion Mayab	www.asociacionmayab.org	•	
Association for Chinese Families of the Disabled	www.acfd-ca.org		
Au Co Vietnamese Cultural Center	www.aucocenter.org	•	
Bay Area Latino Lawyers Fund			
Bindlestiff Studio	www.bindlestiffstudio.org		
Bing Kong Tong Benevolent Association	http://bingkongtong.com		
Caminos Pathways Learning Center		•	
Career Resources Development Center		•	
Casa de la Raza			
Center for Asian American Media	http://caamedia.org		

Nonprofit	Website	Surveyed	Interviewed
Center for Asian Indian Newcomers			
Center on Race, Poverty, and the Environment	www.crpe-ej.org		
Central American Resource Center	http://carecensf.org	•	•
Central Chinese High School in America	www.cchsia.org		
Centro Cultural y de Servicio de las Americas			
Centro del Pueblo			
Centro Latino Cuzcatlán			
Centro Latino de San Francisco	www.centrolatinodesf.org	•	•
Cham Refugee Community of San Francisco		•	
Charity Cultural Services Center	www.sfccsc.org	•	
Chinatown Alleyway Improvement Association			
Chinatown Community Children's Center	www.childrencenter.org	•	
Chinatown Community Development Center	www.chinatowncdc.org	•	
Chinatown Economic Development Group			
Chinatown Neighborhood Association		•	
Chinatown Neighborhood Center			
Chinatown-North Beach Youth Service and Coordinating Center			
Chinese American Citizens Alliance	www.cacanational.org		
Chinese American Voters Education Committee			
Chinese Americans for Freedom and Human Rights			
Chinese Consolidated Women's Association			
Chinese Culture Center of San Francisco	www.c-c-c.org	•	
Chinese Democratic Education Foundation			
Chinese Family Alliance	www.chinesefamilyalliance.org	•	
Chinese for Affirmative Action	www.caasf.org	•	•
Chinese Historical Society of America	www.chsa.org		
Chinese Hospital	www.chinesehospital-sf.org	•	•
Chinese Newcomers Service Center	www.chinesenewcomers.org	•	•
Chinese Performing Arts Foundation	www.chineseamericancf.org		

(Continued)

Nonprofit	Website	Surveyed	Interviewed
Chinese Progressive Association	www.cpasf.org	•	•
Chinese Women's Association of America			
Chung Ngai Dance Troupe	www.chungngai.com		
Círculo de Vida Cancer Support and Resource Center	www.circulodevida.org	•	
Coalition for Immigrant Refugee Rights and Services			
Compañeros Del Barrio			•
Congress of Russian Americans	www.russian-americans.org	•	
Council of Armenian American Organizations			
Council of Asian American Business Associations of California	www.caaba.org		
Croatian American Cultural Center	www.slavonicweb.org	•	
Dolores Street Community Services	www.dscs.org	•	•
Donaldina Cameron House	www.cameronhouse.org	•	•
El Teatro de la Esparanza			
Ellas en Acción			
Ethiopian Nurses Association of California		•	
Eviction Defense Collaborative	www.evictiondefense.org	•	•
Filipino Task Force on AIDS			
Filipino-American Council of San Francisco			
Filipino-American Development Foundation	www.bayanihancc.org/bcc-fadf.html	•	•
Galería de la Raza	www.galeriadelaraza.org		
Good Samaritan Family Resource Center	http://goodsamfrc.org	•	
Grupo Aztlan de San Francisco			
Gum Moon Women's Residence	www.gummoon.org	•	•
Hispanic Scholarship Fund	www.hsf.net		
Hokka Nichi Bei Kai Japanese American Association			
Honduran Association of San Francisco and the Bay Area			
Immigrant Legal Resource Center	www.ilrc.org	•	•
Indochinese Housing Development Corporation	http://ihdcsf.org		
Indochinese Voice			
Indus Women Leaders			

Nonprofit	Website	Surveyed	Interviewed
Institute for Multiracial Justice			
Instituto Familiar de la Raza	http://ifrsf.org	•	•
Instituto Laboral de la Raza	www.ilaboral.org	•	•
Interfaith Coalition for Immigrant Rights	http://icir-clue.blogspot.com	•	•
International Institute of San Francisco (now: International Institute of the Bay Area)	www.iibayarea.org	•	•
Irish Immigration Pastoral Center	www.sfiipc.org	•	•
Italian-American Community Services Agency (now: Italian Community Services)	www.italiancs.com		•
Japanese Community Youth Council	www.jcyc.org	•	•
Japanese Cultural and Community Center of Northern California	www.jcccnc.org		
Japantown Art and Media Workshop			
Japantown Task Force	http://japantowntaskforce.org	•	
Jewish Community Center of San Francisco	www.jccsf.org	•	•
Jewish Community Federation	www.jewishfed.org		
Jewish Family and Children's Services	www.jfcs.org	•	•
Jewish Vocational Service	www.jvs.org	•	•
Kai Ming	www.kaiming.org/newkm	•	
Kearny Street Housing Corporation			
Kiangsu Chekiang Charitable Foundation			
Kimochi	www.kimochi-inc.org	•	•
Korean American Community Center of San Francisco			
Korean American Senior Services		•	•
Korean American Women Artists and Writers Association	www.kawawa.org		
Korean Center	http://koreancentersf.org		
Korean Cultural Preservation Association			
La Casa de las Madres	www.lacasa.org	•	
La Raza Centro Legal	www.lrcl.org	•	•
La Raza Community Resource Center	http://larazacrc.org		•
Lao American Family Resource Center		•	

(Continued)

Nonprofit	Website	Surveyed	Interviewed
Latin American Resource Center and Clearing House			
Latina Breast Cancer Agency	www.latinabca.org	•	
Latino Community Foundation	http://latinocf.org		
Latino Institute for Family and Education			
Latino Marrow Donor Program			
Latinos for Civil Service			
Manilatown Heritage Foundation	http://manilatown-heritage-foundation.org	•	
Manos Unidas Community and Development Center			
Margaret Cruz Latina Breast Cancer Foundation	www.cancerlinks.com/Mujeres/mission.html		
Mexican Cultural Center			
Mi Familia			
Middle Eastern Organization for Women			
Mission Child Care Consortium		•	
Mission Council on Alcohol Abuse for the Spanish Speaking	www.missioncouncil.org		
Mission Cultural Center for Latino Arts	www.missionculturalcenter.org		
Mission Economic and Cultural Association			
Mission Economic Development Agency	http://medasf.org	•	
Mission Hiring Hall	http://missionhiringhall.org	•	
Mission Housing Development Corporation	www.missionhousing.org		
Mission Language and Vocational School	www.mlvs.org	•	
Mission Learning Center		•	
Mission Neighborhood Centers	http://mncsf.org		
Mission Neighborhood Health Center	www.mnhc.org		
Mujeres Unidas y Activas	http://mujeresunidas.net	•	•
National Chinese Welfare Council			
Newcomers Association			
NICOS Chinese Health Coalition	www.nicoschc.org	•	•
Nihonmachi Little Friends	www.nlfchildcare.org	•	
Nobiru-Kai Japanese Newcomers Services		•	•

Nonprofit	Website	Surveyed	Interviewed
Northern California Council of Korean Americans from North Korea			
Northern California Federation of Korean Senior Citizens			
On Lok Senior Health Services	www.onlok.org	•	•
Organization of Chinese Americans			
Organization of Filipino Educators			
Pacific Asian American Women Bay Area Coalition	www.paawbac.org		
Pakistan Association of San Francisco Bay Area	http://pasfbayarea.org		
Partnership for Immigrant Leadership and Action (now: Mobilize the Immigrant Vote)	www.pilaweb.org	•	•
Philippine American Writers and Artists	http://pawainc.com		
Philippine Education Support Committee			
Ping Xuen Tenants Association		•	
POCOVI		•	•
Proyecto Ayuda			
Puebla Soccer Club			
Refugee and Immigrant Services at Catholic Charities	http://community.cccyo.org/page.aspx?pid=269	•	•
Refugee Transitions	www.reftrans.org	•	•
Russian American Community Services	http://racssf.org	•	
Russian American Cultural Foundation			
Russian American Nurses Association			
Russian Center for Emotional Support			
Russian Center of San Francisco	www.russiancentersf.com	•	
Samoan Community Development Center	www.samoancenters.org/www/html/about/about.html	•	
Samoans for Samoans of California			
San Francisco American Chinese Cultural Center			
San Francisco Day Labor Program	www.sfdaylabor.org	•	•
San Francisco Filipino Cultural Center	http://thesffcc.com	•	
San Francisco Mission Chinese Business Improvement Association			
San Francisco Organizing Project	www.sfop.org	•	•
Self-Help for the Elderly	www.selfhelpelderly.org		•

(Continued)

Nonprofit	Website	Surveyed	Interviewed
Society of Asian Women Leaders			
South of Market Child Care		•	
Southeast Asian Community Center	www.seaccusa.org	•	•
Spanish Professionals in America			
St. Peter's Housing Committee (now: Causa Justa/Just Cause)	www.cjjc.org	•	•
Survivors International		•	
Swiss Benevolent Society of San Francisco	www.sbssf.com		
Unidad Nicaraguense de Amistad			
United Irish Societies of San Francisco	www.uissf.org		
Upwardly Global	www.upwardlyglobal.org	•	•
Vietnam Chinese Mutual Aid and Friendship Association		•	
Vietnam Fukien High School Mutual Aid and Friendship Association			
Vietnamese Community Center of San Francisco	http://vietccsf.org/2014	•	•
Vietnamese Elderly Mutual Assistance Association		•	•
Vietnamese Family Services Center			
Vietnamese Veterans Mutual Assistance Association		•	•
Vietnamese Women Mutual Assistance Association		•	
Vietnamese Youth Development Center	www.vydc.org	•	•
Vietnamese-American Chamber of Commerce of San Francisco			
Visitacion Valley Community Center		•	
West Bay Pilipino Center	http://westbaycenter.org	•	•
Women's Initiative for Self Employment (now: Renaissance Entrepreneurship Center)	www.rencenter.org	•	
Wu Yee Children's Services	www.wuyee.org	•	•
Young Workers United	www.youngworkersunited.org	•	•

Note: Websites were last visited on August 21, 2015.

ACKNOWLEDGMENTS

In researching and writing this book, I received support and encouragement from many individuals. I am grateful to my committee members in the Departments of Political Science and Sociology at UC Berkeley, where I earned my doctoral degree. I offer special thanks to Taeku Lee, Irene Bloemraad, Jack Citrin, and Bruce Cain. They gave me the freedom to explore on my own, but on many occasions offered advice, constructive criticisms, and insights to keep me on track, also after I graduated. I could not have asked for a better group of advisors. My interactions with the students and faculty at the Institute of Governmental Studies also provided fertile ground for the development of this book. Special thanks go to the participants of the Interdisciplinary Immigration Workshop, who shaped this project with insightful comments and honest observations. At the Institute for the Study of Societal Issues, Christine Trost, David Minkus, and Deborah Lustig taught me to share my research more effectively across disciplines. And Anne Benker, Ellen Borrowman, Maribel Guillermo, Janeen Jackson, Myra Nieves-Bekele, and Liz Wiener provided essential administrative support, allowing me to complete graduate school as an international student without major bureaucratic headaches.

I was fortunate to be surrounded by colleagues and friends at Berkeley who offered intellectual inspiration, camaraderie, and a sense of community when I needed it the most. A big thank you to Ming Hsu Chen, Francisco Dóñez, Joanna Doran, Erica Kohl-Arenas, Roberto Gonzales, Ken Haig, Rebecca Hamlin, Rahsaan Maxwell, Ben Peacock, Gretchen Purser, and Phil Wolgin for the many suggestions and constructive critiques they offered on my writing. This book would not have been possible without the support of Shannon Gleeson, the best writing partner any scholar could wish for. She read more versions of my work than was good for her, and she was always available for feedback and patiently put up with my drive to get things right. She rocks. My gratitude also goes to Amy Gurowitz and Felicia Wong for providing opportunities to share my research in their classrooms and to Nicole Boyle for teaching me about mapping software.

When I was a postdoc researcher at the Harvard Kennedy School of Government, Archon Fung, Aviva Argote, and Edward Schumacher-Matos provided important encouragement for me to do additional research on municipal ID cards in San Francisco and New Haven. I received valuable comments on my work from participants at the Harvard Migration and Immigrant Integration Workshop. The Institute for the Social Sciences at Cornell University offered a stimulating community of immigration scholars when I was a research associate there. The helpful feedback I received from Amada Armenta, Richard Bensel, Maria Lorena Cook, Kati Griffith, Mary Katzenstein, María Cristina García, Sharon Sassler, and Stephen Yale-Loehr is reflected in the pages that follow. In particular, I want to thank Michael Jones-Correa for his critical feedback and thought-provoking discussions at important points in the writing process. He pushed me past my resistance to make some important changes and refine my ideas, and my book is better because of it. At Cornell, Nij Tontisirin provided assistance in building maps. My work has also benefited from feedback and ideas that Pieter Bevelander, Elizabeth Cohen, Kathleen Coll, Richard DeLeon, Linda Donaldson, Willem Maas, Helen Marrow, Mireille Paquet, David Plotke, Doris Marie Provine, Karthick Ramakrishnan, Rogers Smith, Steven Rathgeb Smith, Floris Vermeulen, and Janelle Wong shared with me at various conferences in the United States and abroad.

At the City University of New York, Thomas Halper and Jeffrey Peck went out of their way to make sure I had time to complete the book manuscript. Héctor Cordero-Guzmán, Nancy Foner, Diana Gordon, Ken Guest, Ron Hayduk, Phil Kasinitz, Anna Law, Lina Newton, Robert Smith, and Monica Varsanyi are top-notch immigration scholars, and I have thrived in their company. I am grateful beyond words to John Mollenkopf, who has cheered me on at every turn. He read the entire manuscript and offered substantive and editorial suggestions that greatly improved the project. He also alerted me to numerous immigration-related events and research opportunities in New York City, instantly making me feel at home. I am very lucky to have him as my friend, colleague, and mentor.

Several institutions have backed my studies and research. With gratitude I acknowledge the funding I received from the Dutch Ministry of Education, Culture, and Science as well as the Netherland-America Foundation, which allowed me to pursue my graduate studies in the United States in the first place. I am thankful for the financial support I received from the Institute for the Study of Societal Issues, the Institute of Governmental Studies, the UC Berkeley Political Science Department, the Hauser Institute for Civil Society, the Cornell Institute for the Social Sciences, and the

Professional Staff Congress at CUNY. Generous support from the Dean's Office at Baruch College supported publication expenses. Thank you also to Michael McGandy, to the rest of the staff at Cornell University Press, and particularly to the anonymous reviewers who provided constructive feedback and concrete suggestions for improving the manuscript.

I received lots of encouragement from friends and family during the writing process. The Khor clan and the other residents of the Pacifica house provided a loving home away from my desk, introduced me to various Asian culinary delights, taught me how to have fun living green, and showed me that charitable endeavors are not just topics of academic interest but also a way of life. Thank you Kathleen Gerson and John Mollenkopf for your friendship, for sharing many of John's delicious meals, and for giving me a home in Brooklyn. The love and support from my immediate family—my mom, dad, Christa, and Arwin—helped me to complete this book. I am especially grateful for their support of my decision to pursue my career on this side of the Atlantic, even though they would rather see me settle within Dutch borders. And in the last year, my dachshund Roxy has warmed my lap and kept me company as I finalized the manuscript revisions. Thank you all for your love, patience, and support.

Finally, I am deeply indebted to the leaders and volunteers of the many immigrant-serving nonprofits and city officials who spoke with me in the course of my research in San Francisco and the other cities where I have studied immigrant integration. They willingly shared with me their deep knowledge about the local political scene and generously gave me hours of their time even when they had much more pressing issues to deal with. Their tireless advocacy to improve the lives of immigrants who struggle in our midst is an inspiration to me. Thank you all for telling me about the important and necessary work you do. I dedicate this book to you.

NOTES

Introduction: The Local Politics of Immigrant Integration

1. The definition of immigrant integration as the process through which immigrants, over time, achieve parity in life chances with native-born Americans is similar to how other scholars have defined immigrant assimilation (Alba and Nee 2003), immigrant adaptation (Ramakrishnan 2005), and immigrant incorporation (Marrow 2005). The term *integration*, however, better connotes that immigrant inclusion is a dynamic, two-way process in which immigrants and the receiving society work together to build stronger, more vibrant, and more cohesive communities. The term *integration* also travels across disciplinary lines more easily and better captures immigrants' inclusion into various aspects of American society, including the economy, housing, education, health care, and civic and political participation. Sociologists primarily use the term *assimilation* to discuss immigrants' economic and socio-cultural mobility. Political scientists often use the term *incorporation* to talk specifically about immigrants' participation in aspects of political life.

2. The federal government has not always been hands-off with immigrant rights and integration. In the 1910s and 1920s, the U.S. Bureau of Naturalization and the Bureau of Education joined private citizen groups, settlement houses, social workers, employers, labor unions, schools, and state and local agencies in a national crusade to Americanize immigrants from eastern and southern Europe (McClymer 1978). These public- and private-sector organizations involved in the Americanization movement coordinated and jointly funded programs to provide English language instruction, civics classes, patriotic naturalization proceedings, and Fourth of July celebrations—all aimed at encouraging immigrants to shed their Old World ways and adopt a singular American identity (Higham 1955; Ziegler-McPherson 2009).

3. The settlement houses and mutual aid societies operating around the turn of the twentieth century did not have the 501(c)(3) designation, a category created only with the establishment of the modern tax code in 1954. Like today's 501(c)(3) nonprofits, however, they did enjoy certain tax exemptions, which the Tariff Act of 1894 established (Arnsberger et al. 2008).

4. Foundations are excluded from the analysis because they do not provide direct services to immigrants but instead make grants to immigrant-serving nonprofits and other public charities. Churches are excluded because their primary mission is to promote religious messages, religious education, and worship activities, not to provide direct services to immigrants or to advocate their issues. Compared with immigrant-serving nonprofits, foundations and churches are also subject to additional IRS restrictions on their political activities. They are not eligible for the 501(h) election, a safe harbor status available to other 501(c)(3) nonprofits that want to en-

gage in substantial lobbying. Additionally, foundations must generally pay an excise tax on any lobbying expenditures they make, which is not the case for other 501(c)(3) nonprofits that abide by federal lobbying regulations (Lunder 2007).

5. This approach to counting immigrant-serving nonprofits draws on techniques used by Cordero-Guzmán (2005), Cortés (1998), Gleeson and Bloemraad (2013), and Hung (2007) but instead emphasizes organizations' client characteristics rather than their names, staff characteristics, or mission statements.

1. Nonprofit Organizations as Immigrant Rights Advocates

1. During the nineteenth century, with a high point around 1875, twenty-two states and territories allowed noncitizens to vote in local, state, and federal elections. Illinois was the first state to withdraw alien suffrage, in 1848; Arkansas was the last to do so, in 1926 (Aylsworth 1931).

2. The 1790 Naturalization Act limited U.S. citizenship to foreigners who were free white persons, excluding indentured servants, slaves, free African Americans, and Asian Americans. Chinese immigrants became eligible for U.S. citizenship in 1943, with repeal of the 1882 Chinese Exclusion Act, and Filipino immigrants in 1946, as a result of the Filipino Naturalization Act. The racial restrictions enacted in 1790 were fully removed only in 1952 when the U.S. Congress enacted the McCarran-Walter Act, which made Japanese immigrants eligible for American citizenship.

3. The 1912 "Bread and Roses Strike" is a notable exception. This labor protest, led by the Industrial Workers of the World, was a strike of immigrant workers in textile mills in Lawrence, Massachusetts. More than half of the strikers were women and included many immigrants from southeastern Europe. The strike was a reaction to one mill owner's decision to lower wages when a new law shortening the work-week took effect. It grew rapidly to include twenty-three thousand workers from fifty-one different countries. The strike lasted more than two months, defying the assumptions of conservative AFL unions that female, unskilled, and ethnically diverse immigrant workers could not be organized. The strike was a success, and workers won pay increases and improvements in working conditions, but most of these gains had disappeared several years later (Cameron 1993; Watson 2005).

4. In recent years, members of the U.S. House of Representatives have enjoyed reelection rates as high as 98 percent and members of the U.S. Senate as high as 90 percent (Ornstein, Mann, and Malbin 2008). According to the Cook Political Report (2004, 2008), only 14 percent of House elections were competitive in 2008, up from 9 percent in 2004.

5. Using data from Verba, Schlozman, and Brady's (1995) Citizen Participation Study, Leighley (2001: 42) finds that 47 percent of non-Hispanic whites were targeted for campaign mobilization, compared with 14 percent of Latinos.

6. Interview, March 29, 2005. PILA closed down in 2011, passed its programs on to sister organizations, and became Mobilize the Immigrant Vote, a 501(c)(3) nonprofit focused on increasing voter and civic participation in immigrant communities across California.

7. Interview, May 25, 2005.

8. The Service Employees International Union (SEIU), which represents workers in health care support services and property services, started the Justice for Jani-

tors campaign in 1985. Since its inception, this campaign has organized more than 225,000 janitors, a heavily immigrant workforce, in more than thirty cities across Canada and the United States (SEIU 2015). Similarly, in 2003, the Hotel Employees and Restaurant Employees Union (HERE) organized the Immigrant Workers Freedom Ride, a national mobilization of tens of thousands of immigrants, to focus public attention on immigrant rights.

9. The seven unions initially part of the Change to Win coalition (and the workers they represent) were the International Brotherhood of Teamsters (freight drivers and warehouse workers), the Laborers' International Union of North America (construction workers and other manual laborers), the Service Employees International Union (health care support workers and workers in property services), UNITE-HERE (workers in manufacturing and the hotel and restaurant industries), the United Brotherhood of Carpenters (carpenters), the United Farm Workers (agricultural workers), and the United Food and Commercial Workers (workers in food retail, meatpacking, and food processing). The United Brotherhood of Carpenters left the coalition in 2009 but did not return to the AFL-CIO. After an internal feud, two-thirds of UNITE-HERE members rejoined the AFL-CIO in 2009 (the other third formed a new union called Workers United) and the Laborers' International Union of North America followed suit in 2010.

10. Interview, April 26, 2005.

11. Interview, May 10, 2005.

12. In 2014, more than two hundred cities and counties across the country had formal or informal policies—collectively referred to as "sanctuary policies"—that limit their cooperation with federal immigration enforcement officials (DHS 2014b). San Francisco became a sanctuary city in 1989, when the Board of Supervisors adopted the City of Refuge Ordinance, a non-cooperation policy that bars city officials from collaborating with federal immigration authorities in all but a few explicit circumstances. The ordinance forbids the use of city resources to enforce federal immigration laws. See chapter 5 for more detail.

13. *American Baptist Churches v. Thornburgh*, commonly referred to as the "ABC case," was a class action lawsuit filed by eight religious organizations in federal court in 1985 against the U.S. Attorney General and the head of the Immigration and Naturalization Service (INS) for allegedly violating domestic (1980 Refugee Act) and international (1951 United Nations Convention Relating to the Status of Refugees and its 1967 Protocol) laws in denying asylum to Guatemalans and Salvadorans who had fled political repression in Central America. The lawsuit was settled before trial in 1991, whereby the INS agreed to use fairer judicial procedures to re-adjudicate the status for ABC class members who had been denied refugee status after 1980. The ABC settlement agreement also contained special provisions regarding employment authorization and detention of eligible ABC class members (Coutin 1998).

14. According to the Pew Forum on Religion and Public Life (2008: 47), 46 percent of today's immigrants are Catholics, 24 percent are Protestants (with 15 percent evangelicals and 7 percent mainliners), 3 percent Hindus, 1.7 percent Muslims, 1.6 percent Buddhists, and 1.5 percent Jews. Sixteen percent of immigrants have no religious affiliation.

15. Hearing of the San Francisco Immigrant Rights Commission, December 12, 2001.

16. The introduction's "Research Design and Data" section explains how I arrived at this number. The appendix includes a complete listing of immigrant-serving nonprofits in San Francisco in 2006.

17. Interview, April 25, 2006.

18. Interview, February 28, 2006.

19. Interview, February 21, 2007.

20. Interview, May 10, 2005.

21. Interview, February 21, 2007.

22. Interview, August 15, 2006.

23. Interview, May 23, 2007.

24. Interview, April 3, 2006.

25. Interview, February 28, 2006.

26. I replicated the quiz that Berry and Arons (2003) used in their study.

27. Interview, February 22, 2006.

28. Interview, February 10, 2006.

29. Interview, February 10, 2006.

30. Interview, August 15, 2006.

31. Some of this city funding is state and federal funding that is channeled through San Francisco. Since city officials decide how this money is allocated, nonprofit advocates see it as local government funding.

32. Interview, July 17, 2006.

33. Interview, February 9, 2005.

34. Interview, March 28, 2006.

35. Interview, February 12, 2009.

36. Interview, May 23, 2007.

37. Interview, May 11, 2007.

2. Immigrants and Politics in San Francisco

1. Unless otherwise noted, population statistics are from the three-year estimates of the 2011–2013 American Community Survey.

2. Immigrants' naturalization rate in San Francisco (60%) is higher than at the national level (46%). There is no evidence to suggest, however, that this contributed to patronage-style politics, where members of the Board of Supervisors enacted immigrant rights and integration policies in exchange for immigrants' votes. In August 2015, immigrants made up only a small proportion (23%) of all 433,000 registered voters in San Francisco ("Online Counts Reports" 2015). Furthermore, the proportion of noncitizen immigrants living in poverty in San Francisco in 2013 (22%) was higher than the proportions of naturalized immigrants and native-born residents (13% each). Immigrants who would benefit the most from immigrant rights and integration policies are the ones without voting rights.

3. Interview, April 26, 2005.

4. Interview, February 9, 2005.

5. Interview, February 22, 2006.

6. English-plus activism emerged in reaction to the English-only movement in the late 1980s. Proponents of English-plus legislation seek to promote greater acceptance of language diversity by encouraging individuals to gain proficiency in English *plus* one or more foreign languages (Jones and Singh 2005).

7. Interview, May 25, 2005.

8. Interview, February 14, 2005.

9. Interview, February 11, 2005.

10. Most public-funded employment services assume that participants have ninth-grade levels of education and basic English skills. Most private-funded training programs target skilled workers and managers (Capps et al. 2003; Tumlin and Zimmermann 2003).

11. Interview, February 3, 2009.

12. Interview, February 9, 2009. In 2010, St. Peter's Housing Committee and Just Cause Oakland merged to form Causa Justa (Just Cause).

13. An estimated 11.2 million undocumented immigrants resided in the United States in 2010, including 6.5 million from Mexico, 2.6 million from other countries in Latin America, and 1.3 million from Asia (Passel and Cohn 2011). According to estimates from the General Accounting Office (2004), between 27 and 57 percent of all undocumented immigrants in the United States are visa violators who overstay their temporary non-resident visas.

14. Interview, August 2, 2006.

15. Interview, February 1, 2006.

16. By law, Newsom can be an ex-officio member of the DCCC as long as he maintains a residence in San Francisco. He lost his DCCC seat after moving to another county just north of San Francisco in the summer of 2011 (Sherbert 2011).

17. Hayduk (2006) provides a more detailed analysis of these measures and why they failed.

18. The 2000 Roper Social Capital Benchmark Survey, a Harvard-based research project measuring Americans' civic engagement, includes a sample of five hundred San Franciscans. This sample mirrored the diversity of the city's population in terms of race, ethnicity, gender, age, and immigration status (272 respondents identified as non-Hispanic white, 42 as African American, 74 as Asian, 67 as Latino; 265 respondents were females; respondents came from all age ranges; 53 respondents were non–U.S. citizens). The survey contained one question on immigration, asking respondents to evaluate the following statement: "Immigrants are getting too demanding in their push for equal rights." Seventy-six percent (374/490) of respondents disagreed (either strongly or somewhat) with this statement, while 22 percent agreed (either strongly or somewhat).

19. City subsidies to redevelopers were common during the administration of Mayor Willie Brown (1996–2004). Brown's pro-growth stance was apparent in 1997, when he announced at the groundbreaking for a new project: "Mayors are known for what they build and not anything else, and I intend to cover every inch of the ground that isn't open space" (King 2004).

20. For example, the Third Street Light Rail—a major north-south transportation corridor connecting downtown with San Francisco's southern boundary—went into service in 2007.

3. Providing Language Access through Nonprofit-Government Collaborations

1. Proposition 38, approved by 72 percent of California voters in 1984, is a statewide advisory initiative that expresses disapproval of the bilingual voting materials mandated by Section 203 of the federal Voting Rights Act. Proposition 63, approved by 74 percent of California voters in 1986, is a state constitutional amendment declaring English the official language of California.

2. Shortly after the U.S. Supreme Court delivered its *Lau v. Nichols* opinion, the U.S. Congress enacted the Equal Educational Opportunities Act of 1974. Also in response to the *Lau* decision, California policymakers enacted the Chacón-Moscone Bilingual-Bicultural Education Act in 1976 to mandate bilingual education for limited English proficient students (Moran 2007).

3. The fourteen departments are: the Adult Probation Department, the Department of Elections, the Department of Human Services, the Department of Public Health, the District Attorney's Office, the Department of Emergency Management, the Fire Department, the Human Services Agency, the Juvenile Probation Department, the Municipal Transportation Agency, the Police Department, the Public Defender's Office, the Residential Rent Stabilization and Arbitration Board, and the Sheriff's Office.

4. In April 2014, Tagalog became the third certified foreign language to be covered under EASO.

5. Interview, August 2, 2006.

6. Interview, August 2, 2006.

7. Interview, July 17, 2006.

8. Interview, July 17, 2006.

9. Interview, August 2, 2006.

10. Interview, September 6, 2006.

11. Interview, July 17, 2006.

12. Interview, August 2, 2006.

13. Interview, August 2, 2006.

14. Interview, August 2, 2006.

15. Interview, August 2, 2006.

16. Interview, July 17, 2006.

17. Interview, July 17, 2006.

18. Interview, July 17, 2006.

19. Interview, July 17, 2006.

20. Interview, July 17, 2006. The runoff election system in place at the time helps explain the surprising outcome of the 2000 elections. Both Mabel Teng (District 7) and Michael Yaki (District 1) defeated their challengers by comfortable margins in the November 2000 elections. Because neither received a majority of the votes, they had to face the respective runners-up in a runoff election in December 2000. After leading her opponent by a 44–22 percent margin in November, Teng suffered a stinging thirty-nine-vote defeat (verified by a recount) to Tony Hall in the December runoffs (Gordon 2001). Similarly, Yaki beat Jake McGoldrick in November 2000 with a 38–28 percent result, but in the December runoffs, McGoldrick beat Yaki with 52 percent of the vote (San Francisco Department of Elections).

21. Interview, September 6, 2006.

22. Interview, July 17, 2006.

23. Interview, July 17, 2006.

24. Interview, July 17, 2006.

25. Interview, July 17, 2006.

26. Interview, July 17, 2006.

27. Interview, September 6, 2006.

28. Memo from the budget analyst to the Board of Supervisors, dated May 23, 2001. On file with the author.

29. Hearing in the full Board of Supervisors, May 29, 2001.

30. Hearing in the full Board of Supervisors, May 29, 2001.

31. Interview, August 2, 2006.

32. Nonprofit advocates commented that Hall's campaign slogan in 2000—which declared that he was "one of us"—sounded "xenophobic" and that he had made "problematic statements" about the immigrant community (Hong 2001). Also, in response to my question why Hall was critical of EASO, Mark Leno responded that Hall "was often a fiscal conservative on the Board. But sometimes that fiscal conservatism was either cover for or interactive with a much more narrow view of life in San Francisco. I think he had campaign signs, which were targeted to more traditional Caucasian voters in the western part of town where he was running against Mabel Teng. I may have the actual wording wrong, but the intent is accurate: 'Vote for Tony Hall. He's one of us.' It was less than an inclusive campaign." Interview, September 6, 2006.

33. Hearing in the full Board of Supervisors, May 29, 2001.

34. CAA also fought back the portrayal of EASO as a racial issue in the media. One CAA advocate submitted a letter to the editor of the *San Francisco Chronicle* on April 13, 2001, negating the paper's statements that policies like EASO result in "a workforce comprised entirely of Asians and Latinos."

35. Hearing in the full Board of Supervisors, May 29, 2001.

36. Interview, September 6, 2006.

37. Interview, July 20, 2006.

38. Interview, July 20, 2006.

39. Interview, July 20, 2006.

40. Interview, July 27, 2006.

41. Interview, August 2, 2006.

42. Interview, July 17, 2006.

43. Interview, July 17, 2006.

44. Interview, July 20, 2006.

45. At this time, Mark Leno—the sponsor of EASO in 2001—was no longer on the Board of Supervisors. He was on the California State Assembly between 2002 and 2008, and he has been a state senator since 2008.

46. Interview, August 15, 2006.

47. Interview, February 21, 2007.

48. Interview, July 20, 2006.

49. Interviews, June 2, 2009 (Asian Law Caucus), and January 23, 2006 (Interfaith Coalition for Immigrant Rights).

50. The additional thirteen departments are: the San Francisco International Airport, the Office of the Assessor-Recorder, the City Hall Building Management

Office, the Department of Building Inspection, the Department of the Environment, the San Francisco Public Library, the Mayor's Office of Economic and Workforce Development, the Planning Department, the Department of Public Works, the Public Utilities Commission, the Recreation and Park Department, the Office of the Treasurer and Tax Collector, and the San Francisco Zoo.

4. Raising Minimum Wages through Nonprofit-Union Collaborations

1. According to Reich, Hall, and Hsu (1999), of all the workers benefitting from MCO, 61 percent are women, 11 percent African American (who make up 11 percent of the labor force), 21 percent Latino (18 percent of the labor force), and 30 percent Asian and Pacific Islander (24 percent of the labor force). The study by Alunan et al. (2000) contains similar estimates.

2. Interview, May 28, 2007.

3. Interview, June 12, 2007.

4. Interview, June 12, 2007.

5. Interview, June 11, 2007.

6. Campaign files from the Living Wage Coalition. On file with the author.

7. Interview, June 19, 2007.

8. Interview, May 26, 2007.

9. Hearing in the Finance Committee of the Board of Supervisors, March 18, 1999.

10. Hearing in the Finance Committee of the Board of Supervisors, March 18, 1999.

11. A group of thirteen nonprofits, including seven serving immigrants, organized a meeting in the Mission district on September 15, 1999, to explain the effect of MCO on immigrant-serving nonprofits and their clients. The Living Wage Coalition also organized a "Living Wage Community Fair and Congress" in the Mission district on October 16, 1999, to build support for MCO among low-wage workers and nonprofit workers. Multilingual flyers advertised these events to immigrants.

12. One of the two directors of the Living Wage Coalition mentioned that unions had learned this from research that Brian Murphy of the San Francisco Urban Institute was working on (interview, May 18, 2007). Although Murphy had not published this research at the time that the Living Wage Coalition came together in 1998, his later work demonstrates that 44 percent of all nonprofits in San Francisco with 100 or more employees are unionized, while 16 percent of those with 51 to 99 employees are (Murphy 2002).

13. Interview, May 18, 2007.

14. Interview, May 9, 2007.

15. Interview, May 14, 2007.

16. Internal NCCIR memo, January 25, 2000. On file with the author.

17. Interview, May 18, 2007.

18. Interview, June 11, 2007.

19. Interview, May 18, 2007.

20. Interview, May 18, 2007.

21. However, pursuant to U.S. Supreme Court decisions in *Communication Workers of America v. Beck* (1988) and *Lehnert v. Ferris Faculty Association* (1991), unions

cannot spend compulsory union dues of non-members on political activities when non-members object.

22. MCO, however, was amended in 2007 (Ordinance 212-07) to allow for automatic wage increases by pegging the MCO wage rate to the previous year's Consumer Price Index for urban wage earners in the San Francisco-Oakland-San Jose metro area.

23. In November 2014, 77 percent of San Francisco voters passed Proposition J, raising the city's minimum wage to $15 by 2018. In January 2015, the San Francisco minimum wage was $11.05 as a result of MWO. In May 2015, it increased to $12.25 as a result of Proposition J.

24. The Office of Labor Standards Enforcement (OLSE) also monitors for-profit businesses and nonprofit organizations that have service contracts with city agencies to ensure their compliance with the requirements of MCO. When for-profit businesses or nonprofit organizations break the contract and fail to pay their employees the wage that MCO mandates, OLSE can charge them a fine and the contracting city agency can terminate the contract.

25. Meeting minutes from the Minimum Wage Coalition, May 21, 2003. On file with the author.

26. Interview, June 12, 2007.

27. Interview, June 12, 2007.

28. Interview, June 3, 2007. Mission Agenda no longer exists.

29. Interview, May 23, 2007.

30. Interview, June 3, 2007.

31. Meeting minutes from the Minimum Wage Coalition, May 21, 2003. On file with the author.

32. Interview, June 12, 2007.

33. Interview, June 12, 2007.

34. Because the city was under severe budget constraints, Barry Hermanson—the former co-chair of the Living Wage Coalition who had been working with Matt Gonzalez on minimum wage legislation since mid-2001—provided $25,000 of his personal funds to pay for the study. The Board of Supervisors issued an "accept and expend resolution" in June 2002 to authorize the study.

35. The Minimum Wage Coalition submitted a total of 21,840 signatures to qualify MWO for the ballot; only 9,735 were needed. Letter dated July 28, 2003, from John Arntz, director of the San Francisco Department of Elections, to Barry Hermanson. On file with the author.

36. Interview, May 11, 2007.

37. Interview, May 11, 2007.

38. Many immigrant-serving nonprofits actually relied on the Minimum Wage Coalition to be paid for their campaign work. According to state financial disclosure statements (Form 410) that the Proposition L campaign committee filed with the San Francisco Ethics Commission, various nonprofit employees and campaign workers recruited by immigrant-serving nonprofits received small amounts of campaign worker salaries.

39. Interview, June 3, 2007.

40. Interview, May 23, 2007.

41. Interview, June 14, 2007.

42. Interview, June 14, 2007.

43. Interview, May 9, 2007.

44. Interview, May 23, 2007.

45. Interview, May 23, 2007.

46. Interview, May 11, 2007.

47. Interview, May 23, 2007.

48. Interview, May 23, 2007.

49. Interview, May 11, 2007.

50. Interview, May 29, 2007.

51. Interview, January 25, 2011.

52. Interview, May 29, 2007.

53. San Francisco Board of Supervisors, Legislative File 060247.

54. Interview, San Francisco Office of Labor Standards Enforcement, January 25, 2011.

55. Interview, May 29, 2007.

56. Interview, May 29, 2007.

57. Interview, May 29, 2007.

58. The Health Care Accountability Ordinance (2001) requires city contractors and certain tenants on city property to offer health plan benefits to their employees or make payments to the city for use by the Department of Public Health. The Health Care Security Ordinance (2006) provides comprehensive health care for the city's seventy-three thousand uninsured adult residents (Katz 2008), a group that includes many immigrants. The Paid Sick Leave Ordinance (2006), legislated via initiative, requires all employers to provide paid sick leave to all employees, including temporary and part-time employees, who work in San Francisco. The Wage Theft Prevention Ordinance (2011) enhances the enforcement powers of OLSE and doubles the fines for employers who retaliate against workers exercising their rights under San Francisco labor laws. Proposition J (2014) gradually increases San Francisco's minimum wage to $15 by 2018.

59. Interview, May 11, 2007.

5. Strategic Framing and Municipal ID Cards

1. California's Proposition 187 from 1994 was declared unconstitutional in 1998 for interfering with the federal government's exclusive power to regulate immigration. Arizona's Proposition 200 from 2004 went into effect in December 2004 after a federal judge lifted the temporary restraining order.

2. The most controversial provisions of Arizona's S.B. 1070 were declared unconstitutional in the 2012 U.S. Supreme Court case of *United States v. Arizona*. The Arizona copycat laws enacted in 2011—Alabama's H.B. 56, Georgia's H.B. 87, Indiana's S.B. 590, South Carolina's S.B. 20, and Utah's H.B. 497—have also been challenged in court.

3. Never enforced, the Hazleton ordinance was declared unconstitutional in 2007.

4. However, the 2012 launch of the Deferred Action for Childhood Arrivals program—a federal administrative directive that offers qualified young undocumented immigrants a two-year renewable stay of deportation and the ability to apply for a legal work permit—has prompted several states to revisit their driver's license

laws. As of July 2015, twelve states (California, Colorado, Connecticut, Delaware, Hawaii, Illinois, Maryland, Nevada, New Mexico, Utah, Vermont, and Washington) and the District of Columbia allow undocumented immigrants to apply for a driver's license (NILC 2015).

5. Other countries that issue consular registration cards are: Argentina (Matrícula Consular Argentina), Brazil (Matrícula de Cidadão Brasileiro), Colombia (Tarjeta de Registro Consular), the Dominican Republic (Localizador de Archivo), Guatemala (Tarjeta de Identificación Consular Guatemalteca), Mali (Carte d'Identité Consulaire), Pakistan (National Identity Card for Overseas Pakistanis), and Senegal (Carte Consulaire) (O'Neil 2003).

6. Email communication with the head of the Consular Coordination and Hispanic Affairs Section of the Embassy of Mexico, February 11, 2015.

7. Email communication with the head of the Consular Coordination and Hispanic Affairs Section of the Embassy of Mexico, February 23, 2015. The nine states are: California, Colorado, Illinois, Maryland, Nevada, New Mexico, Utah, Vermont, and Washington. Utah accepts the matrícula consular for obtaining a driving privilege card, which cannot be used for identification purposes by a government entity.

8. San Francisco, CA—Resolution No. 928-01, "Resolution Recognizing "Matrícula Consular" as Official Identification."

9. San Francisco, CA—Administrative Code Sec. 95.1, Ordinance No. 21-02, "Requiring City Departments to Accept Photo Identification Cards Issued by Other Countries as Personal Identification If the Cards Meet Certain Standards."

10. New Haven and San Francisco issue their own ID cards to city residents regardless of their citizenship and documentation status, and the REAL ID Act— which applies only to states—does not prohibit them from doing so. Oakland started issuing ID cards in February 2013, Richmond (Calif.) in October 2014, and New York City in January 2015. Los Angeles enacted a municipal ID ordinance in November 2012 and Hartford (Conn.) in June 2015, but they have yet to implement their policies. Since 2008, law enforcement officials in three New Jersey municipalities have started to endorse the "community ID cards" issued by local nonprofit organizations in Asbury Park, Freehold, and Mercer County (CPD 2013). The nonprofit FaithAction International House has made a similar community ID card available in Greensboro (N.C.) since 2013 (Rowe 2013).

11. Interview, February 3, 2009.

12. The Social Security Administration (SSA) sends a "no-match letter" to employers when the names or social security numbers listed on a worker's Form W-2 do not match SSA records. The letter serves to provide notice of the discrepancy, which can affect workers' future retirement or disability benefits. No-match letters have come under fire in recent years because of their role in immigration enforcement. Although they make no statement about workers' immigration status and no longer contain any mention of U.S. Immigration and Customs Enforcement (ICE), employers have nonetheless assumed that workers identified in the letters are undocumented immigrants. Because they are liable for civil and criminal penalties for knowingly hiring undocumented workers, many employers have terminated workers with unmatched social security numbers. Many of these terminations are improper, affecting low-wage immigrant workers in particular. Other, more unscrupulous employers have misused the no-match letters to take advantage of workers by undermining their right to organize and by cutting their pay and benefits (Mehta,

Theodore, and Hincapié 2003). The 2006–2007 immigration raids in the Bay Area were part of the federal government's Operation Return to Sender, a massive national sweep of illegal immigrants by ICE that resulted in the arrests of over twenty-three thousand undocumented immigrants (McKinley 2007).

13. Interview, February 3, 2009.

14. Interview, February 12, 2009.

15. The California Health and Safety Code requires local police to report non-citizens who are arrested for drug-related offenses to federal immigration officials.

16. Interviews, February 3, 9, and 12, 2009.

17. Two interviews, February 3, 2009.

18. Interviews, February 4 and 9 and June 2, 2009.

19. Interview, February 4, 2009.

20. Interview, February 4, 2009.

21. Interview, February 9, 2009.

22. Interview, February 9, 2009.

23. Interview, February 12, 2009.

24. Interview, February 12, 2009.

25. Interview, February 12, 2009.

26. Public hearing on the Municipal ID Ordinance in the Finance Committee of the Board of Supervisors, October 24, 2007.

27. Public hearing on the Municipal ID Ordinance in the Finance Committee of the Board of Supervisors, October 24, 2007.

28. Interview, February 9, 2009.

29. Interview, February 4, 2009.

30. Several respondents thought that ALDI had intentionally leaked the story. None could prove this, but the accusation reveals the tensions within the Municipal ID Card Coalition and suggests that at times there was disagreement over campaign strategies and tactics.

31. Interview, February 4, 2009.

32. Interview, February 4, 2009.

33. Interview, June 2, 2009.

34. Public hearing on the New Haven ID card program in the Finance Committee of the Board of Aldermen, May 17, 2007.

35. Interview, June 3, 2009.

36. No one person opposed the policy during public hearings, but the clerk of the Board of Supervisors has on record thirty-two letters and emails criticizing the ordinance. San Francisco, CA—Legislative File 071333.

37. San Francisco, CA—Legislative File 071333.

38. Interview, February 17, 2009.

39. Public hearing in the full Board of Supervisors, November 13, 2007.

40. Interview, February 17, 2009.

41. Interview, February 17, 2009.

42. Interview, February 4, 2009.

43. The Immigration Reform Law Institute is the legal arm of the Federation for American Immigration Reform, an anti-immigrant 501(c)(3) nonprofit located in Washington, D.C.

44. Houston and New York City have been under similar scrutiny from the media, federal officials, and anti-immigrant groups for their immigrant-friendly policies and practices (Gleeson 2012; Murthy 2007).

45. Russoniello, a Republican appointee, had threatened to bring criminal action against San Francisco officials since the City of Refuge Ordinance was enacted in 1989. There is no evidence that this ever translated into an actual prosecution. By 2009, it was evident that the federal grand jury had no intention to act on the matter. In August 2010, Obama appointee Melinda Haag succeeded Russoniello as the U.S. Attorney for the Northern District of California.

46. Interview, February 12, 2009.

47. Interview, February 4, 2009.

48. Interview, February 12, 2009.

49. "Petition for Peremptory Writ of Mandamus; Complaint for Declaratory and Injunctive Relief." Filed by the Immigration Reform Law Institute with the California Superior Court on May 13, 2008, Case No. 08-508341.

50. "Memorandum of Points and Authorities in Support of Respondents' Demurrer to Petition for Peremptory Writ of Mandamus and Complaint for Declaratory and Injunctive Relief." Filed by the City Attorney's Office with the California Superior Court on August 29, 2008, Case No. 08-508341.

51. "Memorandum of Points and Authorities in Support of Respondents' Demurrer to Petition for Peremptory Writ of Mandamus and Complaint for Declaratory and Injunctive Relief." Filed by the City Attorney's Office with the California Superior Court on August 29, 2008, Case No. 08-508341.

52. "Brief of Amici Curiae Coalition on Homelessness, Transgender Law Center, and St. Peter's Housing Committee in Support of Respondents' Demurrer to Petition for Peremptory Writ of Mandamus and Complaint for Declaratory and Injunctive Relief." Filed by the American Civil Liberties Union of Northern California with the California Superior Court on August 29, 2008, Case No. 08-508341.

53. Interview, February 9, 2009.

54. Interview, February 9, 2009.

55. Interview, February 4, 2009.

56. San Francisco took additional steps to make the municipal ID card secure. The city invested in technology allowing the county clerk to verify the authenticity of government-issued documents that card applicants may use to identify themselves. The county clerk also has access to a biometrics program that checks the facial features of card applicants to ensure that the same person is not issued a card under a different identity.

57. Email communication with the county clerk, January 29, 2015.

58. Interview, February 9, 2009.

59. The San Francisco Office of Civic Engagement and Immigrant Affairs (OCEIA) was created in February 2009 through the consolidation of a handful of city offices and administrative positions responsible for implementing immigrant integration programs since 2001. OCEIA also absorbed the functions previously performed by the immigrant rights administrator.

60. Public hearing on the implementation of the Municipal ID Ordinance in the Public Safety Committee of the Board of Supervisors, May 4, 2009.

61. The three legal challenges were: (1) a civil lawsuit (*Fonseca v. Fong*) challenging the San Francisco Police Department's use of the sanctuary policy to shield undocumented drug offenders from federal immigration officials; (2) a federal criminal investigation into the city's practice of harboring and transporting undocumented juvenile offenders; and (3) a civil lawsuit brought by the Bologna family (*Bologna v. City and County of San Francisco*) alleging that the city's sanctuary policy was responsible for the death of three family members by Edwin Ramos, an undocumented immigrant from El Salvador.

62. The Secure Communities program enjoyed the support of California attorney general Jerry Brown and Mayor Newsom, but immigrant rights advocates and the Board of Supervisors backed San Francisco sheriff Michael Hennessey's efforts to find ways for the city to opt out of it (Gordon 2010b).

63. Similarly, in October 2013, California governor Jerry Brown signed the Trust Act into law. This act limits the state's cooperation with the federal Secure Communities program by prohibiting local law enforcement agencies from detaining people for deportation if they are arrested for a minor crime or otherwise are eligible to be released from local jail (Garling 2013).

Conclusion: Making Immigrant Rights Real

1. The language access policies are: Executive Order 4-01 (2001) and Executive Order 9-08 (2009) in Philadelphia, Local Law 73 (2003) and Executive Order 120 (2008) in New York City, and the Language Access Act (2004) in Washington, D.C.

REFERENCES

Abu-Laban, Yasmeen, and Judith A. Garber. 2005. "The Construction of the Geography of Immigration as a Policy Problem: The United States and Canada Compared." *Urban Affairs Review* 40(4): 520–561.

Alba, Richard. 2004. "Language Assimilation Today: Bilingualism Persists More Than in the Past, but English Still Dominates." Working Paper No. 111. San Diego: Center for Comparative Immigration Studies.

Alba, Richard, and Victor Nee. 2003. *Remaking the American Mainstream: Assimilation and Contemporary Immigration*. Cambridge: Harvard University Press.

Aleinikoff, T. Alexander, David A. Martin, and Hiroshi Motomura. 2008. *Immigration and Citizenship: Process and Policy*. St. Paul: Thomson West.

Allen, Jr., John L. 2006. "Mahony on Immigration." *National Catholic Reporter*. April 14. Available at http://natcath.org/NCR_Online/archives2/2006b/041406/041406h.php, last visited August 21, 2015.

Allswang, John M. 1986. *Bosses, Machines, and Urban Voters*. Revised edition. Baltimore: Johns Hopkins University Press.

Alunan, Susan, Lisel Blash, Rowena Mamaradlo, Melissa McElvane, Brian Murphy, Michael J. Potepan, Hadley Roff, and Odilla Sidime-Brazier. 2000. *The Living Wage in San Francisco: Analysis of Economic Impact, Administrative and Policy Issues*. San Francisco: San Francisco Urban Institute, San Francisco State University.

American Federation of Labor–Congress of Industrial Organizations (AFL-CIO). 2001. *A Nation of Immigrants*. Presented at the AFL-CIO 24th Biennial Convention, Las Vegas, Nevada, December 12–6. Available at www.aflcio.org/content/download/6951/75037/file/res5.pdf, last visited August 21, 2015.

Andersen, Kristi. 2010. *New Immigrant Communities: Finding a Place in Local Politics*. Boulder: Lynne Rienner Publishers.

Andrew, Merrindahl. 2010. "Women's Movement Institutionalization: The Need for New Approaches." *Politics and Gender* 6(4): 609–616.

Andrews, Kenneth T., and Bob Edwards. 2004. "Advocacy Organizations in the U.S. Political Process." *Annual Review of Sociology* 30: 479–506.

Applegate, Ron. 2007. "Organizing for Equitable Economic Development: The Significance of Community Empowerment Organizations for Unions." In *Labor in New Urban Battlegrounds: Local Solidarity in a Global Economy*, edited by Lowell Turner and Daniel B. Cornfield, 53–72. Ithaca: Cornell University Press.

Archibold, Randal C. 2007. "Illegal Immigrant Advocate for Families Is Deported." *New York Times*. August 21, A-14.

Arnsberger, Paul, Melissa Ludlum, Margaret Riley, and Mark Stanton. 2008. "A History of the Tax-Exempt Sector: An SOI Perspective." *Statistics of Income Bulletin*. Available at www.irs.gov/pub/irs-soi/tehistory.pdf, last visited August 21, 2015.

Aylsworth, Leon E. 1931. "The Passing of Alien Suffrage." *American Political Science Review* 25(1): 114–116.

Babcock, Phillip. 1999. "Letters to the Editor." *San Francisco Chronicle.* May 27.

Bailey, Melissa. 2007. "City ID Plan Approved." *New Haven Independent.* June 5. Available at http://newhavenindependent.org/archives/2007/06/city_id_plan_ap.php, last visited August 21, 2015.

Bass, Gary D., David F. Aarons, Kay Guinane, Matthew F. Carter, and Susan Rees. 2007. *Seen but Not Heard: Strengthening Nonprofit Advocacy.* Washington, D.C.: Aspen Institute.

Bass, Loretta E., and Lynne M. Casper. 2001. "Differences in Registering and Voting Between Native-Born and Naturalized Americans." *Population Research and Policy Review* 20: 483–511.

Bau, Ignatius. 1994. "Cities of Refuge: No Federal Preemption of Ordinances Restricting Local Government Cooperation with the INS." *La Raza Law Review* 7: 50–71.

Baumgartner, Frank R., and Beth L. Leech. 1998. *Basic Interests: The Importance of Groups in Politics and in Political Science.* Princeton: Princeton University Press.

Bean, Frank D., Mark Leach, and B. Lindsay Lowell. 2004. "Immigrant Job Quality and Mobility in the United States." *Work and Occupations* 31(4): 499–518.

Begin, Brent. 2011. "Illegal Immigrants Leaving San Francisco for Cheaper Pastures." *San Francisco Examiner.* July 21. Available at http://archives.sfexaminer.com/sanfrancisco/illegal-immigrants-leaving-san-francisco-for-cheaper-pastures/Content?oid=2178492, last visited August 21, 2015.

Beito, David T. 2000. *From Mutual Aid to the Welfare State: Fraternal Societies and Social Services, 1890–1967.* Chapel Hill: University of North Carolina Press.

Bender, Steven W. 2003. *Greasers and Gringos: Latinos, Law, and the American Imagination.* New York: New York University Press.

Berk, Marc L., and Claudia Schur. 2001. "The Effect of Fear on Access to Care Among Undocumented Latino Immigrants." *Journal of Immigrant Health* 3(3): 151–156.

Bernhardt, Annette, Ruth Milkman, Nik Theodore, Douglas Heckathorn, Mirabai Auer, James DeFilippis, Ana Luz González, Victor Narro, Jason Perelshteyn, Diana Polson, and Michael Spiller. 2009. *Broken Laws, Unprotected Workers: Violations of Employment and Labor Laws in America's Cities.* National Employment Law Project, the UCLA Institute for Research on Labor and Employment, and the UIC Center for Urban Economic Development.

Bernstein, Hamutal, Julia Gelatt, Devlin Hanson, and William Monson. 2014. *Ten Years of Language Access in Washington, D.C.* Washington, D.C.: Urban Institute.

Berry, Jeffrey M., and David F. Arons. 2003. *A Voice for Nonprofits.* Washington, D.C.: Brookings Institution.

Biles, John, Meyer Burstein, and James Frideres (editors). 2008. *Immigration and Integration in Canada in the Twenty-first Century.* Kingston (Ontario): School of Policy Studies, Queen's University Press.

Bloemraad, Irene. 2006. *Becoming a Citizen: Incorporating Immigrants and Refugees in the United States and Canada.* Berkeley: University of California Press.

Bloemraad, Irene, and Els de Graauw. 2012. "Immigrant Integration and Policy in the United States: A Loosely Stitched Patchwork." In *International Perspectives:*

Integration and Inclusion, edited by James Frideres and John Biles, 205–232. Montreal and Kingston: Queen's Policy Studies Series, McGill-Queen's University Press.

Bobo, Kim. 2008. *Wage Theft in America: Why Millions of Working Americans Are Not Getting Paid—And What We Can Do About It.* New York: New Press.

Bonanno, Michael D. 2009. "Municipal Identity (Card) Crisis: U.S. Citizenship Values and the San Francisco Municipal I.D. Program." *Georgetown Journal of Law and Public Policy* 7: 545–570.

Boris, Elizabeth T., Erwin de Leon, Katie L. Roeger, and Milena Nikolova. 2010. *Human Service Nonprofits and Government Collaboration: Findings from the 2010 National Survey of Nonprofit Government Contracting and Grants.* Washington, D.C.: Urban Institute.

Boris, Elizabeth T., and C. Eugene Steuerle. 2006. "Scope and Dimensions of the Nonprofit Sector." In *The Nonprofit Sector: A Research Handbook*, edited by Walter W. Powell and Richard Steinberg, 66–88. New Haven: Yale University Press.

Brannon, Johnny. 2000. "Compromise Ruled in Living Wage Talks." *The Independent.* July 15, 1-A.

Brazil, Eric. 1999. "Desperation in Demand for a Wage to Live On: Workers Tearfully Tell S.F. Supervisors What It's Like to Get Bare Minimum." *San Francisco Examiner.* March 7, D.

Brettell, Caroline B., and Deborah Reed-Danahay. 2012. *Civic Engagements: The Citizenship Practices of Indian and Vietnamese Immigrants.* Stanford: Stanford University Press.

Brody, Evelyn, and Joseph J. Cordes. 2006. "Tax Treatment of Nonprofit Organizations: Two-Edged Sword?" In *Nonprofits and Government: Collaboration and Conflict*, second edition, edited by Elizabeth T. Boris and C. Eugene Steuerle, 141–180. Washington, D.C.: Urban Institute.

Browning, Rufus P., Dale Rogers Marshall, and David H. Tabb. 1984. *When Protest Is Not Enough: The Struggle of Blacks and Hispanics for Equality in Urban Politics.* Berkeley: University of California Press.

Buchanan, Wyatt. 2007a. "City Has a Plan for Immigrant ID Card." *San Francisco Chronicle.* September 7, B-4.

———. 2007b. "ID Card Plan Would Help Immigrants Get Basic Services." *San Francisco Chronicle.* September 19, B-1.

Budget and Legislative Analyst. 2014. "Policy Analysis Report: Analysis of Language Access Services in San Francisco." San Francisco: Budget and Legislative Analyst's Office. Available at www.sfbos.org/Modules/ShowDocument.aspx?documentid=49561, last visited August 21, 2015.

Burgoon, Brian, Janice Fine, Wade Jacoby, and Daniel Tichenor. 2010. "Immigration and the Transformation of American Unionism." *International Migration Review* 44(4): 933–973.

Cain, Bruce E., D. Roderick Kiewiet, and Carole J. Uhlaner. 1991. "The Acquisition of Partisanship by Latinos and Asian Americans." *American Journal of Political Science* 35: 390–422.

California Budget Project (CBP). 1998. *Making Ends Meet: How Much Does It Cost to Raise a Family in California?* Sacramento: California Budget Project.

California State Auditor. 1999. "Dymally-Alatorre Bilingual Services Act: State and Local Governments Could Do More to Address Their Clients' Needs for Bilingual Services." Report No. 99110. Sacramento: Bureau of State Audits.

Cameron, Ardis. 1993. *Radicals of the Worst Sort: Laboring Women in Lawrence, Massachusetts, 1860–1912.* Urbana: University of Illinois Press.

Capps, Randy, Michael Fix, Jeffrey S. Passel, Jason Ost, and Dan Perez-Lopez. 2003. "A Profile of the Low-Wage Immigrant Workforce." Washington, D.C.: Urban Institute.

Card, David. 2007. "How Immigration Affects U.S. Cities." Centre for Research and Analysis of Migration. Discussion Paper Series, CDP No. 11/07.

Carens, Joseph H. 1989. "Membership and Morality: Admission to Citizenship in Liberal Democratic States." In *Immigration and the Politics of Citizenship in Europe and North America,* edited by William Rogers Brubaker, 31–49. Lanham: University Press of America.

Castells, Manuel. 1983. *The City and the Grassroots: A Cross-Cultural Theory of Urban Social Movements.* Berkeley: University of California Press.

Causa Justa/Just Cause (CJJC). 2014. *Development without Displacement: Resisting Gentrification in the Bay Area.* Oakland: Causa Justa/Just Cause.

Center for Popular Democracy (CPD). 2013. *Who We Are: Municipal ID Cards as a Local Strategy to Promote Belonging and Shared Community Identity.* New York: Center for Popular Democracy.

Chaves, Mark, Laura Stephens, and Joseph Galaskiewicz. 2004. "Does Government Funding Suppress Nonprofits' Political Activity?" *American Sociological Review* 69(April): 292–316.

Chavez, Leo R. 2008. *The Latino Threat: Constructing Immigrants, Citizens, and the Nation.* Stanford: Stanford University Press.

Chen, May, and Kent Wong. 1998. "The Challenge of Diversity and Inclusion in the AFL-CIO." In *A New Labor Movement for the New Century,* edited by Gregory Mantsios, 213–231. New York: Garland Publishing.

Chen, Mei-Zhi. 1999. "If Living Wage Is Enacted, It Will Damage Nonprofits Severely." *Sing Tao Daily.* May 7.

Chinese for Affirmative Action (CAA). 2015. "History." Available at www.caasf.org/about-us/history/, last visited August 21, 2015.

Chinese Progressive Association (CPA). 2010. *Check Please! Health and Working Conditions in San Francisco Chinatown Restaurants.* San Francisco: Chinese Progressive Association.

———. 2015. "Workers Organizing Center." Available at www.cpasf.org/node/14, last visited August 21, 2015.

Chiswick, Barry R., and Paul W. Miller. 2005. "Do Enclaves Matter in Immigrant Adjustment?" *City & Community* 4(1): 5–35.

"Church Growth in 1901: Census Statistics Show Roman Catholics Made Largest Gains." 1902. *New York Times.* January 17.

Cisneros, J. David. 2008. "Contaminated Communities: The Metaphor of "Immigrant as Pollutant" in Media Representations of Immigration." *Rhetoric and Public Affairs* 11(4): 569–602.

"City Hall and Labor Gang Up on Nonprofits." 1998. *San Francisco Chronicle.* July 5. Available at http://articles.sfgate.com/1998-07-05/opinion/177260

85_1_nonprofits-catholic-social-services-service-employees-international-union, last visited August 21, 2015.

Clark, John, and Rachel A. O'Hara. 1999. "Living Wage Task Force: Report to the Board of Supervisors." City and County of San Francisco: Department of Administrative Services.

Cohen, Lizabeth. 1990. *Making a New Deal: Industrial Workers in Chicago, 1919–1939.* New York: Cambridge University Press.

Cook Political Report. 2004. "2004 Competitive House Race Chart." October 29. Available at http://cooktemp.dreamhosters.com/races/report_pdfs/2004_house_chart_oct29.pdf, last visited September 1, 2013.

——. 2008. "2008 Competitive House Race Chart." November 3. Available at http://media.timesfreepress.com/docs/2008/06/2008_house_comp_june12.pdf, last visited August 21, 2015.

Cordero-Guzmán, Héctor R. 2005. "Community-Based Organisations and Migration in New York City." *Journal of Ethnic and Migration Studies* 31(5): 889–909.

Cordero-Guzmán, Héctor R., Nina Martin, Victoria Quiroz-Becerra, and Nik Theodore. 2008. "Voting with Their Feet: Nonprofit Organizations and Immigrant Mobilization." *American Behavioral Scientist* 52(4): 598–617.

Cortés, Michael. 1998. "Counting Latino Nonprofits: A New Strategy for Finding Data." *Nonprofit and Voluntary Sector Quarterly* 27(4): 437–458.

Coté, John. 2008. "Supporters of City ID Card Program Hold Rally." *San Francisco Chronicle.* September 17, B-2.

Coutin, Susan Bibler. 1998. "From Refugees to Immigrants: The Legalization Strategies of Salvadoran Immigrants and Activists." *International Migration Review* 32(4): 901–925.

Coyle, Dennis J. 1988. "The Balkans by the Bay." *Public Interest* 91(Spring): 67–78.

Dahl, Robert A. 1961. *Who Governs? Democracy and Power in an American City.* New Haven: Yale University Press.

Dart, John. 1996. "Church Acknowledges Close Ties to the Christian Coalition." *Los Angeles Times.* March 23, B-9.

Davis, Allen Freeman. 1994. *Spearheads for Reform: The Social Settlements and the Progressive Movement, 1890–1914.* Third edition. New Brunswick: Rutgers University Press.

Davis, Robert C., Edna Erez, and Nancy Avitabile. 2001. "Access to Justice for Immigrants Who Are Victimized: The Perspective of Police and Prosecutors." *Criminal Justice Policy Review* 12(3): 183–196.

Dean, Amy B., and David B. Reynolds. 2009. *A New New Deal: How Regional Activism Will Reshape the American Labor Movement.* Ithaca: Cornell University Press.

DeBare, Ilana. 1999. "One Woman's Trials of Surviving on Low Wage." *San Francisco Chronicle.* April 9, B-1.

De Genova, Nicholas. 2004. "The Legal Production of Mexican/Migrant 'Illegality'." *Latino Studies* 2(2): 160–185.

de Graauw, Els. 2008. "Nonprofit Organizations: Agents of Immigrant Political Incorporation in Urban America." In *Civic Hopes and Political Realities: Immigrants, Community Organizations, and Political Engagement,* edited by S. Karthick Ramakrishnan and Irene Bloemraad, 323–350. New York: Russell Sage Foundation Press.

——. 2013. "Immigrants and Political Incorporation in the United States." In Volume 4 of *Immigrants in American History: Arrival, Adaptation, and Integration*, edited by Elliott Robert Barkan, 1875–1892. Santa Barbara: ABC-CLIO Books.

——. 2014. "Municipal ID Cards for Undocumented Immigrants: Local Bureaucratic Membership in a Federal System." *Politics & Society* 42(3): 309–330.

——. 2015a. "Nonprofits and Cross-Organizational Collaborations to Promote Local Labor Rights Policies." *WorkingUSA: The Journal of Labor and Society* 18(1): 103–126.

——. 2015b. "Polyglot Bureaucracies: Nonprofit Advocacy to Create Inclusive City Governments." *Journal of Immigrant & Refugee Studies* 13(2): 156–178.

de Leon, Erwin, Matthew Maronick, Carol J. De Vita, and Elizabeth T. Boris. 2009. *Community-Based Organizations and Immigrant Integration in the Washington, D.C., Metropolitan Area.* Washington, D.C.: Urban Institute.

DeLeon, Richard E. 1992. *Left Coast City: Progressive Politics in San Francisco, 1975–1991.* Lawrence: University Press of Kansas.

——. 2003. "San Francisco: The Politics of Race, Land Use, and Ideology." In *Racial Politics in American Cities*, third edition, edited by Rufus P. Browning, Dale Rogers Marshall, and David H. Tabb, 167–198. White Plains: Longman.

——. 2008. "Sanfranciscoism." *San Francisco Bay Guardian.* September 3. Available at www.sfbg.com/2008/09/03/sanfranciscoism, last visited August 21, 2015.

DeLeon, Richard E., Steven Hill, and Lisel Blash. 1998. "The Campaign for Proposition H and Preference Voting in San Francisco." *Representation: Journal of Representative Democracy* 35(4): 265–274.

Delgado-Gaitan, Concha. 2004. *Involving Latino Families in Schools: Raising Student Achievement through Home-School Partnerships.* Thousand Oaks: Corwin Press.

Department of Homeland Security (DHS). 2014a. *Yearbook of Immigration Statistics: 2013.* Washington, D.C.: Department of Homeland Security, Office of Immigration Statistics.

——. 2014b. *Law Enforcement Systems & Analysis: Declined Detainer Outcome Report.* Available at http://cis.org/sites/cis.org/files/Declined%20detainers%20report .pdf, last visited August 21, 2015.

Department of Homeland Security (DHS)/Task Force on New Americans. 2008. *Building an Americanization Movement for the Twenty-first Century: A Report to the President of the United States from the Task Force on New Americans.* Washington, D.C.: Department of Homeland Security.

Diamond, Stanley. 1990. "English: The Official Language of California, 1983–1988." In *Perspectives on Official English: The Campaign for English as the Official Language of the USA*, edited by Karen L. Adams and Daniel T. Brink, 111–119. New York: Mouton de Gruyter.

Dolan, Jay P. 1975. *The Immigrant Church: New York's Irish and German Catholics, 1815–1865.* Baltimore: Johns Hopkins University Press.

Donaldson, Linda Plitt. 2007. "Advocacy by Nonprofit Human Service Agencies: Organizational Factors as Correlates to Advocacy Behavior." *Journal of Community Practice* 15(3): 139–158.

Dyrness, Grace, and Clara Irazábal. 2007. "A Haven for Illegal Immigrants: The Sanctuary Movement Hopes that by Sheltering a Few, It Will Highlight the Plight of Millions." *Los Angeles Times*. September 2, M-6.

Egelko, Bob. 2003. "Mexican ID Cards Under Fire: Feds Suspend Pilot Program in S.F." *San Francisco Chronicle*. January 25, A-13.

———. 2008. "Federal Probe into S.F. Sanctuary Policy." *San Francisco Chronicle*. October 4, A-1.

Elshtain, Jean Bethke. 2002. *Jane Addams and the Dream of American Democracy*. New York: Basic Books.

English First. 2015. Available at http://englishfirst.org/d/states, last visited August 21, 2015.

Epp, Charles R. 2010. *Making Rights Real: Activists, Bureaucrats, and the Creation of the Legalistic State*. Chicago: University of Chicago Press.

Epstein, Edward. 1998. "S.F. Board Smiles on Local Businesses." *San Francisco Chronicle*. December 8, A-21.

———. 1999a. "S.F. Refuses to Act Quickly on Living Wage: Labor Activists Deplore Decision to Seek Thorough Financial Analysis." *San Francisco Chronicle*. June 2, A-15.

———. 1999b. "Ammiano Says Feud with S.F. Mayor Spurred His Write-In Candidacy." *San Francisco Chronicle*. October 20, A-19.

———. 1999c. "Brown Raises Pay for Lowest-Paid Airport Workers." *San Francisco Chronicle*. November 22, A-17.

———. 2000. "S.F. Living-Wage Law May Go to Voters: Mayor Probably Won't OK Comprehensive Plan." *San Francisco Chronicle*. May 26, A-21.

Erie, Steven P. 1988. *Rainbow's End: Irish-Americans and the Dilemmas of Urban Machine Politics, 1840–1985*. Berkeley: University of California Press.

Eslinger, Bonnie. 2007. "Immigrants May Be Given City ID Cards." *San Francisco Examiner*. September 7, 1.

Etzioni-Halevy, Eva. 1983. *Bureaucracy and Democracy: A Political Dilemma*. Boston: Routledge and Kegan Paul.

Fabricant, Michael B., and Robert Fisher. 2002. *Settlement Houses under Siege: The Struggle to Sustain Community Organizations in New York City*. New York: Columbia University Press.

Ferman, Barbara. 1985. *Governing the Ungovernable City: Political Skill, Leadership, and the Modern Mayor*. Philadelphia: Temple University Press.

Fine, Janice. 2006. *Worker Centers: Organizing Communities at the Edge of the Dream*. Ithaca: Cornell University Press.

Finnie, Chuck. 1999. "Mayor Says He'll Back S.F. Wage Hike." *San Francisco Examiner*. January 20, A-9.

Firestone, David. 1997. "Mayoral Order on Immigrants Is Struck Down." *New York Times*. July 19, A-21.

Fisher, Claude S., and Michael Hout. 2006. *Century of Difference: How America Changed in the Last One Hundred Years*. New York: Russell Sage Foundation Press.

Fisher, Robert. 2005. "History, Context, and Emerging Issues for Community Practice." In *The Handbook of Community Practice*, edited by Marie Weil, 34–58. Thousand Oaks: Sage Publications.

Fix, Michael E. (editor). 2009. *Immigrants and Welfare: The Impact of Welfare Reform on America's Newcomers.* New York: Russell Sage Foundation Press.

Fix, Michael E., Wendy Zimmermann, and Jeffrey S. Passel. 2001. *The Integration of Immigrant Families in the United States.* Washington, D.C.: Urban Institute.

Foley, Michael W., and Dean R. Hoge. 2007. *Religion and the New Immigrants: How Faith Communities Form Our Newest Citizens.* New York: Oxford University Press.

Frasure, Lorrie A., and Michael Jones-Correa. 2010. "The Logic of Institutional Interdependency: The Case of Day Laborer Policy in Suburbia." *Urban Affairs Review* 45(4): 451–482.

Friedland, Roger, and Donald Palmer. 1984. "Park Place and Main Street: Business and the Urban Power Structure." *Annual Review of Sociology* 10: 393–416.

Fujiwara, Lynn F. 2005. "Immigrant Rights Are Human Rights: The Reframing of Immigrant Entitlement and Welfare." *Social Problems* 52(1): 79–101.

Gammal, Denise L., Caroline Simard, Hokyu Hwang, and Walter W. Powell. 2005. *Managing Through Challenges: A Profile of San Francisco Bay Area Nonprofit Organizations.* Stanford: Stanford Graduate School of Business.

Ganz, Marshall. 2009. *Why David Sometimes Wins: Leadership, Organization, and Strategy in the California Farm Worker Movement.* New York: Oxford University Press.

Garcia, Ken. 2009. "Ms. Fong Goes to Washington." *San Francisco Examiner.* September 18. Available at http://archives.sfexaminer.com/sanfrancisco/ms-fong-goes-to-washington/Content?oid=2142702, last visited August 21, 2015.

García, Mario T. 2005. "PADRES: Latino Community Priests and Social Action." In *Latino Religions and Civic Activism in the United States,* edited by Gastón Espinosa, Virgilio Elizondo, and Jesse Miranda, 77–110. New York: Oxford University Press.

Gardner, Trevor. 2011. "The Threat of Sanctuary: Child Immigrants as Criminal Aliens of San Francisco." *Institute for the Study of Social Change,* University of California, Berkeley. ISSC Fellows Working Papers. Paper ISSC_WP_49.

Garling, Caleb. 2013. "Gov. Brown Signs Law to Limit Immigrant Detentions." *San Francisco Chronicle.* October 5. Available at www.sfgate.com/news/article/Gov-Brown-signs-law-to-limit-immigrant-detentions-4872527.php, last visited August 21, 2015.

Gavit, John Palmer. 1922. *Americans by Choice.* New York: Harper.

Gerber, David A. 1989. *The Making of an American Pluralism: Buffalo, New York, 1825–1860.* Chicago: University of Illinois Press.

German Marshall Fund. 2011. *Transatlantic Trends: Immigration (Key Findings 2011).* Washington, D.C.: German Marshall Fund. Available at http://trends.gmfus.org/files/2011/12/TTImmigration_final_web1.pdf, last visited August 21, 2015.

Gerstle, Gary, and John Mollenkopf (editors). 2001. *E Pluribus Unum? Contemporary and Historical Perspectives on Immigrant Political Incorporation.* New York: Russell Sage Foundation Press.

Gibson, Campbell, and Kay Jung. 2006. "Historical Census Statistics on the Foreign-Born Population of the United States: 1850–2000." Working Paper No. 81. Washington, D.C.: U.S. Bureau of the Census, Population Division.

Gleeson, Shannon. 2012. *Conflicting Commitments: The Politics of Enforcing Immigrant Workers Rights in San Jose and Houston.* Ithaca: Cornell University Press.

Gleeson, Shannon, and Irene Bloemraad. 2013. "Assessing the Scope of Immigrant Organizations: Official Undercounts and Actual Underrepresentation." *Nonprofit and Voluntary Sector Quarterly* 42(2): 344–368.

Gonzales, Roberto G. 2010. "More Than Just Access: Undocumented Students Navigating the Postsecondary Terrain." *Journal of College Admission* 206: 48–52.

Gordon, Rachel. 1998. "Supes OK Living-Wage Study." *San Francisco Examiner.* November 24, A-14.

———. 2000. "Brown Averts Showdown at Ballot on S.F. Living Wage." *San Francisco Examiner.* July 11, A-1.

———. 2001. "S.F. to Recount Votes in District 7 Next Week." *San Francisco Chronicle.* January 6, A-11.

———. 2010a. "Setback to S.F.'s Policy on Sanctuary: Suspects' Prints Must Go to Immigration Officials." *San Francisco Chronicle.* May 6, A-1.

———. 2010b. "Feds Will Consider S.F.'s Bid to Opt Out." *San Francisco Chronicle.* September 2, C-1.

———. 2011. "City Revises Its Stance on Illegal Immigrant Youths." *San Francisco Chronicle.* May 11, A-1.

Government Accountability Office (GAO). 2004. "Border Security: Consular Identification Cards Accepted within the United States, but Consistent Federal Guidance Needed." (GAO-04-881, August.) Washington, D.C.: Government Accountability Office.

General Accounting Office. 2004. "Overstay Tracking: A Key Component of Homeland Security and a Layered Defense." Report No. GAO-04-82. Washington, D.C.: General Accounting Office.

Griffith, Kati L. 2009. "U.S. Migrant Worker Law: The Interstices of Immigration Law and Labor and Employment Law." *Comparative Labor Law and Policy Journal* 31: 125–161.

Grønbjerg, Kirsten A. 1993. *Understanding Nonprofit Funding: Managing Revenues in Social Services and Community Development Organizations.* San Francisco: Jossey-Bass.

Harmon, Gail M., Jessica A. Ladd, and Eleanor A. Evans. 2000. *Being a Player: A Guide to the IRS Lobbying Regulations for Advocacy Charities.* Washington, D.C.: Alliance for Justice.

Hartman, Chester W. 2002. *City for Sale: The Transformation of San Francisco.* Revised and updated edition. Berkeley: University of California Press.

Hayduk, Ronald. 2006. *Democracy for All: Restoring Immigrant Voting Rights in the United States.* New York: Routledge.

Heizer, Robert F., and Alan J. Almquist. 1971. *The Other Californians: Prejudice and Discrimination under Spain, Mexico, and the United States to 1920.* Berkeley: University of California Press.

Hendricks, Tyche. 2009. "Immigration: Obama Urged to Focus on Better Integration." *San Francisco Chronicle.* January 19, A-1.

Heredia, Luisa L. 2008. "Faith in Action: The Catholic Church and the Immigrant Rights Movement, 1980–2007." Ph.D. dissertation, Department of Sociology, Harvard University.

Hessick, Carissa Byrne, and Gabriel J. Chin (editors). 2014. *Strange Neighbors: The Role of States in Immigration Policy.* New York: New York University Press.

Heuchan, Laura M. 1985–1986. "Nonprofit Charitable Organizations, 1982." *Statistics of Income Bulletin* 5(3): 21–40.

Higham, John. 1955. *Strangers in the Land: Patterns of American Nativism, 1860–1925.* New Brunswick: Rutgers University Press.

Hill, Laura E., and Hans P. Johnson. 2011. *Unauthorized Immigrants in California: Estimates for Counties.* San Francisco: Public Policy Institute of California.

Hirsch, Barry T., and David A. Macpherson. 2010. *Union Membership and Coverage Database from the CPS.* Georgia State University and Trinity University. Available at www.unionstats.com, last visited August 21, 2015.

Hirsch, Matthew. 2005. "The Nonprofit Gold Rush." *San Francisco Bay Guardian* 39(23): 16–18.

Hogarth, Paul. 2008a. "Supervisors Run for DCCC: Progressive Slate Formed." *BeyondChron.* March 10. Available at www.beyondchron.org/news/index.php?itemid=5453, last visited August 21, 2015.

———. 2008b. "Progressives Run for DCCC on West Side." *BeyondChron.* May 14. Available at www.beyondchron.org/articles/Progressives_Run_for_DCCC_on_West_Side_5667.html, last visited August 21, 2015.

———. 2010. "S.F. Democratic Races Show Need for Reform." *BeyondChron.* April 12. Available at www.beyondchron.org/news/index.php?itemid=8007, last visited August 21, 2015.

Hong, Joseph. 2001. "Recount On: Big Bucks and Politics behind Teng/Hall Recount." *AsianWeek.* January 12, 13.

Hopkins, Daniel J. 2010. "Politicized Places: Explaining Where and When Immigrants Provoke Local Opposition." *American Political Science Review* 104(1): 40–60.

Hsu, Madeline Y. 2015. *The Good Immigrants: How the Yellow Peril Became the Model Minority.* Princeton: Princeton University Press.

Hung, Chi-Kan Richard. 2007. "Immigrant Nonprofit Organizations in U.S. Metropolitan Areas." *Nonprofit and Voluntary Sector Quarterly* 36(4): 707–729.

Hunter, Floyd. 1953. *Community Power Structure: A Study of Decision Makers.* Chapel Hill: University of North Carolina Press.

Huntington, Samuel P. 2004. "The Hispanic Challenge." *Foreign Policy* (March/April): 30–44.

Iceland, John, and Melissa Scopilliti. 2008. "Immigrant Residential Segregation in U.S. Metropolitan Areas." *Demography* 45(1): 79–94.

Immigrant Rights Commission (IRC). 2008. "Commission Bylaws." Available at www.sfgov2.org/ftp/uploadedfiles/immigrant/AboutUs/IRCBylaws.pdf, last visited August 21, 2015.

Internal Revenue Service (IRS). 2014. *Data Book, 2013.* Available at www.irs.gov/pub/irs-soi/13databk.pdf (table 25), last visited August 21, 2015.

Isaacs, Matt. 1998a. "Living-Wage Plan Moves Forward Amid Protest." *The Independent.* November 10.

———. 1998b. "Supervisors Come to Uneasy Truce on Wage Proposal." *The Independent.* November 28.

Jacobson, Robin, and Kim Geron. 2008. "Unions and the Politics of Immigration." *Socialism and Democracy* 22(3): 105–122.

Jiménez, Tomás R. 2007. "From Newcomers to Americans: An Integration Policy for a Nation of Immigrants." *Immigration Policy in Focus* 5(11). Washington, D.C.: Immigration Policy Center.

———. 2011. *Immigrants in the United States: How Well Are They Integrating Into Society?* Washington, D.C.: Migration Policy Institute.

Johansen, Yliana. 2011. "The Media, Politics, and Policy: Taking Another Look at the Development of San Francisco's Policies on Immigrant Juvenile Offenders." *UC Davis Journal of Juvenile Law & Policy* 15(1): 125–158.

Johnson, Jason B. 1998. "Foes Say Plan to Study Living Wage Concept Only a Political Ploy." *San Francisco Chronicle.* November 10, A-17.

Jones, Mari C., and Ishtla Singh. 2005. *Exploring Language Change.* New York: Routledge.

Jones-Correa, Michael. 1998. *Between Two Nations: The Political Predicament of Latinos in New York City.* Ithaca: Cornell University Press.

———. 2001. "Institutional and Contextual Factors in Immigrant Naturalization and Voting." *Citizenship Studies* 5(1): 41–56.

———. 2008. "Race to the Top? The Politics of Immigrant Education in Suburbia." In *New Faces in New Places: The Changing Geography of American Immigration*, edited by Douglas S. Massey, 308–340. New York: Russell Sage Foundation Press.

———. 2011. *All Immigration Is Local: Receiving Communities and Their Role in Successful Immigrant Integration.* Washington, D.C.: Center for American Progress.

Jones-Correa, Michael, and Els de Graauw. 2013. "The Illegality Trap: The Politics of Immigration and the Lens of Illegality." *Dædalus* 142(3): 185–198.

Jonsson, Patrik. 2006. "To Curb Illegal Immigration, South Cracks Down on Housing Codes." *Christian Science Monitor* 98(36): 3.

Jorae, Wendy Rouse. 2009. *The Children of Chinatown: Growing Up Chinese American in San Francisco, 1850–1920.* Chapel Hill: University of North Carolina Press.

Kasinitz, Philip, John H. Mollenkopf, Mary C. Waters, and Jennifer Holdaway. 2008. *Inheriting the City: The Children of Immigrants Come of Age.* Cambridge: Harvard University Press.

Katz, Mitchell H. 2008. "Golden Gate to Health Care for All? San Francisco's New Universal-Access Program." *New England Journal of Medicine* 358(4): 327–329.

Keesling, Francis V. 1933. *San Francisco Charter of 1931.* San Francisco [Publisher unknown].

Kilroy, Tony. 1999. *Kilroy's Directory of San Francisco's Politically Active Groups.*

King, John. 2004. "The Mayor's Legacy: Willie Brown." *San Francisco Chronicle.* January 24, A-13.

Knight, Heather. 2008a. "S.F. Juvenile Hall Braces for Detainee Surge." *San Francisco Chronicle.* July 4, A-1.

———. 2008b. "Aaron Peskin Wins Vote for Dem County Chair." *San Francisco Chronicle.* July 25, B-1.

———. 2008c. "Minutemen Protest S.F.'s Sanctuary Policy." *San Francisco Chronicle.* July 31, B-1.

——. 2008d. "Illegal Youth Issue Goes to Attorney General." *San Francisco Chronicle.* August 7, B-3.

——. 2009a. "Hundreds Wait for Hours to Buy ID Card." *San Francisco Chronicle.* January 16, B-1.

——. 2009b. "New Top Cop Looks to Be Tailor Made." *San Francisco Chronicle.* June 21, A-1.

——. 2009c. "With Veto Annulled, Legal Fight Possible." *San Francisco Chronicle.* November 11, C-1.

Koerin, Beverly. 2003. "The Settlement House Tradition: Current Trends and Future Concerns." *Journal of Sociology and Social Welfare* 30(2): 53–68.

Kymlicka, Will. 1998. *Finding Our Way: Rethinking Ethnocultural Relations in Canada.* Toronto: Oxford University Press.

La Ganga, Maria L. 2008. "'Sanctuary City' No Haven for a Family and Its Grief." *Los Angeles Times.* July 26.

——. 2009. "San Francisco Board Overrides Mayor's Veto of Sanctuary Expansion." *Los Angeles Times.* November 11.

La Luz, José, and Paula Finn. 1998. "Getting Serious about Inclusion: A Comprehensive Approach." In *A New Labor Movement for the New Century*, edited by Gregory Mantsios, 197–211. New York: Garland Publishing.

Laglagaron, Laureen, Cristina Rodríguez, Alexa Silver, and Sirithon Thanasombat. 2008. *Regulating Immigration at the State Level: Highlights from the Database of 2007 State Immigration Legislation and the Methodology.* Washington, D.C.: Migration Policy Institute.

Laguerre, Michel S. 2000. *The Global Ethnopolis: Chinatown, Japantown and Manilatown in American Society.* New York: St. Martin's Press.

Lee, James. 2011. *U.S. Naturalizations: 2010.* Washington, D.C.: Department of Homeland Security. Available at www.dhs.gov/xlibrary/assets/statistics/publications/natz_fr_2010.pdf, last visited August 21, 2015.

Lee, Patricia. 1988. "Asian Immigrant Women & HERE Local 2." *Labor Research Review* 1(11): 29–38.

Leighley, Jan E. 2001. *Strength in Numbers? The Political Mobilization of Racial and Ethnic Minorities.* Princeton: Princeton University Press.

Lelchuk, Ilene. 2000. "S.F. Approves Living Wage Law." *San Francisco Examiner.* August 22.

Levada, William J. 1999. "A Plea for Living Wages." *San Francisco Chronicle.* November 1, A-25.

Levitt, Peggy. 2007. *God Needs No Passport: Immigrants and the Changing American Religious Landscape.* New York: New Press.

Lewis, Gregory. 1999a. "Three Quit S.F.'s Living Wage Task Force: Trio Frustrated by Calls to Extend Work for 6 Months." *San Francisco Examiner.* May 27, C.

——. 1999b. "Voters in S.F. Strongly Support Living Wage Plan, Poll Shows." *San Francisco Examiner.* August 19, A.

Lewis, Paul G., and Doris Marie Provine. 2011. "No Changing the Conversation? Immigrant Integration Efforts in Metropolitan Phoenix." Paper presented at the annual meeting of the Western Political Science Association, San Antonio, Texas, April 21.

Lewis, Paul G., and S. Karthick Ramakrishnan. 2007. "Police Practices in Immigrant-Destination Cities: Political Control or Bureaucratic Professionalism?" *Urban Affairs Review* 42(6): 874–900.

Lineberry, Robert L. 1977. *Equality and Public Policy: The Distribution of Municipal Public Services.* Beverly Hills: Sage Publications.

Linton, April. 2009. "Language Politics and Policy in the United States: Implications for the Immigration Debate." *International Journal of the Sociology of Language* 199(September): 9–37.

Lipsky, Michael. 1980. *Street-Level Bureaucracy: Dilemmas of the Individual in Public Service.* New York: Russell Sage Foundation Press.

Lissak, Rivka Shpak. 1989. *Pluralism and Progressives: Hull House and the New Immigrants, 1890–1919.* Chicago: University of Chicago Press.

Logan, John R., and Harvey L. Molotch. 1987. *Urban Fortunes: The Political Economy of Place.* Berkeley: University of California Press.

"Long-overdue Paychecks." 2005. Editorial. *San Francisco Chronicle.* March 25, B-8.

Lovett, Ian. 2014. "As Housing Costs Soar, San Francisco Seeks Ballot Solution." *New York Times.* October 2, A-12.

Luce, Stephanie. 2004. *Fighting for a Living Wage.* Ithaca: Cornell University Press.

——. 2005. "The Role of Community Involvement in Implementing Living Wage Ordinances." *Industrial Relations* 44(1): 32–58.

Lunder, Erika. 2007. "Tax-Exempt Organizations: Political Activity Restrictions and Disclosure Requirements." *Congressional Research Service* (RL33377; September 11). Available at http://assets.opencrs.com/rpts/RL33377_20070911.pdf, last visited August 21, 2015.

Majic, Samantha. 2011. "Serving Sex Workers and Promoting Democratic Engagement: Rethinking Nonprofits' Role in American Civic and Political Life." *Perspectives on Politics* 9(4): 821–839.

Mar, Eric. 1999. "Letters to the Editor." *San Francisco Examiner.* March 25.

Marrow, Helen B. 2005. "New Destinations and Immigrant Incorporation." *Perspectives on Politics* 3(4): 781–799.

——. 2009. "Immigrant Bureaucratic Incorporation: The Dual Roles of Government Policies and Professional Missions." *American Sociological Review* 74(5): 756–776.

——. 2011. "Deserving to a Point: Unauthorized Immigrants in San Francisco's Universal Access Healthcare Model." *Social Science & Medicine* 74(6): 846–854.

Martin, Nina. 2012. "'There Is Abuse Everywhere': Migrant Nonprofit Organizations and the Problem of Precarious Work." *Urban Affairs Review* 48(3): 389–416.

Marwell, Nicole P. 2004. "Privatizing the Welfare State: Nonprofit Community-Based Organizations as Political Actors." *American Sociological Review* 69(2): 265–291.

Matos, Kica. 2008. "The Elm City Resident Card: New Haven Reaches Out to Immigrants." *New England Community Developments* 1: 1–7.

McCann, Michael W. 1994. *Rights at Work: Pay Equity Reform and the Politics of Legal Mobilization.* Chicago: University of Chicago Press.

McClymer, John F. 1978. "The Federal Government and the Americanization Movement, 1914–1925." *Prologue: The Journal of the National Archives* 10(1): 23–41.

McDonald, Terrence J. 1987. *The Parameters of Urban Fiscal Policy: Socioeconomic Change and Political Culture in San Francisco, 1860–1906.* Berkeley: University of California Press.

McGerr, Michael. 1986. *The Decline of Popular Politics: The American North, 1865–1928.* New York: Oxford University Press.

McKinley, Jesse. 2007. "San Francisco Bay Area Reacts Angrily to Series of Immigration Raids." *New York Times.* April 28, A-14.

McMenamin, Dan. 2013. "Mayor Signs Off on Rule Prohibiting SF Cops from Complying with Most Federal Immigration Hold Requests." *San Francisco Appeal.* October 9. Available at http://sfappeal.com/2013/10/mayor-signs-off-on-rule-prohibiting-sf-cops-from-complying-with-most-federal-immigration-hold-requests/, last visited August 21, 2015.

Mehan, Hugh. 1997. "The Discourse of the Illegal Immigration Debate: A Case Study in the Politics of Representation." *Discourse and Society* 8: 249–270.

Mehta, Chirag, Nik Theodore, and Marielena Hincapié. 2003. "Social Security Administration's No-Match Letter Program: Implications for Immigration Enforcement and Workers' Rights." Chicago: Center for Urban Economic Development.

Migration Policy Institute (MPI). 2014. "National and County Estimates of Populations Eligible for DAPA and DACA Programs, 2009–2013." Washington, D.C.: Migration Policy Institute/Data Hub.

Milkman, Ruth. 2006. *L.A. Story: Immigrant Workers and the Future of the U.S. Labor Movement.* New York: Russell Sage Foundation Press.

Milkman, Ruth, and Laura Braslow. 2011. *The State of the Unions 2011: A Profile of Organized Labor in New York City, New York State, and the United States.* New York: The Joseph S. Murphy Institute for Worker Education and Labor Studies, Center for Urban Research, and the NYC Labor Market Information Services, CUNY.

Milkman, Ruth, and Daisy Rooks. 2003. "California Union Membership: A Turn-of-the-Century Portrait." Institute for Labor and Employment, UC Berkeley. Available at http://escholarship.org/uc/item/94x791km, last visited August 21, 2015.

Mink, Gwendolyn. 1986. *Old Labor and New Immigrants in American Political Development: Union, Party, and State, 1875–1920.* Ithaca: Cornell University Press.

Minkoff, Debra C. 1995. *Organizing for Equality: The Evolution of Women's and Racial-Ethnic Organizations in America, 1955–1985.* New Brunswick: Rutgers University Press.

Modares, Ali, and Jennifer Kitson. 2008. *Nonprofit Organizations as Facilitators of Immigrant Integration in Los Angeles County, California.* Los Angeles: The Edmund G. "Pat" Brown Institute of Public Affairs.

Mollenkopf, John. 1983. *The Contested City.* Princeton: Princeton University Press.

Mooney, Margarita. 2007. "The Catholic Church's Institutional Responses to Immigration: From Supranational to Local Engagement." In *Religion and Social Justice for Immigrants,* edited by Pierrette Hondagneu-Sotelo, 157–171. New Brunswick: Rutgers University Press.

Moran, Rachel F. 2007. "The Story of *Lau v. Nichols*: Breaking the Silence in Chinatown." In *Education Law Stories,* edited by Michael A. Olivas and Ronna Greff Schneider, 111–157. New York: Foundation Press.

Mosley, Jennifer E. 2010. "Organizational Resources and Environmental Incentives: Understanding the Policy Advocacy Involvement of Human Service Non-profits." *Social Service Review* 84(1): 57–76.

Mosley, Jennifer E., and Alejandra Ros. 2011. "Nonprofit Agencies in Public Child Welfare: Their Role and Involvement in Policy Advocacy." *Journal of Public Child Welfare* 5: 297–317.

Mullin, Megan, Gillian Peele, and Bruce E. Cain. 2004. "City Caesars? Institutional Structure and Mayoral Success in Three California Cities." *Urban Affairs Review* 40(1): 19–43.

Murphy, Brian M. 2002. *A Comprehensive Profile of San Francisco's Nonprofit Human Service Providers*. San Francisco: San Francisco Urban Institute, San Francisco State University.

Murphy, Pat. 2006. "Translated City Websites Soon to Make Sense." *Fog City Journal*. September 8.

Murthy, Hamsa M. 2007. "Cities, Citizenship, and Undocumented Aliens: Dilemmas of Law and Political Community in Contemporary America." *Institute for the Study of Social Change*, University of California, Berkeley. ISSC Fellows Working Papers. Paper ISSC_W P_10.

Najam, Adil. 2000. "The Four-C's of Third Sector-Government Relations: Cooperation, Confrontation, Complementarity, and Co-optation." *Nonprofit Management and Leadership* 10(4): 375–396.

National Center for Charitable Statistics (NCCS). 2006. "Business Master File, 01/2006, 501(c)(3) Data Extract."

National Conference of State Legislatures (NCSL). 2013. "2013 Immigration Report." Washington, D.C.: National Conference of State Legislatures.

National Employment Law Project (NELP). 2015. "City Minimum Wage Laws: Recent Trends and Economic Evidence." New York: National Employment Law Project. Available at www.nelp.org/content/uploads/City-Minimum-Wage-Laws-Recent-Trends-Economic-Evidence.pdf, last visited August 21, 2015.

National Immigration Law Center (NILC). 2002. "Driver's Licenses for Immigrants: Broad Diversity Characterizes States' Requirements." *Immigrant Rights Update* 16(7). Available at www.nilc.org/pubs/iru/2002/iru7-02.pdf, last visited July 20, 2011.

———. 2015. "Infographic: State Laws on Driver's Licenses for Immigrants, July 2015." Available at www.nilc.org/DLaccesstoolkit2.html#table, last visited August 21, 2015.

Needleman, Ruth. 1998. "Building Relations for the Long Haul: Unions and Community-Based Groups Working Together to Organize Low-Wage Workers." In *Organizing to Win: New Research on Union Strategies*, edited by Kate Bronfenbrenner, Sheldon Friedman, Richard W. Hurd, Rudolph A. Oswald, and Ronald L. Seeber, 71–86. Ithaca: Cornell University Press.

Ness, Immanuel. 2005. *Immigrants, Unions, and the New U.S. Labor Market*. Philadelphia: Temple University Press.

Nevius, Chuck W. 2010. "City's Far Left Gets Beating at Ballot Box." *San Francisco Chronicle*. November 18, C-1.

New York Immigration Coalition (NYIC). 2010. *Still Lost in Translation: City Agencies' Compliance with Local Law 73 and Executive Order 120—Examining Progress and Work Still to Be Done.* New York: New York Immigration Coalition.

Nieves, Evelyn. 1999. "In Old Mission District, Changing Grit to Gold." *New York Times.* January 21.

Nishioka, Joyce. 1999. "S.F. Mulls Cost of a Living Wage." *AsianWeek* 20(29): 10.

Nishioka, Joyce, and Perla Ni. 1999. "$11 Wage Put on the Table." *AsianWeek* 20(36): 10.

Nissen, Bruce. 2004. "The Effectiveness and Limits of Labor-Community Coalitions: Evidence from South Florida." *Labor Studies Journal* 29(1): 67–88.

North, David S. 1987. "The Long Grey Welcome: A Study of the American Naturalization Program." *International Migration Review* 21(2): 311–326.

O'Connor, Edwin. 1956. *The Last Hurrah.* Boston: Little, Brown.

Odem, Mary E. 2008. "Unsettled in the Suburbs: Latino Immigration and Ethnic Diversity in Metro Atlanta." In *Twenty-First-Century Gateways: Immigrant Incorporation in Suburban America,* edited by Audrey Singer, Susan W. Hardwick, and Caroline B. Brettell, 105–136. Washington, D.C.: Brookings Institution.

Office of Labor Standards Enforcement (OLSE). 2013. *Minimum Wage Ordinance: Annual Report, FY 2012–2013.* Available at http://sfgsa.org/modules/showdocument.aspx?documentid=11225, last visited August 21, 2015.

——. 2015. "Minimum Compensation Ordinance (MCO)." Available at http://sfgsa.org/index.aspx?page=403, last visited November 22, 2015.

O'Leary, Mary E. 2007. "Group Files FOI Request for ID Card Info." *New Haven Register.* July 21.

——. 2008. "Elm City ID Holder Names Protected: Safety at Risk, Says Homeland Security." *New Haven Register.* March 5.

O'Neil, Kevin. 2003. "Consular ID Cards: Mexico and Beyond." Washington, D.C.: Migration Policy Institute.

——. 2010. "Hazleton and Beyond: Why Communities Try to Restrict Immigration." Washington, D.C.: Migration Policy Institute.

Onishi, Norimitsu. 2012. "San Francisco Tech Boom Brings Jobs and Worries." *New York Times.* June 5, A-15.

"Online Counts Reports." 2015. Available at http://politicaldata.com/online-counts-reports/, last visited August 21, 2015.

Ornstein, Norman J., Thomas E. Mann, and Michael J. Malbin. 2008. *Vital Statistics on Congress 2008.* Washington, D.C.: Brookings Institution.

O'Rourke, Dara. 2002. "Motivating a Conflicted Environmental State: Community-Driven Regulation in Vietnam." In *The Environmental State Under Pressure,* edited by Arthur P. J. Mol and Frederick H. Buttel, 221–244. Amsterdam: Elsevier.

Pallares, Amalia, and Nilda Flores-González. 2010. *¡Marcha! Latino Chicago and the Immigrant Rights Movement.* Urbana: University of Illinois Press.

Park, Julie, and Dowell Myers. 2010. "Intergenerational Mobility in the Post-1965 Immigration Era: Estimates by an Immigration Cohort Method." *Demography* 47(2): 369–392.

Passel, Jeffrey S. 2006. "The Size and Characteristics of the Unauthorized Migrant Population in the U.S.: Estimates Based on the March 2005 Current Population Survey." Washington, D.C.: Pew Hispanic Center.

Passel, Jeffrey S., and D'Vera Cohn. 2009. "A Portrait of Unauthorized Immigrants in the United States." Washington, D.C.: Pew Hispanic Center.

———. 2011. "Unauthorized Immigrant Population: National and State Trends, 2010." Washington, D.C.: Pew Hispanic Center.

———. 2013. "A Nation of Immigrants: A Portrait of the 40 Million, Including 11 Million Unauthorized." Washington, D.C.: Pew Hispanic Center.

Passel, Jeffrey S., D'Vera Cohn, Jens Manuel Krogstad, and Ana Gonzalez-Barrera. 2014. "As Growth Stalls, Unauthorized Immigrant Population Becomes More Settled." Washington, D.C.: Pew Research Center's Hispanic Trends Project.

Peel, Roy V. 1935. *The Political Clubs of New York City*. New York: G. P. Putnam's Sons.

Pekkanen, Robert J., Steven Rathgeb Smith, and Yutaka Tsujinaka. 2014. *Nonprofits and Advocacy: Engaging Community and Government in an Era of Retrenchment*. Baltimore: Johns Hopkins University Press.

Peterson, Paul E. 1981. *City Limits*. Chicago: University of Chicago Press.

Pew Forum on Religion and Public Life. 2008. "U.S. Religious Landscape Survey." Washington, D.C.: Pew Research Center.

Pickus, Noah. 2005. *True Faith and Allegiance: Immigration and American Civic Nationalism*. Princeton: Princeton University Press.

Piven, Frances Fox, and Richard A. Cloward. 1977. *Poor People's Movements: Why They Succeed, How They Fail*. New York: Pantheon Books.

Plotke, David. 1999. "Immigration and Political Incorporation in the Contemporary United States." In *The Handbook of International Migration: The American Experience*, edited by Charles Hirschman, Philip Kasinitz, and Josh DeWind, 294–318. New York: Russell Sage Foundation Press.

Pollin, Robert, and Stephanie Luce. 1998. *The Living Wage: Building a Fair Economy*. New York: New Press.

Portes, Alejandro, and John W. Curtis. 1987. "Changing Flags: Naturalization and Its Determinants among Mexican Immigrants." *International Migration Review* 21(2): 352–371.

Portes, Alejandro, and Rubén G. Rumbaut. 2001. *Legacies: The Story of the Immigrant Second Generation*. Berkeley/New York: University of California Press and Russell Sage Foundation Press.

Portes, Alejandro, and Min Zhou. 1993. "The New Second Generation: Segmented Assimilation and Its Variants." *Annals of the American Academy of Political and Social Science* 530: 74–96.

Qian, Zhenchao, and Daniel T. Lichter. 2011. "Changing Patterns of Interracial Marriage in a Multiracial Society." *Journal of Marriage and Family* 73(5): 1065–1084.

Ramakrishnan, S. Karthick. 2005. *Democracy in Immigrant America: Changing Demographics and Political Participation*. Stanford: Stanford University Press.

Ramakrishnan, S. Karthick, and Irene Bloemraad (editors). 2008. *Civic Hopes and Political Realities: Immigrants, Community Organizations, and Political Engagement*. New York: Russell Sage Foundation Press.

Ramakrishnan, S. Karthick, and Thomas J. Espenshade. 2001. "Immigrant Incorporation and Political Participation in the United States." *International Migration Review* 35(3): 870–907.

Ramakrishnan, S. Karthick, and Tom Wong. 2010. "Partisanship, Not Spanish: Explaining Municipal Ordinances Affecting Undocumented Immigrants." In *Taking Local Control: Immigration Policy Activism in U.S. Cities and States*, edited by Monica W. Varsanyi, 73–93. Stanford: Stanford University Press.

Reich, Michael, Peter Hall, and Fiona Hsu. 1999. "Living Wages and the San Francisco Economy: The Benefits and Costs." Berkeley: Institute of Industrial Relations.

Reich, Michael, and Amy Laitinen. 2003. "Raising Low Pay in a High Income Economy: The Economics of a San Francisco Minimum Wage." Working Paper No. 99, Institute for Labor and Employment, UC Berkeley. Available at http://escholarship.org/uc/item/7336j74k, last visited August 21, 2015.

Reichley, A. James. 1992. *The Life of the Parties: A History of American Political Parties.* New York: Free Press.

Reynolds, David B. 2001. "Living Wage Campaigns as Social Movements: Experiences from Nine Cities." *Labor Studies Journal* 26(2): 31–64.

———. 2004. "The Living Wage Movement Mushrooms in the United States." In *Living Wage Movements: Global Perspectives*, edited by Deborah M. Figart, 69–84. New York: Routledge.

Ridgley, Jennifer. 2008. "Cities of Refuge: Immigration Enforcement, Police, and the Insurgent Genealogies of Citizenship in U.S. Sanctuary Cities." *Urban Geography* 29(1): 53–77.

Rodríguez, Cristina M. 2008. "The Significance of the Local in Immigration Regulation." *Michigan Law Review* 106: 567–642.

Rogers, Reuel R. 2006. *Afro-Caribbean Immigrants and the Politics of Incorporation: Ethnicity, Exception, or Exit.* New York: Cambridge University Press.

Romero, Tom I. 2008. "No Brown Towns: Anti-Immigrant Ordinances and Equal Educational Opportunities for Latinos/as." *Journal of Gender, Race, and Justice* 12(1): 13–56.

Rosenstone, Steven J., and John Mark Hansen. 1993. *Mobilization, Participation, and Democracy in America.* New York: Macmillan.

Rowe, Jeri. 2013. "Creating a Bond of Trust and Understanding." *Greensboro News & Record*, August 4.

Sabatini, Joshua. 2006. "City Vows to Fix Translations." *San Francisco Examiner.* September 8.

Salamon, Lester M. 1981. "Rethinking Public Management: Third-Party Government and the Changing Forms of Government Action." *Public Policy* 29(3): 255–275.

———. 1995. *Partners in Public Service: Government-Nonprofit Relations in the Modern Welfare State.* Baltimore: Johns Hopkins University Press.

———. 1999. *America's Nonprofit Sector: A Primer.* Second edition. New York: Foundation Center.

Sammon, Peter J. 2000. "The Living Wage Movement." *America: The National Catholic Weekly* 183(5): 16–19.

San Francisco (California). 2006a. "Report Concerning the Status of San Francisco's Equal Access to Services Ordinance." City and County of San Francisco: Immigrant Rights Commission.

——. 2006b. "Cultural Competency Task Force Report." City and County of San Francisco: Office of the Mayor.

——. 2008. "2008 Equal Employment Opportunity Workforce Utilization Analysis." City and County of San Francisco: Department of Human Resources.

San Francisco Department of Human Resources. 2008. "Appendix B: City & County of San Francisco Workforce Composition Percentages by Race/Ethnicity and Gender, 1972–2008." On file with the author.

San Francisco Labor Council (SFLC). 2006. "Resolution in Support of Immigrant Workers." April 3. Available at www.sflaborcouncil.org/ViewUpload/36, last visited January 19, 2010.

——. 2007. "Resolution for Organizing a Response to the Department of Homeland Security's New Rules Regarding No-Match Letters." September 10. Available at http://sflaborcouncil.org/sites/labor/uploads/09-10-07ResReNo-Match Ltrs.pdf, last visited August 21, 2015.

——. 2009a. "Resolution in Support of the May Day 2009 March and Rally in San Francisco for Worker and Immigrant Rights and in Support of ILWU Local 10 Decision to Stop Work in Bay Area Ports on May 1, 2009 to Protest Repression of Port Workers and Immigrants by the Department of Homeland Security." April 27. Available at http://sflaborcouncil.org/sites/labor/uploads/04-27-09ResSptMayDay+ILWUActions.pdf, last visited August 21, 2015.

——. 2009b. "Resolution to Defend Immigrant Youth and Our Families." November 9. Available at http://sflc.live2.radicaldesigns.org/wp-content/uploads/sites/sflaborcouncil/uploads/11-09-09ResDefendingImmigrantYth+Famil ies.pdf, last visited August 21, 2015.

——. 2010a. "Resolution in Support of 2010 May Day March & Rally in San Francisco." April 12. Available at http://sflaborcouncil.org/sites/labor/uploads/04-12-10ResSptMayDay2010.pdf, last visited August 21, 2015.

——. 2010b. "Resolution to Oppose Arizona's Apartheid-like Laws and Support the National Boycott of Arizona." May 24. Available at http://sflaborcouncil.org/sites/labor/uploads/05-24-10ResOppAZImmLaw+SptBoycott.pdf, last visited August 21, 2015.

——. 2010c. "Resolution to Support an Immigration Policy Based on Labor and Human Rights." July 12. Available at http://sflaborcouncil.org/sites/labor/uploads/07-12-10ResReImmigrationPolicy.pdf, last visited August 21, 2015.

Santa Ana, Otto. 2002. *Brown Tide Rising: Metaphors of Latinos in Contemporary American Public Discourse.* Austin: University of Texas Press.

Sassen, Saskia. 2001. *The Global City: New York, Tokyo, London.* Second edition. Princeton: Princeton University Press.

Saucedo, Renee. 2003. "Yes! on Proposition L and No! on Proposition M." *El Tecolote.* October 23.

Saunders, Debra J. 2008a. "Sanctuary Policy Made City Less Safe." *San Francisco Chronicle.* July 22, B-7.

——. 2008b. "GOP Would Make Sanctuary Cities Pay." *San Francisco Chronicle.* September 1, B-5.

Schattschneider, Elmer E. 1960. *The Semisovereign People: A Realist's View of Democracy in America.* New York: Holt, Rinehart, and Winston.

Schmid, Carol L. 2001. *The Politics of Language: Conflict, Identity, and Cultural Pluralism in Comparative Perspective.* New York: Oxford University Press.

Schmid, Hillel, Michal Bar, and Ronit Nirel. 2008. "Advocacy Activities in Non-profit Human Service Organizations: Implications for Policy." *Nonprofit and Voluntary Sector Quarterly* 37(4): 581–602.

Schmidt Sr., Ron. 2007. "Comparing Federal Government Immigrant Settlement Polices in Canada and the United States." *American Review of Canadian Studies* 37(1): 103–122.

Schmidt, Sr., Ron, Yvette M. Alex-Assensoh, Andrew L. Aoki, and Rodney E. Hero. 2010. *Newcomers, Outsiders, and Insiders: Immigrants and American Racial Politics in the Early Twenty-first Century.* Ann Arbor: University of Michigan Press.

Schneider, Anne, and Helen Ingram. 1993. "Social Construction of Target Populations: Implications for Politics and Policy." *American Political Science Review* 87(2): 334–347.

Schneider, Dorothee. 2001. "Naturalization and United States Citizenship in Two Periods of Mass Migration: 1894–1930, 1965–2000." *Journal of Ethnic History* 21(1): 50–76.

Schneider, Robert L., and Lori Lester. 2001. *Social Work Advocacy: A New Framework for Action.* Belmont: Brooks/Cole.

Scrivner, Gary N. 1990. "100 Years of Tax Policy Changes Affecting Charitable Organizations." In *The Nonprofit Organization: Essential Readings*, edited by David L. Gies, J. Steven Ott, and Jay M. Shafritz, 126–137. Pacific Grove: Brooks/Cole.

Service Employees International Union (SEIU). 2015. "A Look Back and a Look Forward: 25 Years of Organizing Janitors." Available at www.seiu-illinois. org/a/justice-for-janitors/justice-for-janitors-20-years-of-organizing.php, last visited August 21, 2015.

Shaw, Randy. 2006. "San Francisco Fails to Mobilize for Immigrant Rights." *BeyondChron.* March 27. Available at www.beyondchron.org/news/index. php?itemid=3083, last visited August 21, 2015.

——. 2007. "SF Irish Mobilize for Legalization of Immigrants." *BeyondChron.* March 15. Available at www.beyondchron.org/news/index.php?itemid=4301, last visited August 21, 2015.

Sherbert, Erin. 2011. "Gavin Newsom Booted from S.F. Democratic Party." *SF Weekly.* July 29. Available at http://blogs.sfweekly.com/thesnitch/2011/07/ gavin_newsom_dccc_aaron_peskin.php, last visited August 21, 2015.

Sherman, Rachel, and Kim Voss. 2000. "Organize or Die: Labor's New Tactics and Immigrant Workers." In *Organizing Immigrants: The Challenge for Unions in Contemporary California*, edited by Ruth Milkman, 81–108. Ithaca: Cornell University Press.

Singer, Audrey. 2004. *The Rise of New Immigrant Gateways.* Washington, D.C.: The Brookings Institution.

Skocpol, Theda. 1991. "Targeting within Universalism: Politically Viable Policies to Combat Poverty in the United States." In *The Urban Underclass*, edited by Christopher Jencks and Paul E. Peterson, 411–436. Washington, D.C.: Brookings Institution.

Skrentny, John D. 2002. *The Minority Rights Revolution.* Cambridge: Harvard University Press.

Smith, Heather A., and Owen J. Furuseth. 2008. "The "Nuevo South": Latino Place Making and Community Building in the Middle Ring Suburbs of Charlotte." In *Twenty-First-Century Gateways: Immigrant Incorporation in Suburban America*, edited by Audrey Singer, Susan W. Hardwick, and Caroline B. Brettell, 281–307. Washington, D.C.: Brookings Institution.

Smith, Rebecca. 2007. "Human Rights at Home: Human Rights as an Organizing and Legal Tool in Low-Wage Worker Communities." *Stanford Journal of Civil Rights and Civil Liberties* 3: 285–315.

Smith, Steven Rathgeb, and Michael Lipsky. 1993. *Nonprofits for Hire: The Welfare State in the Age of Contracting*. Cambridge: Harvard University Press.

Sonenshein, Raphael J. 1993. *The Politics of Black and White: Race and Power in Los Angeles*. Princeton: Princeton University Press.

Soyer, David. 2006. "Mutual Aid Societies and Fraternal Orders." In *A Companion to American Immigration*, edited by Reed Ueda, 528–546. Malden: Blackwell Publishers.

Soysal, Yasemin N. 1994. *Limits of Citizenship: Migrants and Postnational Membership in Europe*. Princeton: Princeton University Press.

Sterne, Evelyn Savidge. 2001. "Beyond the Boss: Immigration and American Political Culture from 1880 to 1940." In *E Pluribus Unum? Contemporary and Historical Perspectives on Immigrant Political Incorporation*, edited by Gary Gerstle and John Mollenkopf, 33–66. New York: Russell Sage Foundation Press.

Stillwell, Cinnamon. 2008. "San Francisco: Sanctuary Gone Awry." *San Francisco Chronicle*. July 16.

Stone, Clarence N. 1989. *Regime Politics: Governing Atlanta, 1946–1988*. Lawrence: University of Kansas Press.

———. 1993. "Urban Regimes and the Capacity to Govern: A Political Economy Approach." *Journal of Urban Affairs* 15(1): 1–28.

———. 1996. "Urban Political Machines: Taking Stock." *PS: Political Science and Politics* 29(3): 446–450.

Streiff, Meg. 2005. "Boston's Settlement Housing: Social Reform in an Industrial City." Ph.D. dissertation, Department of Geography and Anthropology, Louisiana State University.

Suro, Roberto, Jill H. Wilson, and Audrey Singer. 2011. *Immigration and Poverty in America's Suburbs*. Washington, D.C.: Brookings Institution.

Tarrow, Sidney. 1996. "Social Movements in Contentious Politics: A Review Article." *American Political Science Review* 4(90): 874–883.

———. 2011. *Power in Movement: Social Movements and Contentious Politics*. Third edition. New York: Cambridge University Press.

Tattersall, Amanda. 2005. "There is Power in Coalition: A Framework for Assessing How and When Union-Community Coalitions Are Effective and Enhance Union Power." *Labor and Industry: A Journal of the Social and Economic Relations of Work* 16(2): 97–112.

Tattersall, Amanda, and David Reynolds. 2007. "The Shifting Power of Labor-Community Coalitions: Identifying Common Elements of Powerful Coalitions in Australia and the U.S." *WorkingUSA: The Journal of Labor and Society* 10(1): 77–102.

Taylor, Marilyn, Gary Craig, and Mick Wilkinson. 2002. "Co-option or Empowerment? The Changing Relationship between the State and the Voluntary and Community Sectors." *Local Governance* 28(1): 1–11.

Telles, Edward E., and Vilma Ortiz. 2008. *Generations of Exclusion: Mexican Americans, Assimilation, and Race.* New York: Russell Sage Foundation Press.

Tentler, Leslie Woodcock. 1997. "Present at the Creation: Working-Class Catholics in the United States." In *American Exceptionalism? U.S. Working-Class Formation in an International Context,* edited by Rick Halpern and Jonathan Morris, 134–157. New York: St. Martin's Press.

Theodore, Nik, and Nina Martin. 2007. "Migrant Civil Society: New Voices in the Struggle over Community Development." *Journal of Urban Affairs* 29(3): 269–287.

Thompson, A. Clay. 1999. "Asking for a Raise." *San Francisco Bay Guardian.* March 24.

Tilly, Charles. 1998. "Where Do Rights Come From?" In *Democracy, Revolution, and History,* edited by Theda Skocpol, 55–72. Ithaca: Cornell University Press.

Trolander, Judith Ann. 1987. *Professionalism and Social Change: From the Settlement House Movement to Neighborhood Centers, 1886 to the Present.* New York: Columbia University Press.

Tucker, James T. 2006. *The ESL Logjam: Waiting Times for Adult ESL Classes and the Impact on English Learners.* Los Angeles: NALEO Educational Fund.

Tumlin, Karen C., and Wendy Zimmermann. 2003. *Immigrants and TANF: A Look at Immigrant Welfare Recipients in Three Cities.* Occasional Paper No. 69. Washington, D.C.: Urban Institute.

U.S. Census Bureau. 2012. "Current Population Survey: Voting and Registration Supplement." Table 11 ("Reported Voting and Registration among Native and Naturalized Citizens, by Race, Hispanic Origin, and Region of Birth: November 2012"). Available at www.census.gov/hhes/www/socdemo/voting/publications/p20/2012/tables.html, last visited August 21, 2015.

———. 2013a. "2013 American Community Survey, 1-Year Estimates." Table S0501 ("Selected Characteristics of the Native and Foreign-Born Populations") for the United States and various cities. Available at http://factfinder2.census.gov.

———. 2013b. "2013 American Community Survey, 3-Year Estimates." Tables S0501 ("Selected Characteristics of the Native and Foreign-Born Populations") and S0502 ("Selected Characteristics of the Foreign-Born Population by Period of Entry into the United States) for San Francisco. Available at http://factfinder2.census.gov.

Valelly, Richard M. 2005. "Why Then But Not Now? Immigrant Incorporation in Historical Perspective." Paper presented at the Center for the Study of Democratic Politics. Princeton University, Princeton, New Jersey, April 14.

Van Derbeken, Jaxon. 2008a. "City's Shield of Migrants Probed: Feds Say Drug Lords 'Gaming the System'." *San Francisco Chronicle.* June 29, A-1.

———. 2008b. "8 Young Migrant Crack Dealers Escape." *San Francisco Chronicle.* July 1, A-1.

———. 2008c. "S.F. Mayor Reverses Policy on Illegals." *San Francisco Chronicle.* July 3, A-1.

———. 2008d. "New City Protocol in Works to Deal with Teen Illegals." *San Francisco Chronicle.* July 10, B-3.

———. 2008e. "S.F. IDs 10 Possible Illegal Youths to Feds." *San Francisco Chronicle.* July 12, B-1.

——. 2008f. "Feds Deny S.F. Claims on Cooperation on Illegal Juveniles." *San Francisco Chronicle.* July 20, A-15.

——. 2008g. "Slaying Suspect Once Found S.F. Sanctuary." *San Francisco Chronicle.* July 20, A-1.

——. 2008h. "Another Illegal Immigrant Offender Flees Group Home." *San Francisco Chronicle.* July 23, B-1.

——. 2008i. "S.F. Fund Aids Teen Felons Who Are Illegal." *San Francisco Chronicle.* August 3, A-1.

——. 2008j. "Panel Sticks Up for Immigrant Juvenile Felons." *San Francisco Chronicle.* August 19, A-1.

——. 2008k. "Family Blames Sanctuary Policy in 3 Slayings." *San Francisco Chronicle.* August 23, A-1.

——. 2008l. "S.F. Court Lets Teenager in Drug Case Stay in U.S." *San Francisco Chronicle.* August 26, A-1.

——. 2008m. "S.F. Gives Teen Drug Suspect to Immigration." *San Francisco Chronicle.* August 28, A-1.

——. 2008n. "Immigrant Drug Suspect Gamed S.F.'s Juvie System." *San Francisco Chronicle.* August 31, A-1.

Varsanyi, Monica W. 2007. "Documenting Undocumented Migrants: The *Matrículas Consulares* as Neoliberal Local Membership." *Geopolitics* 12(2): 299–319.

——. 2008. "Immigration Policing Through the Backdoor: City Ordinances, the "Right to the City," and the Exclusion of Undocumented Day Laborers." *Urban Geography* 29(1): 29–52.

——. 2010a. "Immigration Policy Activism in U.S. States and Cities: Interdisciplinary Perspectives." In *Taking Local Control: Immigration Policy Activism in U.S. Cities and States,* edited by Monica W. Varsanyi, 1–27. Stanford: Stanford University Press.

—— (editor). 2010b. *Taking Local Control: Immigration Policy Activism in U.S. Cities and States.* Stanford: Stanford University Press.

Vega, Cecilia M. 2007. "Newsom Freezes Hiring, Orders Cuts in Face of $229 Million Deficit." *San Francisco Chronicle.* November 29, B-1.

Verba, Sidney, Kay Lehman Schlozman, and Henry E. Brady. 1995. *Voice and Equality: Civic Voluntarism in American Politics.* Cambridge: Harvard University Press.

Voss, Kim, and Irene Bloemraad (editors). 2011. *Rallying for Immigrant Rights: The Fight for Inclusion in 21st Century America.* Berkeley: University of California Press.

Voss, Kim, and Rachel Sherman. 2000. "Breaking the Iron Law of Oligarchy: Union Revitalization in the American Labor Movement." *American Journal of Sociology* 106(2): 303–349.

Wang, L. Ling-Chi. 1994. "*Lau v. Nichols:* History of a Struggle for Equal and Quality Education." In *Chinese Immigrants and American Law,* edited by Charles McClain, 422–445. New York: Garland Publishing.

Watson, Bruce. 2005. *Bread and Roses: Mills, Migrants, and the Struggle for the American Dream.* New York: Viking.

Wattenberg, Martin P. 1996. *The Decline of American Political Parties, 1952–1994.* Cambridge: Harvard University Press.

———. 2001. *The Rise of Candidate-Centered Politics.* Cambridge: Harvard University Press.

Wells, Miriam J. 2000. "Unionization and Immigrant Incorporation in San Francisco Hotels." *Social Problems* 47(2): 241–265.

White House Task Force on New Americans. 2015. *Strengthening Communities by Welcoming All Residents: A Federal Strategic Action Plan of Immigrant & Refugee Integration.* Available at www.whitehouse.gov/sites/default/files/docs/final_tf_newamericans_report_4-14-15_clean.pdf, last visited August 21, 2015.

Wilson, Catherine E. 2013. "Language Access Policies in Philadelphia: Municipal Directives and Nonprofit Collaboration." *Nonprofit and Voluntary Sector Quarterly* 42(5): 963–984.

Wilson, William Julius. 1987. *The Truly Disadvantaged: The Inner City, the Underclass, and Public Policy.* Chicago: University of Chicago Press.

Wilson, Yumi. 1999. "Union Poll Says Voters Back Living-Wage Plan." *San Francisco Chronicle.* August 17, A-14.

Wirt, Frederick M. 1974. *Power in the City: Decision Making in San Francisco.* Berkeley: Institute of Governmental Studies Press.

Wolch, Jennifer R. 1990. *The Shadow State: Government and Voluntary Sector in Transition.* New York: Foundation Center.

Wolfinger, Raymond, and Steven J. Rosenstone. 1980. *Who Votes?* New Haven: Yale University Press.

Wong, Janelle S. 2002. "The Role of Community Organizations in the Political Incorporation of Asian American and Latino Immigrants." Paper prepared for the Conference on Race and Civil Society, Racine, Wisconsin, January 11–12.

———. 2006. *Democracy's Promise: Immigrants and American Civic Institutions.* Ann Arbor: University of Michigan Press.

Woolard, Kathryn A. 1990. "Voting Rights, Liberal Voters and the Official English Movement: An Analysis of Campaign Rhetoric in San Francisco's Proposition 'O'." In *Perspectives on Official English: The Campaign for English as the Official Language of the USA*, edited by Karen L. Adams and Daniel T. Brink, 125–137. New York: Mouton de Gruyter.

Yang, Philip Q. 1994. "Explaining Immigrant Naturalization." *International Migration Review* 28(3): 449–477.

Ziegler-McPherson, Christina A. 2009. *Americanization in the States: Immigrant Social Welfare Policy, Citizenship, and National Identity in the United States, 1908–1929.* Gainesville: University of Florida Press.

Index

Lightning Source UK Ltd.
Milton Keynes UK
UKHW01f1450131018
330428UK00001B/166/P

9 781501 700194